Communication
Problem Solving

Communication Problem Solving

The Language of Effective Management

IAN McCALL
McCall Consultancy Services

JOHN COUSINS
Glasgow College

JOHN WILEY & SONS
Chichester · New York · Brisbane · Toronto · Singapore

Other Wiley Editorial Offices

John Wiley & Sons, Inc., 605 Third Avenue,
New York, NY 10158-0012, USA

Jacaranda Wiley Ltd, G.P.O. Box 859, Brisbane,
Queensland 4001, Australia

John Wiley & Sons (Canada) Ltd, 22 Worcester Road,
Rexdale, Ontario M9W 1L1, Canada

John Wiley & Sons (SEA) Pte Ltd, 37 Jalan Pemimpin 05-04,
Block B, Union Industrial Building, Singapore 2057

Library of Congress Cataloging-in-Publication Data:

McCall, J. B.
Communication problem solving: the language of effective
  management/Ian McCall, John Cousins.
    p. cm.
Includes bibliographical references.
ISBN 0-471-92026-6
1. Communication in management. 2. Interorganizational relations.
3. Problem solving. I. Cousins, John. II. Title.
HD30.3.M398 1989
658.4′5—dc20   89–70684
                                                              CIP

British Library Cataloguing in Publication Data:

McCall, Ian
  Communication problem solving.
  1. Management. Communication
  I. Title II. Cousins, John
  658.4′5

ISBN 0-471-92026-6

Phototypeset by Dobbie Typesetting Limited, Plymouth, Devon
Printed and bound in Great Britain by Courier International Ltd, Tiptree, Essex

Contents

Preface

Research into management in the last decade has turned upside down our earlier ideas of what managers do. This has led to a new emphasis on communication in management education. As a result we have seen, rightly, a burgeoning of organizational communication as a subject of study. In order to understand better how to communicate within organizations, we need to know more about organizational processes and the forces which make them what they are. No longer can subjects like marketing, or operations management, or human resource management, afford to develop outside the mainstream of organizational behaviour. If they do it is at the risk of being perceived as less than relevant. For its part, organizational behaviour has to take account of what is happening in communication which gives it greater relevance. Organizational communication has, in turn, to take on board the fact that what happens between organizations affects, and is affected by, what goes on within them.

It is a characteristic of latter-day organizations that they develop interdependent associations with other organizations whether as suppliers, customers or intermediaries, or as partners in some form of joint enterprise—formal or informal. This view is reflected in the idea of markets as networks of interacting organizations which have a mutual, but not necessarily equal, resource dependence. The perspective is one which views the making of relationships with other organizations as a necessary condition for the effective harnessing of resources across organizations. It is equally true for both the public and private sectors. The skills needed to handle such developments are also applicable to professional occupations like lawyers, accountants and surveyors. Organizations have to relate to other organizations who can assist them to competitive advantage by performing key activities better, quicker, or more cheaply than competitors. All these activities depend for their successful development and maintenance on communication—all the more so when many of the activities take place across national boundaries.

To do these things well, organizations need a good dispute settlement mechanism—how good it may be depending on the effectiveness of communication. They also need the kind of skills training that reflects the knowledge that—despite the received wisdom which tells us that structure follows strategy—structure in fact represents a barrier to the integration of the specialized functions set up to create efficiency. Co-ordination of disparate specialisms is difficult under conditions in which people are increasingly given responsibility for carrying out tasks through other people whose compliance they cannot require because they have no direct authority over them. Organization structure compounds the problem of the manager trying to reconcile the need for differentiation, to carry out operations efficiently, with the co-ordination of these separate inputs in order to achieve outcomes contracted, legally or implicitly, with customers or partner institutions.

These changing directions are linked to what people say and how they say it. It is through communication between individuals that relations in and between organizations are established, reinforced and nurtured. Similarly, it is through the skills of 'indirect management', which rely heavily on interpersonal communication, that managers at different levels in an organization can get the co-operation of others outside their immediate hierarchy in order to help fulfil their own task requirements. In addressing the communication skills required, it is necessary to explode the myth of rationality in problem solving and decision making; to know something of the cultures that can evolve in an organization and influence perceptions— and how those cultures interact with national cultures; and to identify the networks through which information is obtained to supplement or replace formal systems when the latter fail to deliver.

In approaching the development of communication skills, we are not concerned with pathways of communication in an organization, whether formal or informal. Nor do we feel it appropriate to consider direct communication with the public, or the effects of new applications in information technology. Our concern is rather with how people create meaning; the politics arising from different meanings; and the behaviours and strategies people can employ to handle these political situations. It is about influence, persuasion and negotiation. We make no apology for basing practical communication skills in conceptual frameworks. The view that everything should be distilled, simplified, categorized in 'how-to-do-it' terms—and, by implication, trivialized—is not one to which we subscribe. Managers, and students aspiring to be managers, are normal, bright people whose intelligence we have sought to respect. What we have done is to provide them with frames of reference, in a key area of managerial performance, which will allow them to interpret past experience and respond in a creative way when confronted with unforeseen problems.

We are indebted for advice, comments and contributions from various people. In particular, we should like to thank Arthur Morrison of Napier Polytechnic of Edinburgh, Bob Robertson of the Scottish College of Textiles and Tony Seaton of Newcastle Business School. Our thanks also go to the students, businessmen and public officials who made the time to talk over communication issues with us. Any deficiencies are our own responsibility.

J. B. McCALL
McCall Consultancy Services
Eyemouth, Berwickshire, TD14 5LS

J. Y. COUSINS
Glasgow College, Glasgow, G4 0BA

February 1990

Part 1
Concepts in Communication Problem Solving

1
Introduction

Everybody communicates. They do so to bring meaning to what they do. It is at the centre of their very existence, whether in the home, in the organizations in which they work or in the groups where they find their leisure or other interest. Communication is a dynamic process of interaction and change. If we wish to exercise a measure of control in this process it is helpful if we can isolate the nature of communication and the ingredients it comprises.

This chapter sets out to identify these elements as a basis for defining communication and to provide a framework for the remainder of the book.

COMMUNICATION

No one person is an island. It is only through communication that people make links with others who bring meaning to what they do—within the family, within groups to which they belong or within organizations. The process of communication is central to all our lives. It is the means by which personal bonds are established and nurtured, change in any form of organization is spelt out, people attain mutual gratifications and manage the conflicts that punctuate personal and community living. In order to adapt to changing circumstances people are constantly relearning their means of communication. It is a process involving change and interaction and is in a constant state of flux.

The Communication Framework

Transactional Nature

If one person communicates with another there has to be some sharing of meaning between the two. What is said by one person to another will affect the future messages that will be sent. If you are addressing another person (say, a colleague at work) you look for a reaction to what you have said. That reaction will take the form of an oral response to the sender, which will be accompanied by gestures such as a smile or a frown, the raising of an eyebrow or an inflection of the language used. This response and accompanying clues provide the sender with feedback as to how the message has been received. Without this feedback it would be difficult to establish just how effective the message has been. Similarly, in making a reply the colleague becomes the sender and seeks from you an indication of how his or her message has been received. You, in turn, will provide your interpretation of that message by what you convey. So the dialogue will continue until the exchange gives an outcome.

The point is made by Mangham (1978) that, in any situation, what others do or are perceived to be doing are important clues to the definition of that situation. If a communicator puts together a set of behaviours which can be inferred to be the expression of his preferred goal, he is presenting himself and creates a part for the other in the developing interaction. What he is saying in effect is 'This is whom I want to be taken for and this is whom I take you to be'. The other communicator's interpretation of the situation consists in attempting to take the first communicator's role and in understanding the implications of it for himself, just as the first communicator has to define the other's behaviour and intentions. The significance of the process of definition is that it involves trying to understand the implications of the actions of each of the parties for the other. From this stems patterns of behaviour and imputation of roles for each. Such mutual role taking is a necessary preliminary for effective communication.

It is for these reasons that communication outcomes are said to be interaction dependent. This dependence is thrown into greater relief if the model of dyadic interaction is considered. In this, there is an interplay of factors external and internal to the individuals involved in the exchanges. External influences show up in the relation between a person's actions and the previous actions of the other, while internal influences can be seen in the relation between an act and previous actions by the same person (Clarke, 1983).

The responses given by a receiver can change the behaviour of the sender (who is the receiver when the other person is speaking). For example, if enough negative feedback is given about a belief or a position on an issue, pressure for change is clearly present. If, at the end of that transaction or interaction episode, a particular outcome results, that outcome will colour and affect any subsequent episode. Such outcomes can be brought about by the individual behaviours in which people indulge. We are all given to subjective evaluations about what others have communicated, and very often our responses to such communications can impact on what happens. In other words, people often respond to what others say on the basis of how they feel about it, not what an objective analysis tells them. Messages are often perceived as threats to positions or ambitions or self-images.

There is an old ploy among communication instructors when meeting a group of trainees for the first time in which they highlight how people's behaviour can affect others in a way that sometimes inhibits the objectives explicitly or implicitly aimed for. One instructor known to the senior author starts off by telling trainees that they will get on with him provided they specifically avoid talking about '*a phenomena*', '*a criteria*' or '*a media*' and use the appropriate Greek or Latin singular form. He goes on in this vein until the students begin to take exception and become restive or complain. He then invites them to consider whether they themselves do not in fact annoy other people with whom they seek to communicate in order to achieve a preferred outcome. Then follows a number of examples of the kinds of situations, characteristics or perceptions which induce threats to positions or aspirations or embody values which are anathema to the hearer. The trainees thereafter pay the greatest attention to their own performance.

Instrumental Nature

As hinted in the previous section, we have to accept that communication is used instrumentally, that is, as a tool to reach certain ends if we are concerned with communication problem solving. By doing this, people are able to achieve some measure of control over situations in which they would wish to gain the compliance of the other party. It is maintained that people involved in business communications, either within organizations or between them, should first define objectives for a particular interaction followed by communicative action which is in line with these objectives (Honey, 1979). The objectives may be to elicit information, to solve problems and make decisions, to amuse or inform. Strategies may be planned to meet specific objectives in the most effective manner.

In the process of communicating with someone else in an instrumental or persuasive way that person is likely to adopt just such a persuasive manner in responding to an issue over which a communicative issue has been initiated. There is therefore the necessity for the parties involved in a communication exchange to devise strategies to resist such manipulation and influence (see page 96).

From time to time people may wish to deviate from their instrumental behaviours and indulge in modes of behaviour which are self-satisfying and have no intentional thrust. They do not always keep their messages related strictly to their objectives for it. Sometimes they are highly individual, with widely differing personality traits, and may wish to express agreement with another party's concerns, boast about their achievements and abilities or give enhanced versions of themselves. Nevertheless, within the overall pattern of an interaction they seek to meet specifically defined or implicit objectives.

Interpersonal Nature

The more we know of people and the more frequently we meet them, the more interpersonal our communication becomes. By interacting on a regular basis with other people, as we do in organizations in order to perform our jobs, we have a greater awareness of their uniqueness. It is claimed that this awareness of others involved in any communication exchange is the criterion of whether the communication is interpersonal (Ruffner and Burgoon, 1981).

By getting to know people, we are better able to predict their behaviour. As a result, we are able to devise communication strategies which are more likely to meet their instrumental purposes as well as our own. At the earlier stages of a relationship people call on more general data to enable them to do this through prescribed roles. These are the roles determined by rules and norms that are external to the communication transaction and to any relationship which at this point is merely incipient. Such rules and norms are exemplified within organizations by the various cultures which evolve in them. Handy (1985) classifies organizations into four cultures which represent different philosophies of management, i.e. 'club', 'role', 'task' and 'existential'. In the existential culture for example, organizations achieve their ends through individuals achieving theirs. This is so in organizations such as advertising agencies or consultancy firms. It is best in these cultures to appeal to the talent and skills of individual members.

In inter-organizational communication situations, communicators in the initial stages of a relationship can equally be guided by general data external to the transaction as in the identification of the role culture of the organization to which the other party belongs. In terms of international transactions, the four cultural universals identified by Hofstede (1984) give an interesting and useful means of predicting behaviour at this early stage. These universals are power distance, uncertainty avoidance, individualism and masculinity. Hofstede's research clusters countries on each of these dimensions and also draws conclusions from correlations of the indices which he develops. In communicating with Frenchmen, for example, who have been identified as combining the characteristics strong uncertainty avoidance and weak masculinity (greater modesty than assertiveness), appeals to their risk-avoiding, culturally induced behaviour are more likely to assist positive outcomes than other behaviours.

As the relationship develops we can attempt to predict the behaviour of those with whom we are communicating on the basis of club membership, learned societies or organizational, functional or interest groups, and communicate with them more meaningfully as a result. Nevertheless, the cultural or group characteristics persist, although there will always be those people who do not have the cultural or group traits to the same extent as the majority. It is part of the information-seeking behaviour of communicators to establish when this is so and to adopt other strategies.

Most communications in society in general as well as in the workplace reflect mature relationships. As we become more familiar with people, and progressively know more about them, negotiated roles take precedence in our communications. Such roles are agreed upon by the participants in communication, regardless of those prescribed for them by society or organizations. These agreements can be explicit or implicit. An example of explicit agreeement would be where, for example, two persons in an informal sports group agree to share the burdens of running the group, one to look after the monies collected from members to further their activities and the other to take responsibility for joint activities with similar groups, contacts with the press and training sessions. An implicit agreement might be where a subordinate in an organization uses initiative to solve a problem which could be construed as the prerogative of his or her superior but which the superior ignores as such and further condones by not wresting the initiative from a subordinate in subsequent issues.

Role negotiation is, however, a step towards understanding and accepting enacted roles. Enacted roles are those which people assume as being appropriate for themselves. The individuality of people is recognized, as is also the fact that a person can play multiple roles and indeed assume new ones. An interpersonal relationship takes account of such factors. At this level people are most concerned to understand and explain enacted roles. Thus behaviours become more predictable and hence it is easier to select a strategy for them. They are the individual basis for the transfer of meaning.

The Transactional Model of Communication

What applies in relation to the transactional, instrumental and interpersonal nature of communication within societies and organizations has equal legitimacy between them. This is complicated by the fact that the person(s) being communicated with may well work within a different organizational culture or a part of an organization which views an issue very differently. Such people may also operate within another national culture. To that extent, the skills required of a communicator are very wide indeed. A communicator approaching another organization will be conditioned to a greater or lesser degree by the kind of society or organization of which he or she is a member. Whether within or between societies or organizations, the transactional model shown in Figure 1.1 is the most appropriate for face-to-face encounters in which communication occurs through speech and non-verbal behaviours (Daniels and Spiker, 1987). To the extent that each participant in such an encounter has awareness of self and others in the situation, the sender and receiver aspects are enacted at the same time. Both sender and receiver are simultaneously receiver and sender, encoding and decoding messages and providing feedback to the other.

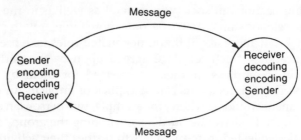

Figure 1.1 *Transaction model of communication (From Daniels and Spiker, 1987, reproduced by permission)*

The process is facilitated at the level of national and organizational cultures by the assumptions which the parties share as a result of being members of that particular culture. At the individual level, it is assisted by knowledge of the other individual obtained from frequent interactions and a growing understanding of what is meaningful to the other in the other's terms. In all cases, the meaning arises when information is placed within a context. Human communication is concerned with the meaning of verbal and non-verbal information.

The Elements of Communication

Communication is usually regarded as having a number of ingredients. Porter and Samovar (1988) first define communication in order to identify the elements. Bearing in mind that we are concerned to develop communication skills which will be applied with conscious intent, they define communication as follows:

> Communication is a dynamic transactional, behaviour-affecting process in which sources and receivers intentionally code their behaviours to produce messages that they transmit through a channel in order to induce or elicit particular attitudes or behaviours.

Having defined communication, Porter and Samovar identify eight specific elements of communication:

1 *A source*. This is a person who has a need to communicate. Such a need may vary from a desire for recognition as an individual to a wish to share information with others or to influence their attitudes and behaviours.
2 *Encoding*. In this process verbal and non-verbal behaviours are selected and arranged within the grammatical rules of the language being used.
3 *The message*. This is what must pass between a source and a receiver if the former is to influence the latter.

4 *The channel*. This provides the connection between the source and the receiver.

5 *A receiver*. This is usually a person intended by the source to be the object of the message.

6 *Decoding*. Like the act of encoding, this is an activity internal to the individual. It processes the message and attributes meaning to the source's behaviours.

7 *Receiver response*. This is what the receiver decides to do about the message. It may vary along a continuum from nothing to a substantial amount.

8 *Feedback*. This is information available to a source which permits qualitative judgements about communication effectiveness in order to adjust and adapt to an ongoing situation.

If reference is made to Figure 1.1 it will serve as a reminder that, when we speak of receivers and sources, both parties are simultaneously source and receiver, encoding and decoding messages and providing feedback at the same time. The channel will normally be the face-to-face one which is most appropriate to the kind of problem-solving activity being addressed. There will be occasions on which telephone or electronic means may be employed, in which case the non-verbal element will have less impact.

THE STRUCTURE OF THIS BOOK

It is against the background of the communication framework outlined above and the transaction model described that the rest of this book is written. Part 1 examines the concepts of communication using a variety of sources and loosely relates these to organizations. It utilizes in adapted form a multi-dimensional approach developed by Mortensen (1972) and illustrated in Figure 1.2 as a basis for the following chapters.

The multi-dimensional approach eliminates the difficulties of trying to fit all the complexities of communicative behaviour into a single all-encompassing criterion such as whether the message is designed to persuade or to inform. Nor does it force us to choose among competing theoretical orientations such as functional versus structural or psychological versus anthropological. We are, as a result, able to derive insights into communication, calling on contributions from whatever discipline has something to offer. We are mindful that the object of the book is to give managers in the broadest sense of the term and those aspiring to being managers, an understanding of communicative processes as a basis for the development of the requisite skills through which they can become more effective in their jobs.

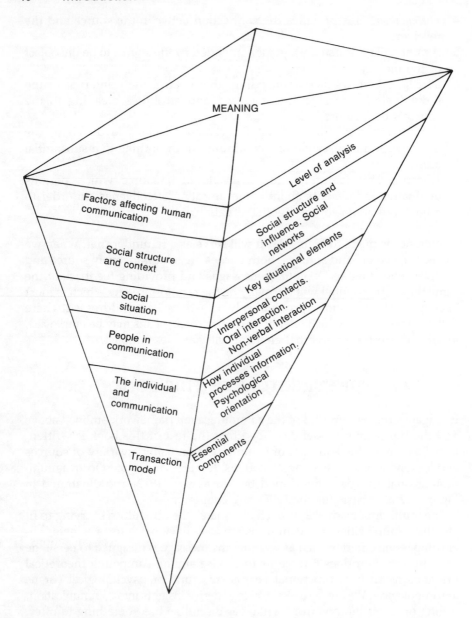

Figure 1.2 Factors influencing meaning in human interaction. Each of the higher and successively more complex dimensions of behaviour depends on the cumulative influences of the other factors. There may, however, be a reverse influence from the lower to the higher factors. For example, social structure and context may determine the nature of the interaction or situation. (Adapted from Mortensen, 1972)

Chapter 2 considers communicating individuals and identifies their uniqueness and the complex human functions which interpret issues and events in ways consistent with past experience and their psychological states. Human information processing seeks to offer a perspective on what happens when raw, sensory data are translated into conscious experience. Busy managers may wish to read the summaries at the middle and end of the chapter, as much of what is written is covered implicitly in the chapters that follow. What is treated in this chapter is, however, necessary to a full understanding of the communicative processes.

When people are in oral communication they use language and accompanying non-verbal signs to convey meaning. Chapter 3 describes the way people are predisposed to interpret messages and how their different perceptions can distort them unless they couch their communications in a manner that addresses these predispositions and perceptions.

Chapter 4 considers the different situational factors which mediate verbal and non-verbal behaviour and provide pointers as to how messages are most effectively conveyed. Sometimes situational factors are determined by contextual and social structural factors, and this is covered in Chapter 5.

Part 2 is very much a treatment of communication in an organizational and inter-organizational setting. Chapter 6 provides frameworks and models for tackling the communication problems presented by the diverse goals, values and outlooks of people in different parts of an organization and in different organizations. It is complicated by the fact that they are inter-dependent and have the capacity to assist or block the attempts of colleagues to carry out their tasks where they have the responsibility but not the hierarchical authority to request their compliance.

Chapter 7 addresses the reality of groups and individuals seeking to promote their own ends either in their capacities of leaders or as subordinates in situations of high political activity. Chapter 8 acknowledges that much communication of importance in organizations is carried out in lateral relationships. Effectiveness in such circumstances is largely a function of informal networks the maintenance of which demand particular communication skills.

There is a relationship between events within and between organizations. Chapter 9 examines the linkages that bind organizations together and the communication strategies they can pursue in furtherance of their joint aims. They evolve a network of interdependent relationships within which conflict is always likely to arise and which have to be resolved by various communication strategies.

When communication takes place within a foreign organization or between personnel of organizations of different national origins the difficulties of encoding and decoding speech and behavioural patterns are multiplied. Chapter 10 sets out to provide frameworks which will assist people who have to communicate across national borders to interact in a positive and sensitive manner.

Chapter 11 puts in perspective the training implications of the previous chapters and seeks to derive a basis from which the skills identified can be built into a management development programme.

The chapters which follow are an attempt to throw light on the processes of communication within and between organizations and on the ways these two are interconnected. They underline the importance for managers at all levels of solving problems through, and arising from communication. It is through the use of appropriate oral and non-verbal skills within different contexts that this takes place. It is applicable in a host of situations. Even where cognitive skills take precedence, as when developing a strategy for an organization, these may count for little if the communicative competence does not exist to counter strong advocacy or political influence. The best plans, based on a sound strategy, might as well never have been put together if their implementation fails due to a lack of the communication skills on which it largely rests.

SUMMARY

1   Communication between individuals is transactional in that outcomes are interaction dependent; is instrumental in that they seek to achieve some control over situations by gaining compliance of the other party; is interpersonal insofar as interacting regularly with people permits the development of relationships which, in turn, facilitate better communication because of greater awareness of their interests and perceptions.

2   As people get to know each other better, so negotiated roles—which can be explicit or implicit—assume precedence. Such roles are a step towards enacted roles which are those people see as being appropriate for themselves. Individuality is recognized and behaviours become more predictable, making it easier to select an appropriate communication strategy.

3   The transactional model of communication is the most suitable for face-to-face encounters. In the model, both sender and receiver are simultaneously receiver and sender, encoding and decoding messages and providing feedback to each other.

4   Communication is defined as a dynamic, transactional, behaviour-affecting process in which people as senders and receivers intentionally code their behaviours to produce messages in order to induce particular attitudes or behaviours in others.

REFERENCES

Clarke, D. D. *Language and Action: A Structural Model of Behaviour*, Pergamon Press, Oxford (1983).
Daniels, T. D. and Spiker, B. K. *Perspectives on Organisational Communication*, William C. Brown, Dubuque, IA (1987).
Handy, C. *Understanding Organisations*, Penguin Books, Harmondsworth (1985).
Hofstede, G. *Culture's Consequences: International Differences in Work-related Values*, Sage, Beverly Hills, CA (1984).
Honey, P. *Solving People Problems*, McGraw-Hill, New York (1979).
Mangham, I. L. *Interactions and Interventions in Organisations*, John Wiley, New York (1978).
Mortensen, T. D. *Communication: The Study of Human Interaction*, McGraw-Hill, New York (1972).
Porter, R. E. and Samovar, L. A. Approaching intercultural communication. In Samovar, L. A. and Porter, R. E. (eds), *Intercultural Communication: A Reader*, Wadsworth, New York (1988).
Ruffner, M. and Burgoon, M. *Interpersonal Communication*, Holt Rinehart and Winston, New York (1981).

2
Communication and the Individual

People are exposed all the time to a flood of physical and social influences. The human organism is geared to complex and interdependent functions designed to interpret events and issues in ways that are consistent with past experience and one's physical and psychological state. It is the aim of information processing to provide a consistent perspective in tracing what happens when raw, sensory data are translated into conscious experience. It assumes that an act of communication results from the interaction of forces inside and outside the nervous systems of the communicating parties.

Communication in a social situation may result from what we expect to happen just as much as it does from what we find. However close the match between what we expect and what we find, the process of interpreting events within one's frame of reference is a central dimension of communication.

To make sense of how people communicate with each other it is first necessary to understand how they handle the messages, experiences and influences that daily bombard their senses. It is also useful to understand how people are predisposed to bring a particular viewpoint or 'frame of reference, 'mind set' or 'personal construct' to bear on their interpretation of events. These two aspects of what the individual brings to an interaction with one or more individuals are respectively termed *information processing* and *psychological orientation.**

HOW PEOPLE PROCESS INFORMATION

How an individual translates these sensory data into meaningful experience is a function of information processing. This aims to provide a perspective consistent with everything that has previously been experienced in creating this conscious interpretation.

---

*This chapter draws heavily on Mortensen (1972).

While everyone is unique in terms of his or her own experience, that experience has been energized by interaction with other individuals. People create in the process of reacting to others, but this is as much because of external forces as of their own personalities and predispositions.

In responding to cues from the environment, human information processing transfers sensory data into any psychological state that affects some change in uncertainty. Since potential sources of perceived change in uncertainty include most variations in the physical world and any changes in one's psychological state, the range of possibilities is wide. In accounting for man's capacity to generate and then control the use of rules or strategies in handling information, it is considered useful to know what happens to a cue or signal once it is received into the nervous system. Why is it, for example, that individuals react so differently to the same cue in the way they create meaning yet the cue and the circumstances remain stable over time? An answer seems to be that people exhibit different types of thinking and also think at different levels. The latter implies an ability to learn and generate different levels of meaning and identify possible alternatives in viewing the interrelationships of sensory data within particular sets of meanings. The former is accounted for by the fact that people have different *integration levels* of information processing.

Generally, low-level integration limits the ability of an individual to think in terms of complex interrelationships. The tendency is to avoid different or alternative meanings. Uncertainty is reduced, subtle distinctions ignored. People and events are categorized in black and white terms. The rule is simple and straightforward—and highly personalized. For example, if a person holds a fixed attitude towards salesmen and classifies them in a simple way, all salesmen will be integrated by a single rule of a judgemental nature: e.g. 'pushy,' 'talkative,' 'self-interested', 'slick'.

As integration moves to more complex levels, significant changes take place in information processing. There is a departure from the rigid either–or ways of thinking. The number of rules and interconnections formed among thought patterns increases and permits a wider range of perspectives that guide the transfer of the data to meaningful thought. With such higher levels of integration come greater flexibility and a need for more information prior to making decisions. As a result, the individual has the capacity to view a social situation in terms of the relationship of two points of view. This maximizes opportunity for the use of alternative rules and strategies and creates the possibility of abstract thinking.

Environmental Impact

According to Schroder *et al.* (1967), environmental complexity is a function of three factors, namely information load, diversity of information and the rate at which information registers on the sense organs. *Information overload* is the number of informational units to which an individual is exposed. The nervous system can only handle so much information at a time. Beyond a certain point necessary to prevent psychological atrophy, further increases in information load stimulate more complex processing activity until a level is reached where the system becomes overloaded, leading to confused thinking and inefficiency in information exchange with others. *Information diversity and rate* complements information load in that while load deals with the number of incoming signals, it does not take account of the diversity of sensory data or the rate at which they arrive.

The theory of information processing put forward by Schroder and his associates goes beyond environmental impact to embrace psychological factors insofar as they mediate the effect of external signals on the activity of the nervous system. This will be examined later in the chapter.

THE DECODING/ENCODING PROCESS

As noted above, information processing is a set of interrelated neurological and psychological functions. These fall into stages of activity known as *encoding* and *decoding*. Decoding embraces all those activities necessary to transfer raw sensory data into what we experience as meaningful information. Encoding is the opposite process, including all activities required to transform information into some behavioural response. The two processes occur simultaneously and continuously, and are major elements of the system by which individuals process information.

The encoding/decoding process can usefully be considered in terms of a chain of events which connect the nervous system in four stages, namely the acquisition of sensory data, the activity of central processing units, information storage and recall.

Acquisition of Sensory Data

Our senses are impinged upon principally by light waves and sound vibrations. Eyes and ears are the main sensors by which we build up our picture of the external world. The other senses are merely an adjunct to reinforce what we interpret via our ears and eyes.

The human receptor system is restricted, however, in the amount of physical energy it can track at any one time. The selective nature of the human receptor system is largely a result of:

1 The nature of *arousal thresholds*. Nerve cells known as *neurons* transmit a pulse of energy through the nerve when energized, but only when a

lower limit has been reached. For any signal to be sent, it must be stronger than the arousal threshold to transmit sensory data to the brain because there is also some impedance of energy transmission from one neuron to another due to the nature of some nerve fibres.

2 *Channel capacity.* There is a clear limit to the amount of information which the human organism can identify accurately. For example, in recognizing a series of numbers the span of absolute judgement lies somewhere in the region of seven items of information (Miller, 1968). According to Norman (1969), it appears that the acquisition of information occurs at two levels. As shown above, the first centres on the sensory system itself and the second on the way an individual's central storage system works. This operates so that attention to and selection of signals is further mediated by expectations, the grammatical meaning and the effect and relevance of incoming signals.

3 *Mechanisms for analysing stimuli.* There is growing evidence that people have powerful detectors for analysing the stimuli most relevant to their social and biological needs. While there is disagreement about how analysis takes place, what is not in dispute is that the sensory system does rearrange raw sensory data. The picture which emerges is of a sensory system in which information about incoming signals is abstracted and combined at increasingly higher levels of processing. When this analysis is complete, the work of the central nervous system takes over.

CENTRAL PROCESSING UNITS

A human being's sensory units carry out the task of transforming raw data into an economical form for transmission to the spinal cord and from there to the brain. The cortex of the brain is an elaborate storage system which can handle several streams of independent activity simultaneously.

The signals picked up by the sensors in the cerebral cortex are transferred as electrical impulses from the sense organs to the appropriate processing units. The central processing units of the brain are then involved in a cross-current of activities involving data gathering, sorting, decision making, monitoring, storing, recalling and integrating the messages into the synchronized activity we call conscious experience. This interplay between stimulus and the organism is the central processing stage of the encoding/decoding process.

Perceptual Organization

Even the simplest of experiences requires some means by which order is imposed on what would appear to be a collection of disconnected elements.

People attempt to order this experience in a way that has given rise to a number of rules or laws.

It has been found, for example, that they organize in ways that give priority to what is most noticeable. Also, they order in a manner that is simple or has regularity or symmetry. This reduces environmental stimuli to manageable proportions. Additionally, they strive for 'closure', that is, they cause incomplete forms or patterns to be 'complete' by filling in the gap or missing details.

When people speak to each other, they focus on sounds that stand out from the background of noise. Closely associated with this is the tendency to filter sound according to the rule of simplicity and closure. These 'laws' of perception act as a kind of psychological filter to enable the interacting parties to attend to what they consider the most strategic aspect of the interaction.

Effect of Attitudes

Generally, the central nervous system separates out the incoming signals on the basis of those feelings, needs, attitudes and motives that happen to be dominant at the moment. The existence of attitudes suggests a readiness to respond to signals in consistent ways. Typically, the state of readiness is grounded in a judgemental bias, either positive or negative, towards categories of ideas, events or issues. Attitudes enable each participant in a dialogue to respond to whatever features of an environment he or she views as pertinent while ignoring features perceived as having little import.

We all tend to perceive what we unconsciously want to. The more partisan the views, the greater will be the degree of *selective perception*. This is why there is always more than one view of a problem, why opposing supporters in a football crowd see a particular incident differently, and why personnel in different departments of an organization often interpret a problem in different ways.

All this does not mean that people will invariably fashion the significance of what they observe in a way that suits their own viewpoints. It has been observed that people are a little selective all the time and very selective sometimes.

Effect of Motivation

Research has shown that motivation is a notable contributory factor to the perception of vague or ambiguous stimuli that is partly or wholly determined by the individual's needs and drives of the moment. Generally, the stronger the emotional state, the more will motivational factors determine what is to be perceived and how much perceptual distortion occurs. Fear-related motives have also been shown to have a marked bearing on perception.

The effects of motives on unambiguous objects and events were seen to distort perceptions only when items or events at issue are not highly valued or when motivation is low. When a situation is clear cut, any possible distortion of perception gives way to a greater concern for ascertaining what is relevant to further information processing.

STORING INFORMATION

Memory cannot be recalled in a mechanistic way as on a computer data disc. The organization, storage and reconstruction of events by human beings are closely interlinked. We saw earlier in considering integration levels that individuals execute a sequence or hierarchy of tests to decide what gets stored and what type of organization is imposed on the stored information. Incoming signals, as we saw, attain meaning only in relation to their place at various levels of integration.

If this hierarchy of processing information can be assumed, then it is reasonable to assume also that the notion of hierarchy implies an underlying order. A pile of bricks does not indicate deliberately made plans, but a wall of bricks does. A plan is an overall process which controls the order in which a sequence of organization and storage is to be performed. Plans suggest a sequence of testing operations that determine which operating phase is appropriate for processing incoming signals. Some plans will be routine, as where signals at the lowest level are being processed. As circumstances become more complex, and signals are handled at the higher levels, people increasingly rely on strategies to solve problems. On the whole, strategies contribute to efficient problem solving.

Memory and Plans

The ancient art of *mnemonics* is an obvious example of plans and strategies in information storage.

Most complex social situations cannot, however, be reduced to simple, ready-made plans such as that of the colour code for resistors (see p. 20). It usually takes a person a considerable length of time to formulate the preliminary mapping strategy. Also, immediate memory tasks are not always of the same nature as the requirements for storing information over extended periods of time. It is therefore useful to separate out short-term memory problems from those of the long term.

Short-term Memory

In the immediate or short-term storage of information we recognize far more information than can be recalled only for an instant later. Only a fraction

---

Mnemonic

Before the advent of the microchip and the printed circuit board, electronic circuitry depended on the combining, together with other elements, of capacitors and resistors. The latter key values, which were indicated on the body of the resistor by means of a colour code, were vividly brought to the memory of trainee naval technicians by the following mnemonic:

Word	Colour	Value
bad	black	0
boys	brown	1
ravish	red	2
often	orange	3
young	yellow	4
girls	green	5
before	blue	6
virginity	violet	7
gets	grey	8
working	white	9

---

of a second is required for rapid loss of information. It is complicated, however, by the *rate* and *sequence* in which signals appear and by the strategies used in storing and recalling them.

The faster signals or images appear and impinge on the individual's sensors, the more likely one signal will obscure or distort the immediate memory of other items. Rate of presentation of signals also appears to have a direct bearing on the degree to which information fades in short-term memory. Sequence has also been studied but results of research are inconclusive.

Some people adopt characteristic strategies of reception and recall. Some maintain a consistent tracking of incoming signals at a rate which approximates the presentation. Others use a strategy of delaying the decoding of operations until more information in a sequence is available. The more redundant the incoming signals, the more apt a person is to employ some delaying strategy, focusing on groups and clusters of words. In short, creative alternative strategies in accordance with the demands of the situation and the psychological make-up of the respective parties fits well into the transactional view of the decoding/encoding process. This was mentioned in Chapter 1 and is addressed in more detail in the appropriate context in Chapter 3. We need now to understand the dynamics of the transformation of information once processed into an encoded response.

RECALL

The idea of a memory system is the direct link between the decoding and encoding stages of information processing. Occurring events can be explained as being the most readily available for immediate response, but analysis of how items of past experience issue from the memory is more difficult. The complexity of information recall is central to establishing what is available for encoding.

It seems that people rarely give an accurate report of what was seen. So great is the distortion of the original remembered material that people actually reconstruct it rather than remember it. The greater the time lapse since the recalled event, the more evident becomes the constructed aspect of the recollections. The organization that individuals seek to impose on stored material has a significant bearing on specific details of recall. This organization or schema is an active assembling of past reactions and experience. It is an enactment which places a premium on the constructive aspects of recalling complex events.

How far, we may ask, do these four stages of information processing account for what we experience in an act of communication? The answer appears to be that information processing is not sufficient of itself. It has to be seen in relation to the dynamic forces that create personal awareness. This will be addressed in the next section.

SUMMARY OF MAIN POINTS SO FAR

1 To understand how people communicate it is necessary to know how they handle the signals which impinge continuously on their senses.
2 How people translate these signals into meaningful experience consistent with their own expectations of an interaction is accounted for by the fact that people can process information at different levels. Low-level integration ignores subtle distinctions and classifies it in a simple way. Higher-level integration sees wider perspectives, provides for greater ambiguity and makes creative solutions possible. All parties to an interaction have to handle information overload and diversity.
3 Decoding is about how sensory data are translated into meaningful information. Encoding is all those activities which create a behavioural response. The encoding/decoding process can be regarded as a series of events connecting the nervous system in four stages. These are acquisition of data, central processing, information storage and recall.
4 Central processing is the interplay between message or stimulus and the organism. It is characterized by the need of people to impose order on signals by giving priority to what for them is salient, at the same time

eliminating what is perceived as unimportant. Attitudes reinforce this and encourage selective perception.

5 People rely on strategies to store received signals. Some track signals as they come in, others delay until more relevant information is at hand and seem to rely on groups and clusters of words.

6 In recalling information, individuals reconstruct rather remember, so great is the distortion of the original remembered material. The longer the information is stored, the greater the constructive aspects of recalling complex events.

PSYCHOLOGY AND
THE COMMUNICATING INDIVIDUAL

The predispositions or 'frames of reference', mentioned earlier, which people bring to any interaction mean that they communicate as much from what they expect to happen as from what is found out or established. The individual ever seeks to make sense according to these frames of reference. These are developed from early childhood through interpersonal contacts which result in learning to approach every communication situation with characteristic feelings of trust or suspicion, openness or defensiveness, commitment or detachment, co-operativeness or competitiveness. Given the breadth of learning situations and the random events to which we are all exposed, it is not surprising that we try to survive in unique and distinctive ways.

The elements of consciousness whereby a person attempts to impose a frame of reference are the cumulative impact of forces that work to make particular sense out of social encounters and unfolding events. People may have deeply religious upbringings and bring to their dialogue with others the particular values (say, of right and wrong) which they have embraced and which might conflict with those of the other parties to the interaction, who may have been brought up to esteem more materialistic values. They may have been influenced by the culture of the organizations or those parts of the organization in which they work or have worked.

It has been cogently argued that people carry mental programmes that are developed in institutions and that these form the basis of national culture. These programmes affect not only individual thought but the behaviour of people in institutions in which they work and play. People working as public servants or as members of private organizations are affected in their behaviour along four universal dimensions of 'power distance', 'uncertainty avoidance', 'individualism' and 'masculinity' (Hofstede, 1984). Power distance is concerned with the extent to which members of a society accept that power in institutions is distributed unequally. Uncertainty avoidance is the degree to which members of a society feel uncomfortable with uncertainty and ambiguity. Individualism reflects the ways in which people live and work together, either in a loosely knit framework where individuals care for themselves and immediate family or in one where the community is the primary concern. Masculinity measures how both sexes in a society tend to embrace goals more popular among men or women. These factors interact with, and affect, the predispositions of individuals entering a communication interaction.

Within this general framework, people can have expectations or mind sets which are largely determined by the way they become accustomed to view issues in their place of work. They construct their own social reality and yet regard it as something external to themselves (see Chapter 7 for a more detailed examination of this phenomenon). In the process they come to share assumptions which bring meaning to their everyday encounters. Different organizations develop different rationalities or logics. In order to function as a group, either as a total organization or as a separate part of it, the individuals who come together must establish a system of communication that allows an acceptable interpretation of what is going on. Because people cannot stand too much uncertainty, categories of meaning which filter out what is considered unimportant, while focusing on what is important, become a major means of reducing uncertainty. Such organizational factors bring to the interaction situation a rich diversity of influences which make the communication of meaning something that goes far beyond the words used, whether plain or fancy.

While these aspects are treated in more detail in Chapters 6–8, it is necessary to mention them here because they are such a significant factor in how people communicate.

Self-awareness

All of us as individuals have an awareness of and towards self which can occur with or without the presence of others. There is an implication in this of some sort of inner dialogue which is mirrored in such phrases as 'consoling herself', 'making New Year resolutions' or 'setting one's goals'.

While the capacity to act towards oneself does not require the presence of another person, the proactive nature of self is most strongly expressed in all interpersonal contact. It is through this contact with others that people learn to think of themselves from the viewpoint of others. This is encapsulated in the phrase of Mead (1934)—'taking the role of the other'.

Not only does communication heighten one's self-awareness, it also serves to guide future behaviour. A change in self-awareness can be said to imply that some kind of social exchange has altered the way people think of themselves. If, for example, a bright recruit to an organization has a problem of self-confidence, one of the management development ploys is to create situations in which, in interaction with others, he proves to himself that he is actually capable of making good decisions and exhibiting traits of leadership in the situations so created.

It is possible to integrate and conceptualize the dynamics of self-oriented psychological states in terms of a single working proposition (Mortensen, 1972): *the self-directed orientations of people engaged in communication tend to make each interactant unique, integrated, internally consistent and active.*

The *uniqueness* of individuals stems from the ways in which we differ—in terms of the type of communication we experience, of roles we play out while engaging in communication, of what we remember and expect, of the sense of risk and trust we feel and of the extent of the sensitivity we show to others. It is through these interactions that we adopt, learn and define or redefine our unique sense of self. A large number of dialogue situations can arise, therefore, in which much of the meaning we construct must remain within the private domain of our inner thoughts.

The unique feelings, attitudes and expectations do not just fly around willy-nilly within the individual's consciousness. People have characteristic ways of organizing these intermittent and diverse impressions of self into meaningful patterns. This *integration* into a stable sense of self has important consequences for communication. Some people have a more stable and more fully integrated sense of self than others. They are better able to become orientated to problems outside of themselves and are more likely to attain an increased measure of autonomy, a freshness of perspective, more creativity and a greater ability to resist pressures to conform (Maslow, 1954). Such people are also less likely to be afraid of behaving co-operatively as a way of achieving preferred communication outcomes, and they show less hostility to, as well as a greater tolerance of, uncertainty. People who have a strong concept of self are not exposed to the defensiveness and denial that prevent people from hearing others. They are thus in a position to find common ground with others because they have the ability to see others' values and perceptions with empathy. Those with a strong self concept have the capacity to become good communicators.

The idea of *consistency* is useful in explaining how notions of self are organized along lines that are free of ambiguity and inconsistency. According to various writers, it appears that nature abhors inconsistency. The more information is incompatible with consistency, the greater is the pressure to resolve inner conflict. The tendency to be self-consistent constrains communication. People often avoid situations where marked inconsistencies with one's psychological orientation are most likely to happen. The concept of cognitive dissonance (Festinger, 1957) supports the idea that, given a choice, people tend to avoid information inconsistent with their attitudes. A further instance of the consistency principle is illustrated when people elect to interact in the main with those they perceive to be most like themselves. When avoidance is not a viable alternative, they tend to adopt some form of perceptual distortion of incompatible information. Discounting the material or selective forgetting are the simplest ways in which this is done.

There is considerable pressure exerted on this self-oriented stability by the accelerating rate of change and the wider variety of interpersonal relationships to which one is exposed. People have a vested interest in not giving up or changing radically their sense of self. The problem to which they are exposed in interacting with others is how to make an *active* effort in constructing a significance that is personally acceptable. People have the capacity to change perceptions and overt behaviour within this framework.

The concept of self assists in defining who we are, and is the central mechanism the humanism organism uses to interpret the actions of others. In so doing, the individual sense of self is constantly taking on new shape and immediacy.

Awareness of Others

As soon as we move to communicating fully with others we are making a shift from the comfort of self-preoccupation to a frame of reference that embraces the experience and perceptions of others. One might expect a sense of mutuality in this situation. Yet this mutuality is, at best, only uneven and sporadic. Most interpersonal contacts are affected by what individuals see as the risk of self-disclosure. A focus on the behaviour of others serves to remind us of what they say we are and are not—the self-delusions, misguided commitments and outright failures we would rather not think about.

As a result, individuals are reluctant to disclose too much about themselves at any one time due to perceived threats to one's status, querying of motives and a variety of other psychological questioning. However, social bonds can grow over time.

Nevertheless, the human organism has the capacity to interact with others in very profound ways, despite the imperfections and risks noted above. How, then, do individual communicators maintain a stable and integrated frame of reference in face of the words, actions and perceptions of those others who comprise the stuff of everyday experience?

Source Credibility

Source credibility is a concept that is a loose collection of factors which, added together, give a total impression of a source. For example, the manner in which persons carry themselves, the words they use and the way they put them together and articulate them, the social distance they maintain or the difficulties they present in terms of their approach, the warmth or otherwise of their tone, all influence the images of communicators. Some people sound highly credible or conduct themselves in a way that makes them look credible. People who sound unsure of what they are saying are often deemed not to be authoritative. Impressions of authority are helped by certain kinds of statements. Sometimes when people are given objective proof that a speaker is a gifted professional they still tend to allow such features as a 'low-class' accent or a black skin to colour their impressions of authoritativeness.

Various studies have shown authoritativeness and trustworthiness to be two factors which form the basis of credibility. A person rated highly on authoritativeness would be viewed as reliable, informed, expert and intelligent. The opposite would apply when the rating is low. Trustworthiness is unconnected with authoritativeness and is concerned with being perceived as honest, friendly, sincere, etc. A person rated highly on trustworthiness may score low on authoritativeness and vice versa.

Factors other than authoritativeness and trustworthiness contribute to perceptions of credibility. Dynamism, extroversion, skill and openness have all been reported as significant variables together to hear and understand the other side of an argument.

Source Credibility and Attitude Change

Over the years studies have indicated that a credible source is more persuasive than one which is not. Yet there is no evidence of a linear relationship between persuasive influence and degree of credibility.

When the views of a speaker are at variance with those of a person or persons listening we have reason to expect that any increase in credibility will yield a proportionate gain in attitude change on the part of the listener(s). A person high in credibility in one situation may fare less well in another. An academic researcher may unearth new perspectives in, and potentially good solutions to, a particular range of industrial problems. He or she may convince academic colleagues by the quality of methodology and the degree by which the frontiers of knowledge have been pushed back. Industrialists may not be so easily persuaded by the academic, whereas if the work is achieved by only one industrialist, his or her industrial peers are the more likely to be convinced.

The Limits to Credibility

Earlier writers have suggested that impressions of credibility were formed in a stable and fixed way. People were either credible with individuals or with particular groups or they were not. This concept of credibility has today been discredited, and new models now take account of the dynamic effects of time and situation on impressions of credibility. Our judgements, even after years of maintaining a given impression of someone, are in fact subject to considerable and sudden change.

When we enter a potential relationship with someone we use all available information to form personal impressions. In doing this, we even use data which have not been received in the course of the social exchange. The anticipation of contact is enough to create some vague, general impression of a person regarding what he or she will be like and how he or she will react to us. One set of expectations could be associated with people we might meet in our places of work and another quite different set with fellow members at the golf club. When we know or assume the views of an expected acquaintance, the urge to personalize is even stronger.

For these reasons, impressions of credibility are as much a function of subjective expectations as is the meaning hearers attribute to the speech behaviour of a given source, as we shall see in Chapter 3. As soon as two people meet in a communication situation a torrent of personal cues pours in for interpretation. What would otherwise be seen to be neutral in emotive terms becomes personalized. Evaluative judgements are made on the basis of manner, interest and expectations together with signals taken from the environment such as seating arrangements, how much is at stake and whether some sort of policy exists which will act as a constraint.

In the majority of situations hearers will not make judgements immediately but will wait for further indications. If the speaker's presentation is too hesitant, the image hearers have of him may have to be revised, particularly if the presentation becomes progressively more halting. If the speaker's presentation is too fluent, he is likely to be seen in the USA as insincere. Sincerity, certainly in the European view, is the norm in the USA, and anything perceived to be too 'smooth', as in situations where the speaker sounds as if he were using an autocue, gives an impression of insincerity. Generally, only a few minutes of speaking time are required to alter impressions of a given source.

How far situation and time factors limit the effect of credibility varies from person to person. In predicting the effects of credibility it is useful to know just how sensitive hearers are to the credibility of a speaker. People who are strongly authoritarian appear to be particularly sensitive to who is talking and less attentive to what is being said. Those who are not particularly authoritarian tend to perceive messages irrespective of who the source is.

Credibility and Interpersonal Interaction

So far, we have seen that credibility has been useful in providing us with general impressions which the parties to an interaction maintain in relation to each other. Even the knowledge that people form impressions of credibility on the basis of authoritativeness and trustworthiness and sometimes along other lines such as dynamism, extroversion and openness merely refines the general description. Usually, the factors commonly associated with credibility may not always be important determinants of impressions maintained towards other interacting parties. Such factors operate only within the wider context of interpersonal orientation.

Imagine a situation in which two researchers have worked together on a project for two years and have just seen it through to a successful conclusion. They are having an informal meeting over a drink to discuss the form of an article on their research for a professional journal. Their conversation is not likely to depend on their impressions of each other's expertise or dynamism. In such circumstances a sense of mutual trust, feelings of a common bond and confidence in each other's declared intentions are the factors most likely to apply.

In another situation the significant factor may simply be the amount of social power which a given person can exert over others. Examples might include commercial negotiations between buying and selling companies, labour/management bargaining, a negotiation between a student protest group and university authorities or an attempt by an employee to talk his boss into giving him the post left vacant by his immediate superior's departure to another firm. One's perception can be raised by such a wide variety of factors that it is more appropriate to dwell on trust and power as being representative of the wider influences at work in face-to-face encounters.

Trust

The question of trust goes well beyond impressions of a person's friendliness, reliability, amiability and so on. It is not, as was thought at one time, something that is defined solely by one-sided, internalized impressions of others. Rather, it is an orientation that grows out of a reciprocal pattern of interrelationships. What is internalized is the result of orientations towards oneself and towards another, including expectations built up over a series of interactions and norms of how to behave towards one another (Deutsch, 1960). Violations of trust built up through these expectations in the form of a perceived attack after co-operative sessions resulted in a sharp decrease in the outcomes which both participants sought (Hornstein and Deutsch, 1968).

When the interacting persons have not previously met they must take certain actions that relate to the type and sequence of choices each makes to the reactions of the other. If neither is willing to exercise limited choices involving some degree of risk or personal loss, a trusting relationship is unlikely to be forthcoming. If the response is rejection, the relationship freezes at that point, and is either terminated or testing begins again. As Schein (1981) neatly put it:

> One way in which a relationship becomes more intimate is through successive minimal self-revelations which constitute interpersonal tests of acceptance. 'If you accept this much of me, then perhaps I can risk revealing a bit more about myself.' Total openness may be safe and creatively productive when acceptance is guaranteed. It can be highly dangerous when goals are not compatible and acceptance is therefore not guaranteed at all.

Development of trust is indeed an incremental process resting on the actions and reactions of the parties.

The impressions which interacting parties form in respect of each other are also tied to judgements they make regarding the similarity of their stands on an issue. As a rule, people are more willing to interact with those others whom they expect to exhibit a manner and attitude like their own. The research literature is replete with communicative situations in which perceptions of similarity influence the course of verbal exchange. However, studies in similarities between two individuals have either not shown a meaningful relationship between similarity and communicative effectiveness or have revealed only a low correlation. Similarity is therefore best considered as an indicator only affecting trust, not an exacting determinant of its creation.

Power

In interpersonal relations power has a considerable bearing on the level of participation and the flow of verbal exchange that takes place between the parties. It can decide who will talk, how much conversation they will make and what they will talk about. Those people who enjoy a high measure of social power generally direct comments to others, initiate directives and make known decisions. They tend to have a high sense of self-esteem and demonstrate willingness to accept messages from their peers. Low-power individuals recognize the ability of those in a higher position to make them do what otherwise they may not. They tend to perceive power figures in negative terms and seek to avoid contact with them. Low power is often associated with low motivation, aggression and ineffectual work. Even in organizations characterized by a strong supportive climate, prolonged exposure to coercive power figures often results in distrust and hostility. The concept of social power is examined more closely in Chapter 6. No more need be said at this stage.

Interpersonal Orientation

In any social encounter there is a blurring of the distinction between self and the external world. Even the simplest conversational exchange involves a mixture of the personal and the interpersonal that blends into the broader frame of conscious experience. The greater this interpersonal communication, the greater is the likelihood that participants' psychological orientations are interdependent. Beyond this, social science does not yet go, except to suggest that the growing research on involvement may well provide an indication of the forces which determine this orientation.

We can say, in communication terms, that the more interaction bears on matters which the participants find highly involving, the more beliefs of personal relevance function as a determinant of their interpersonal orientation. Personal relevance includes basic 'truths' about physical reality, or about social reality and the individual's perception as to what constitutes this; and about the nature of self. By knowing how central a discussion issue is to a participant, the greater the probability of predicting the outcome of an inter-action. The more involving the interaction is, the greater the possibility that the sense of personal involvement and commitment will become the central determinant of other facets of the encounter. A high personal involvement functions as the basis on which people judge all other aspects of a social situation. It therefore affects resistance to change, impression of credibility and a multiplicity of other factors affecting interaction outcomes.

The variables comprising our psychological orientation together present a complex picture. Despite this, people apparently have a vested interest in seeing that everything fits together. Where it does not, pressure is exerted to restore order to the interaction of self and the world outside.

Temperament and Communication

A useful framework exists for being more thoughtful in communication and conflict situations. This is the Myers–Briggs Psychological Type. Type theory has become widely used in various fields. According to the theory as interpreted all persons develop preferences which determine their personalities. The authors develop the theory around a four-part framework. There are eight possible preferences on four separate bi-polar scales.

Extraversion .... Introversion
Sensing .... Intuition
Thinking .... Feeling
Judgement .... Perception

A person's type is a combination of four of the initial letters of the words on the bi-polar scales. These combinations represent people's preferences. It has been related to negotiation by Barkai (1989) but applies equally to communicators seeking to achieve their instrumental purposes. These 'temperaments' go a long way to explaining basic differences in personality style. Communication problem solving can be assisted by paying heed to what other people recognize as important and what motivates and influences them.

SUMMARY OF MAIN POINTS OF
THE PSYCHOLOGY OF COMMUNICATION

1 People are predisposed to think in a particular way which has been conditioned by family, schools and organizations but has also been affected by the individual's unique experience. All these, taken together, constitute a person's frame of reference.

2 It is through interacting with others that we define our concept of self. These interactions are unique communication experiences which are integrated into meaningful patterns or a stable sense of self. People dislike inconsistency and ambiguity and act to construct a significance that is personally acceptable.

3 Despite the perceived risks of self-disclosure, and the words and actions of interacting others, people are helped in maintaining a stable frame of reference by relying on source credibility. Perception of credibility is principally created by authoritativeness and trustworthiness.

4 Credibility varies with the situations in which individuals find themselves and can vary over time, even over a very short span. Because individuals personalize data about others, impressions of credibility are mediated by subjective expectations, interpersonal orientation and social power.

5 Trust is an incremental process which depends on interacting parties gradually revealing more about themselves. Total openness is only safe when acceptance by the other party is guaranteed. It is dangerous when goals are incompatible and acceptance is in no way guaranteed.

REFERENCES

Barkai, J. Psychological types and negotiations. Conflicts and solutions as suggested by the Myers–Briggs classification, working draft, University of Hawaii, November 1989.

Deutsch, M. Trust, trustworthiness and the F Scale. *Journal of Abnormal and Social Psychology*, **61** (1960).

Festinger, L. *A Theory of Cognitive Dissonance*, Row Peterson, Evanston, Ill (1957).

Hofstede, G. *Culture's Consequences: International Differences in Work-related Values*, Sage, Beverly Hills, CA (1984).

Hornstein, H. A. and Deutsch, M. Tendencies to compete and to attack as a function of inspection, incentive and available alternatives. *Journal of Personality and Social Psychology*, **4** (1968).

Maslow, A. H. *Motivation and Personality*, Harper and Row, New York (1954).

Mead, G. H. *Mind, Self and Society,* University of Chicago, Chicago, Ill (1934).

Miller, G. A. The magical number seven, plus or minus two: some limits on our capacity to process information. In Miller, G. A., *The Psychology of Communication,* Penguin Books, Harmondsworth (1968).

Mortensen, C. D. *Communication: The Study of Human Interaction,* McGraw-Hill, New York (1972).

Norman, D. *Introduction to Human Information Processing,* John Wiley, New York (1969).

Schroder, H. M., Driver, M. J. and Streufert, S. *Human Information Systems,* Holt Rinehart and Winston, New York (1967).

3
People in Communication

When people take part in normal conversation, words have little meaning of themselves in that their dialogue has a host of predispositions and perceptions through which they interpret what has been said. If we wish to communicate well, we have to know these predispositions and perceptions so that we can couch our messages in a way which addresses them.

Communication is a simultaneous process of, on the one hand, sending messages and noting the reception of them and, on the other, of receiving messages and noting the intent which the messages convey. The exchange is made up of verbal and non-verbal elements which are wide and varied, and are mediated by the inferences which people often confuse with fact but which are an inevitable and necessary part of the process.

LANGUAGE AND COMMUNICATION

That meaning lies in people and not in words and grammar is nicely illustrated in a story recounted by the late Dominic Behan of how his poet-uncle tried to correct his nephews' and nieces' English by fable.

Behan's uncle was wont to relate the tale of Father Brogan comforting Cockney Cohen just before his execution: 'Tomorrow, my son, you will be eternally grateful for the happenings of these last few days. Thank God you will soon be with your Creator.'

Cockney was not actually pushing to jump the queue for the hereafter. Instead, the concentrated mind complained 'But temorra fauvver, I'm goin' ter be 'ung'.

And Father Brogan, hiding his contempt for Mr Cohen's ignorance, sent the condemned man to his Maker with a compassionate ' "hanged", my son'.

It is a common belief instilled in schools and reinforced in work and voluntary organizations that meaning is contained in words, the accuracy of which can always be found by reference to a good dictionary. Nothing could be further from the truth. The language we use and the non-verbal language

33

inevitably associated with it in giving information and conveying meaning can be easily misunderstood. We bring to our interactions certain filters which colour our perceptions, including our experience of people and organizations, our values and other factors. So the more we know of the process of communication and the more skilled we become in its practice, the less likely we are to misunderstand or be misunderstood.

Sometimes it is quite clear what is meaningful to an individual and what his interests and motivations are. A good communicator can turn this to advantage by couching language in a way that gives it meaning in terms of those interests and motivations.

Sandy Gall of ITN News, London, was one of the foreign press corps who stayed on in Saigon after the fall of the South Vietnamese capital and the withdrawal of the American forces. He had eight hours of film recording the last days, including the arrival of the Viet Cong carrying their rice and rockets, the beaten South Vietnamese stripping off their uniforms and using their helmets to fill up the tanks of stolen cars, refugees fighting to get on a helicopter that would never come and a young Communist commissar in black pyjamas drilling the youth, making them march on the spot and chant Communist slogans.

The North Vietnam authorities had severed all communications with the outside world. Official channels could do nothing to assist despite the combined appeals of the foreign press correspondents. Gall's principal concern was to get his film home while it was still 'hot' news. At a party thrown by the victors to which the overseas press were invited, Gall politely approached the North Vietnamese commanding general and addressed him.

'General,' he said in French, 'I'm Sandy Gall of Independent Television News, London. We correspondents have a problem. We have historic film of your arrival in Saigon. This is a great victory for you and the world waits to see it. But, since we cannot get the film out, no one has actually seen the pictures of your triumph. Can you help us with a plane so that we can fly the film out?' After discussion with an official in Vietnamese he replied, also in French, 'We shall try to get you a plane'. And so it transpired.

(Adapted from Sandy Gall, *Don't Worry about the Money Now*, Hamish Hamilton, 1983. Used with the permission of Sandy Gall Enterprises Ltd)

Spoken Behaviour

Verbal behaviour includes speaking and writing in the code of a language system. The emphasis here will be on the spoken component of that verbal behaviour. It includes these expressions which any group of people commonly use and which come to represent rules for that particular group. When a cost accountant says that 'sales will have to generate a production sufficiently high to reduce unit costs to a competitive level by recovering the fixed costs over at least 90% of capacity' a layman may not understand its full import. It will, however, make perfect sense to another cost accountant or business executive acquainted with the use of such terms, who uses the same kind of language.

All the words used in a language are *symbols*. According to Pollio (1974), a symbol is representational, freely created and culturally transmitted. It is representational to the extent that it stands for something else. Words are symbols which provide labels for objects, actions, experiences and ideas. A word represents an object by providing a link to the notion of that object. It has been reported by Koch and Deetz (1981) that language systems in organizations reveal 'root metaphors' which members use to make sense of their experiences. For example, members might think of their organization as being geared to the needs of its customers (service metaphor) or as a winning team (sport metaphor). Language in relation to metaphor will be explored further in Chapter 7.

Symbols are freely created in that the relationship between them and the objects they represent arise out of the way in which people using a particular language choose the actual symbols. In the 1990s publishers say 'Let's have your hard disc' rather than 'Let's have your manuscript'. The term is invested with a meaning that did not exist even 10 years ago. Similarly, a word like 'twin-deck', which has a special meaning today in relation to stereo systems, might have symbolized in an earlier era the notion of a revolutionary form of sea-going vessel.

When we say symbols are culturally transmitted we mean that these symbols are passed on over time. Sometimes they may be created or changed, pushed by the pressure of new technologies or ideas, or fall into disuse. Generally, however, much of language and the symbols it bears persists through cultural transmission. The symbols which the words represent and the language rules associated with them give a certain order to the world into which we are born. This is equally true whether we talk about interacting with other people in other lands (which is the basis of cross-cultural studies) or people in other organizations or other parts of the same organization to which the cross-cultural approach could equally apply. Because of its importance as a basis for predicting the behaviour of others and adopting appropriate message strategies for communicating effectively with these others, we shall be looking at this more closely in Chapter 5.

Language and Gender Differences

Verbal behaviour towards women in what, in organizational terms, is a male-dominated world creates for women a dilemma in which their professionalism and their femininity are in conflict. If they respond with protest to emphasis by their male colleagues on their femininity ('Give us

---

The contention is made that women make the conversational effort but men determine what is talked about. Throughout the following transcript, male conversation is encouraged at the expense of the female.

Female: Did he have the papers ready for you?
Male: Mmm.
Female: And were they all right . . . was anything missing?
Male: Not that I could see.
Female: That must have been a relief anyway . . . I suppose everything went well after that?
Male: Almost.
Female: Oh, was there something else?
Male: Yes, actually.
Female: It wasn't X . . . was it? He didn't forget again?
Male: I'd say he did.
Female: He really is irresponsible, you know. He will . . .
Male: I'll do something about it. It was the last straw today. How often does that make it this week?

(From Spender, 1980, quoted by Marshall, 1984)

---

the woman's view on this, Dorothy') they are perceived as over-reacting; if they accept the focus on gender, they compound the diminution of their professionalism.

The point has been made that women's support provides an active endorsement of male supremacy in which women are required to be seen willingly to support male control. This is apparently necessary for a smooth operation of activities. It is claimed that women comply with male dominance because they are so effectively socialized into male values through cultural mechanisms which include language that they are involuntary victims of a social system which constantly devalues them (Marshall, 1984). In seeking a solution Marshall comes to the conclusion that, in order to revitalize our modes of being or generate new life strategies, men will have to mitigate agency (control, independence, action, change resistance, achievement) with communion (interdependence, co-operation, being, tolerance, trust, acceptance of change). The path ahead for women, she concludes, lies in enhancing communion with agency. Education and training should be to this end.

Spoken Language and Ambiguity

Ambiguity is an aspect of rhetoric and will be put in the context of the management of meaning in Chapter 5. It is a common problem in society as well as in organizations. Ambiguity arises from the use of abstract terms, lack of specific detail and the confusing use of qualifying and modifying phrases. It appears to be used when issues arise for whatever reason between people or groups, or tasks have to be performed and resolution and/or positive outcomes are sought.

Consider, for example, a situation in which a superior in an organization is requested by a subordinate for advice with regard to an issue which, the superior believes, is part of the work the subordinate is required to perform as laid down in the job description. Let us say it is concerned with how the subordinate should act in relation to 'confidential payments' to an intermediary who, according to the company's agent in the territory concerned for which the subordinate is responsible, can help to obtain a major contract. In return for the intermediary's influence, a substantial payment has to be made. In the circumstances, the superior might say something like 'We have to remember that we have legal responsibility to do our best for our shareholders consistent with a policy in which we are seen to be acting above board'. This advice may be proffered by the superior either as a form of staff development whereby the subordinate is encouraged to think through the problem on the basis of the cardinal principles or as a means of avoiding the direct order which might rebound on the superior at a later date if the payment were made public. If the manager responsible for the territory then goes out and arranges for price and agent's commission to be increased to enable the agent to 'cover his high expenses in pursuing the order', and so help him to make the special payment as if it were his own money he was spending, then *strategic ambiguity* has been successfully applied.

According to Eisenberg (1984) such ambiguity helps to promote cohesion by highlighting the agreement of members of an organization on abstract general ideas, in this case the principles of the legal responsibilities to shareholders and the policy of the company not to involve itself in payments which, if divulged, might be interpreted by stakeholders as doubtful. At the same time, it allows members to apply their own values in the interpretation of the principles, because as a group they might otherwise find themselves in disagreement over specific circumstances.

There is another kind of ambiguity which arises in day-to-day situations. This is the ambiguity that exists between different groups and between different levels in an organization. A sales manager may see the purchase of an expensive new piece of labour-saving capital equipment as the source of opportunities in that it will bring prices down to a more competitive level; the production manager may see it as a means to increase his department's productivity; the financial controller may see it as the price of greater profitability and long-term viability; and the personnel manager may see it as an industrial relations time bomb. Furthermore, the staff of these company officers are likely to share their seniors' viewpoints for the reason that the special language which evolves in groups reinforces and nurtures them. This is sometimes referred to as a *group-restricted code*. Groups and organizations often try to ensure that shared meaning will occur by adopting such a code. To people outside the particular group it can be quite confusing. The interpretation of a message of a proposed purchase is clear only so far as a symbol or group of words constituting a message has the same meaning for different people, which is patently not so in our example. Whether ambiguity is inherent in the nature of a situation (as in the proposed purchase of new equipment) or a deliberate strategy (as in the case of a superior responding to his or her subordinate), communicators have to learn to handle it.

Spoken Language and Differences in Meaning

The Bi-polar Trap

As we all know, situations are rarely black and white. Reality is to be found in some shade of grey. Yet so much do we rely on bi-polar terms that force us to choose between extremes that the very act of so doing precludes other alternatives that may lie between.

Who has not heard of the 'disinterested' student who, categorized as lazy, nevertheless demonstrated considerable industriousness when allowed to use his or her own initiative? The trouble is that we tend to push people into either/or categories. Consider the following questions:

'Is your boss a good or bad leader?'
'Is it simple or complex?'
'Is he disciplined or emotional?'
'Are they hawks or doves?'

The appropriate reply to these would be very much like that of the university professor who, when asked how his wife was, replied 'In relation to what?' It is usually less simplistic and more accurate to think in terms of degrees or comparisons. Our credibility can be damaged if we are identified by listeners as users of oversimplified language structures.

Softening the Impact

Officials announcing increased charges, public relations staff of drug or chemical manufacturers reacting to accusations of side effects or environmental pollution, accountants seeking to explain away to shareholders a poor dividend for the year, principals of educational institutions defending a higher than usual failure rate, striking transport workers seeking to dignify their behaviour, all endeavour to create a less objectionable association in the minds of those affected by the use of euphemism. Some examples follow:

Euphemism	*Real meaning*
Creative accounting	Cooking the books
Adjusting the price	Putting the price up
Adverse trading conditions	Failure to forecast
The experiment was successful but the animals died	We learned what not to do
The risk of contamination is minimal	People can sometimes be infected
The negative swing on an increasingly successful cycle	The results were poor
Industrial action	Industrial inaction

Creating Mental Images

Figures of speech such as simile and metaphor are often used to give added effect to a statement. *Simile* can be used to create effect by drawing a striking comparison with something else, as in:

'As welcome as a porcupine in a balloon factory.'
'The new additive is about as much use as the "p" in "pneumonia".'
'Her parting was like the towpath at Henley on the day after the Boat Race.'
'He looks as intense as a short-sighted man reading an auto-cue'.

We can all learn much from politicians' attempts to lessen the impact of proposed unpopular measures.

People who were not even born in the 1930s have heard about pre-war Britons being refused medical help until they had proved their poverty—the means test man searching their homes in case they had held on to grandmother's hand-carved chiffonier.

When the former Chancellor of the Exchequer Nigel Lawson said at a briefing of journalists that pensioners' income was rising much faster than the average wage, he also implied that those less well off—'a tiny minority'—should be 'targeted'. The journalists assumed this statement was to some point and interpreted it as means testing pensioners to give extra benefits to some at the expense of others.

Lawson claimed he was misinterpreted and the furore lasted for weeks. On this occasion, even the avoidance of the evocative words did not prevent ensuing uproar.

Good simile is less striking than good *metaphor*. This is a kind of explosion of the imagination. When Hamlet tells Rosencrantz and Guildenstern that they live in the middle of Fortune's favour, he does not mean that the two men inhabit the private parts of some mythological woman. What he does is to set the image of this woman against that of the two courtiers as useless ornaments, and the meeting creates a new image in our minds—that of an obscene and fairly pitiable servility. It could be said that the making of a metaphor releases new energy in our imagination, as when two particles are made to collide with each other in a nuclear fusion experiment.

Here are some examples of the use of metaphor heard at some time by one or other of the authors:

'It may be a dirty ball game, but it's the only game in town.'
'Your ideas were hellish in concept and execrable in execution.'
'He is a Shiite in argument.'
'Nail your scrotum to the chair.'
'The greatest love story since Paris put the heartlock on Helen of Troy'.

Sharing Mental Images

Concepts are continually emerging in language, none more so than in the areas of management and systems behaviour. Even educated people, who normally have a larger stock of concepts with which to express themselves than those less well educated, may not have available to them some of these emerging concepts. Such concepts become encapsulated in crisp expressions which people operating in specific areas of work are expected to know and understand in the normal course of events. Failure to convey such a familiarity makes people less easy to communicate with and more likely to be perceived as inadequate for the jobs they are doing.

A selection of such concepts and their linguistic expression have been given us by de Bono (1979) to assist people to share these concepts and gain greater acceptability among associates by expressing a relatively complex idea that is captured in a single condensed expression. The idea of 'trade-off', for example, implies that you may want two different things. You may wish to have a house near your work and yet you may want a large house. If you live in a town, you may not be able to realize both your wants. You may have to trade off one against the other, giving up your nearness to work in order to get the house you are looking for. The concept can be explained in a roundabout way, but the term 'trade-off' provides a simple means of describing the whole situation.

Spoken Language and Speech Sounds

The meaning of a spoken expression often depends on the way in which it is articulated. Rhythm, intonation, pitch, stress and rate of speech are all factors which mediate what is said to give a particular meaning to a phrase or sentence. Take, for example, the statement

'I didn't say he stole it.'

The meaning taken from the statement will depend on the word on which the stress falls.

Emphasis	*Meaning*
I didn't say he stole it	'Please, I wasn't the one who said it'
I *didn't* say he stole it	'I deny absolutely having said it'
I didn't *say* he stole it	'I may have thought it but it isn't what I said'
I didn't say *he* stole it	'Perhaps he didn't but somebody did'
I didn't say he *stole* it	'But he has otherwise managed to obtain it'
I didn't say he stole *it*	'But other things have disappeared'

As can be seen, there is a range of meanings which can be imputed to the statement depending on which word is stressed.

The name given to these factors related to the way in which words are spoken is *paralanguage*, which provides cues to meaning in various ways. Interpersonal attitudes and feelings are indicated primarily by paralanguage. It regulates dialogue in that a pause can signal the end of a particular line of thought or indicate that another person can take a turn at speaking. The difference between a statement and a question can sometimes only be detected through paralanguage, as in the sentences 'This is the way you're going to do it' and 'This is the way you're going to do it?' It is at the heart of dialect and accent, and various studies have shown that, for example, perceptions of an individual's competence can be shaped by it.

Pitch relates to the voice range within which a person normally speaks. With some individuals the range is quite wide and with others fairly narrow. There is always a voice range above that of usual speech which has been called the 'squeak' range, and a range below what has been called the 'growl' range (Brown, 1977) which is not used at all in 'unmarked' or normal range speech. Attitudes can sometimes be inferred from this pitch span used. A wide span in pitch, as where speaker A meets speaker B and says 'Hello' in a way which starts high in the normal speaking range or even in the 'squeak' range, indicates an attitude. If said with a smile or a breathy quality, this might be interpreted as happy or excited. If, in addition, eyebrows are raised and eyes are wide open, it might be excitedly surprised. If instead of the breathy voice and the smile we replace it with turned-down corners of the mouth, it might be disagreeably surprised. If, on the other hand, A meets B and says 'Hello', starting high in the range with a large fall, and particularly if it is accompanied by friendly gestures such as a smile and a warm tone of voice, the expectation is a warm response. If it is uttered on a low fall the speaker is declining to expose any positive attitude.

If the normal span is lowered into the lower part of the normal speaking range, or even into the 'growl' range, this appears to coincide with the desire to express involvement, sincerity, responsibility, sympathy or commitment. *Tempo* is often associated with this kind of speech behaviour. A slow tempo cannot be associated with a specific set of attitudes; people may speak slowly because they are thinking carefully about what they are saying. Equally, they may speak slowly because they wish to give the impression that they are thinking carefully about what they are saying.

Rapid speech may be used to suggest that time is pressing. It may also be used in situations that have nothing to do with time (for example, to get a distasteful message delivered as quickly as possible). Just as pitch variation cannot be related to any specific attitude or emotion, so rapidity of speech cannot be confined to a single attitude.

Articulatory precision is used slowly and precisely when a speaker is enunciating words to make a significant remark. It is a stylistic device and it functions to mark the word or word being articulated in this manner as standing quite apart from the surrounding utterance. The stylistic effect depends on the fact that the sudden precision contrasts with the normal articulatory habits of the speaker.

Apart from the function to mark an appropriate place for the other person to speak and to give the speaker time to think, the *pause* can be used stylistically. It can be manipulated to put a second speaker at a disadvantage. Speaker A makes what sounds like a final comment and reinforces this with a slight pause, which B takes as a cue to enter the dialogue. As B opens his mouth to speak A chooses this moment to continue what he was saying. B is left with the uncomfortable feeling that he has been discourteous in interrupting A; also he has a feeling of frustration in that what he had prepared to say is no longer appropriate, as A has moved the topic of discussion to a fresh point.

Pause or hesitation can also be used in conjunction with other paralinguistic features to lend emphasis to a point. When Ronald Reagan was President of the USA he gave innumerable examples of the masterly use of paralanguage. Using the lower part of the speaking range which betokens sincerity, and appropriate pauses for telling effect, he could have listeners hanging on his every word, as in

'We have [PAUSE] done what we [PAUSE] had to do.'

It appears that when a speaker has a central point to an argument he will emphasize its significance to make it clear to his listener(s) by paralinguistic marking, which will include extended pitch range, slow tempo, precise articulation and extended timing (Brown, 1977). He may speak low in his pitch range, often with a 'creaky' voice; but if the remark is to be perceived as important he must either utter the whole remark slowly or extend the timing of words which contain large pitch movement and are also always stressed, as in

'. . . atTEMPTS to disCREDit the product+have been CLEARLY SHOWN+to be a TISSUE of+LIES' (+indicates a pause between one stretch of speech and another).

So far, examination of paralinguistic features has been confined to features which are directly connected with the speech process. In a sense, this is an artificial constraint in that many facial and bodily features contribute to the meaning of a message. What we have attempted to do so far is to consider some of the aspects that can be noted merely by listening to what has been said, and which can assist in the identification of such speech behaviours and provide a basis for more effective use of the spoken word.

Paralanguage refers to non-verbal aspects of speech-related behaviour. However, occasions can arise where the words can mean one thing and the way in which they are used may imply the opposite, as in Mark Anthony's '. . . for Brutus is an honourable man' or the uncertainty avoider's '. . . but I'm only a simple engineer'. On other occasions deliberate non-verbal gestures can be made which can alter the perceived meaning or significance of what is said.

Some odd non-verbal gestures have been observed which can radically alter the apparent meaning.

'A defence lawyer in Sonora, California, is to appeal in the case of a client convicted of breaking and entering, because, he contends, the prosecuting attorney "farted about 100 times" during his closing speech to the jury.

Defence attorney Clark Head complained: "The closing speech is supposed to be sacred. It's like the defendant's last chance and you aren't supposed to interrupt it. Certainly not by farting and making the jury laugh."

According to *The Lawyer's Weekly*, a Californian legal magazine, Mr Head is considering basing his appeal on "misconduct" by the Tuolumne County Assistant District Attorney, Ned Lowenbach. His client, Gary Davenport, 37, was convicted of five felony counts and one misdemeanour stemming from a break-in at the state highway maintenance yard in September 1986.

continued

continued ——————

> Mr Head says that Mr Lowenbach apologized once claiming that it was an accident. "I don't think it was. He just kept doing it, as if to show disrespect for me, my case and my client. He continually moved around and ripped pieces of paper throughout the trial. And then he would fart again. It was impossible to concentrate. I have been through 50 jury trials and I have never heard anything like this."
>
> Mr Lowenbach remains tight-lipped about the incident. But Eric de Temple, the District Attorney, dismissed the charge as absurd. "We are not going to dignify it with a response." '
>
> (From Robert Rice, 'An ill wind in court brings gales of laughter,' *The Independent*, 14 December 1988, reproduced by permission)

To try to make out the other party's position as laughable is a legitimate tactic, whether the other party is a defendant at a jury trial, a commercial opponent or a colleague at work. To make someone else's advocacy seem trivial by treating it as a joke is part of the armoury of the good communicator. However, it is likely to be viewed as a breach of trust if used to a valued colleague.

SUMMARY OF MAIN POINTS SO FAR

1 Meaning is not in words and grammar but in the minds of people and their perceptions and interpretations of a message.

2 Words used in a language are symbols which provide labels for objects, actions, experiences and ideas. These are freely created and passed on over time. They give, together with associated language rules, an order to our world.

3 Strategic ambiguity promotes group cohesion by highlighting the agreement of members on abstract, general ideas, allowing individuals to apply their own values within these general ideas.

4 Different forms of speech affect meaning greatly. The use of bi-polar terms tends to exclude shades of meaning; euphemism seeks to minimize an unfavourable or undesired impact by an apparently less emotive expression; figures of speech such as simile and metaphor are used to make language more striking and effective.

5 Paralanguage is employed to provide cues to meaning by indicating interpersonal attitudes and feelings, to regulate dialogue, to promote sympathy and others preferred responses and to make emphasis. It is deliberate speech-related use of non-verbal communication.

6 Some non-verbal behaviours can be used intentionally to convey a meaning other than the normal one of the words to which they are an accompaniment.

NON-VERBAL COMMUNICATION

Thus far we have touched on non-verbal communication in that we have consid   ech-related aspects as pitch, stress, pause and tempo as w   te non-verbal behaviours to change the listener's perce   is said.

Ther   variety of non-verbal behaviours that occur largely uncon   rallel with spoken language which have the effect of enhancing understanding of the message being conveyed. Translation of meaning is not confined to the spoken word. Speech is but one of a host of graphic, olfactory, tactile, spatial, temporal and symbolic means of communication. There are signals which cannot be identified by speech. What is sometimes ambiguous in language can be clarified when read together with these non-verbal signs.

Expression of Emotion

In certain circumstances the non-verbal aspects of communication can be of more importance than oral statements. When a communicator going about his or her instrumental purposes finds another communicator, also bent on achieving interaction objectives, to be unreasonably resistant to suggestions or unduly demanding it is likely that intangible issues related to self-esteem will emerge.

If the interaction concerns the implementation of a particular task, for example, as defined by a peer group or someone in authority in an organization, then anxiety can manifest itself in a stream of non-verbal signals about the inner state. These are mainly facial expressions and other gestures, sometimes supplemented by vocal sounds.

Sensitivity to these emotions is a rare quality in a communicator. An understanding of the other's concerns is a first step to communicating meaningfully. Emotions can be difficult enough to handle without the added problem of failing to identify their source. Insensitive behaviour can drive away the other when the interaction goals of both are still attainable.

Communicating Interpersonal Attitudes and Feelings

If we want to communicate effectively with someone else it is necessary to obtain information about that person's attitudes towards us in terms of degree of co-operativeness or competitiveness, and what that person's true feelings, preferences and social perceptions are. If these are held strongly, it is not rational argument that is going to convince him but a statement or appeal in terms of his perceptions.

Traditionally, studies of interpersonal attitudes have been focused on the affiliative/aggressive and dominant/submissive dimensions:

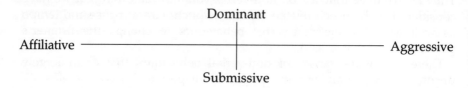

Affiliatives tend to exhibit a greater degree of gaze, a facial expression often incorporating a smile, a soft tone of voice, a direct orientation and bodily relaxation. Such people seek and need acceptance and warmth. Aggressives reject any attempt at the establishment of a relationship. Because such attitudes are often counterproductive, their hostility is often concealed, making it difficult to identify.

People with the motivation to be dominant, especially where there is no status or power difference, exhibit this tendency by a general pattern of bodily relaxation (dominance relations are also characterized by relaxation) accompanied by asymmetrical positions of arms and legs, leaning backwards away from the vertical, and by a tendency to speak more than the other party.

When people meet to achieve some sort of objective they bring to their interaction their own social skills and drives. Consideration of attitudes is significant in such situations. If both persist in asking questions and generally seeking to be dominant, their interaction will be limited. For a dialogue to be successful, there has to be a co-ordination of dominance and submissiveness, affiliation and hostility. If one party insists on using his own preferred social skills, which usually reflect his personality, then the other party has to adopt a corresponding behaviour (Argyle, 1983). If both parties insist on using their own preferred skills and styles, they are not likely to find a perfect fit. The conflict of techniques will lead to discomfort and disharmony. A good communicator will, in the circumstances, adjust his or her behaviour accordingly.

Caveat

Attitudes, feelings and emotions are not always what they seem. Sometimes messages are sent which are not genuine. A member of a music society, famous for having recordings made of its major events and broadcast on national radio, may advocate a particular piece of modern music, but in reality wants to help a friend who is an exponent of that kind of music. A pork-hating guest at a dinner party who finds that her least favourite dish is the main course of the evening is unlikely, except perhaps for religious reasons, to reveal her true feelings to her host at the end of the evening. A salesman of capital equipment is unlikely to convey how much his company needs a particular sale nor will a buyer reveal how keen he is to have a particular product lest the other's objectives for the outcome are raised as a result. Deception is frequently practised in all social interaction, and communication is its agent. People who feel it necessary to practise deception should be able to do it well, for it is a fact of social life. They can learn to do this by first learning to see it in others.

When a person practises deception, that person's behaviour begins to fragment. The words and the non-verbal content say different things. As a result, it is possible to detect the deception. Non-verbal leakage of deception has been studied, and the findings are important for all communicators with purposes to achieve. Indeed, not only has important research been conducted in the area but a book has been written, based on research carried out, on the telling of lies and their detection (Ekman, 1986).

When contradictory signals are received it is the non-verbal one which should be relied upon. Below is a seven-point scale to assist detection in decreasing order of certainty.

1 *Body stress signals.* These are signals resulting from stress to which the nervous system automatically reacts and produces involuntary changes in the body. Sweating, licking of dry lips and heightened pitch of the voice are all signals indicating stress, which may stem from lying, fear or excitement.

2 *Lower body signals.* It is the lower parts of the body that are least easily controlled. Foot-tapping, for example, can indicate impatience when the words spoken and the facial expressions accompanying them apparently show interest.

3 *Body posture signals.* General body posture is often a giveaway, as when one person nods, murmurs accord and even leans forward in an attentive position, but his body slumps or sags, betokening boredom.

4 *Unidentified gestures.* Many hand actions are indefinite movements to which no names have become attached. The communicator who makes aggressive gestures with his hands while talking of the need to do things together is contradicting his verbal claim.

5 *Identified hand gestures.* Many hand gestures are deliberate and definite. Such actions are not to be trusted if they appear as part of a contradictory signal.

6 *Facial expression.* People are so aware of their faces that they can exercise considerable control over them to reinforce spoken deceptive behaviour.

7 *Verbalizations.* When oral messages are given, these can only be trusted when there is no contradictory behaviour.

(Adapted from Morris, 1977)

People often manipulate clues to give an enhanced view of self to maintain a positive and satisfying self-image. Goffman (1972) has shown that interactors need information on intangible as well as tangible issues to allow the parties to gauge each other's attributes, preferences and intentions and so know how to deal with each other. Attributes are not always directly evident; one has often to rely on non-verbal signals associated with such attributes. For example, an individual operating on behalf of his organization might wish to convey the impression that he holds a higher position than he does in reality.

The individual who tries to project an image, either as a person of importance or as a competent communicator, has to be treated as such. A person who believes that he is seen to be capable of effective communication or to be important within his own organization may be expected to behave in an increasingly co-operative manner. If we destroy his 'face', we destroy the relationship.

Parallel Behaviour of Oral and Non-verbal Communication

We claimed at the beginning of this section that what is sometimes ambiguous can be clarified when read together with the non-verbal sign systems. While it is important to know that non-verbal communications can, in certain circumstances, be more meaningful than oral behaviours, it is at least equally important to understand that most of the time each complements the other and loses meaning in isolation.

Birdwhistell (1973) developed the idea that body movement paralleled language. He called his study of body movements 'kinesics'. Anyone turning down the sound on their television set can see that the movements have an expressiveness of their own. Considerable insights into the functions of body movement in human communication have been provided by Ekman and Friesen (1972) in their categorization of these functions. Their taxonomy includes emblems, illustrators, regulators, affect displays and adaptors.

Emblems are kinesic substitutes for oral behaviour. An emblem is intended to transmit a particular message. Examples of these are the cross for Christianity and the clenched fist for black power.

Illustrators are mediating cues clarifying speech behaviour. The politician leaning his head forward, lifting his forearms with palms turned upward as he asks a rhetorical question; the schoolboy shaking his head and crossing his heart while denying a teacher's accusation; the buyer giving a quizzical look with one corner of his mouth turned up slightly, questioning the validity of a salesman's claim; the traffic policeman pointing his arm in a particular direction and outlining the shape of a particular landmark while giving assistance to a lost visitor; all these are examples of illustrators. Enthusiasts use more illustrators than others and give the impression of animation.

Regulators assist in the controlling of dialogue. Such behaviours include the use of eye movement, head positioning and generally those actions which signal the taking of turns in a conversation. Eye contact is particularly significant as a signal for initiating and terminating conversations and in seeking feedback.

Affect displays are cues to what people are feeling. Emotional states may be indicated by smiles, frowns, grunts and other facial movements.

Adaptors are the means by which tension is released or are the results of such tension release. For example, a shudder is the usual release to an episode which has been spine chilling.

COMPLETING THE COMMUNICATION LOOP

Listening and Observing

It is implicit in the transactional model of communication which we have adopted that people are not only able to send messages with adequate verbal and non-verbal fluency, but are equally capable of studying the non-verbal reactions of the party addressed while they are speaking. When it becomes the turn of the other party to speak they should be able to listen to the words and note their non-verbal accompaniment. Without the combination of the two in simultaneous sending and receiving it is not possible to bridge the gap between utterance and felt meaning.

This point is tellingly made by Hall (1983), when he says:

> . . . . human beings live in a single world of communication but they divide that world into two parts: words and behaviour [verbal and non-verbal]. Words, representing perhaps 10 per cent of the total, emphasize the uni-directional aspects of communication—advocacy, law and adversarial relationships—while behaviour, the other 90 per cent, stresses feedback on how people are feeling, ways of avoiding confrontation, and the inherent logic that is the birthright of all people. Words are the medium of business, politicians and our world leaders, all of whom in the final analysis deal in power, so that words become the instruments of power. The non-verbal, behavioural part of communication is the provenance of the common man and the core culture that guides his life. This complex of feedback, local wisdom and feelings is generally ignored or disparaged by our leaders. The question is: How is it possible to maintain a stable world in the absence of the feedback from the other 90 per cent of communication?

Others may claim that Hall has not got his percentages right. This is irrelevant. Whether the non-verbal is 90% or 50%, it is still of considerable significance. Knapp (1978) gives good insights into observing non-verbal behaviour. A classic article on listening is by Rogers and Farson (1977).

Active listening, as propounded by Rogers and Farson, emphasizes the responsibility of the hearer to grasp the facts and feelings of what he or she hears and to help the speaker to work out his or her own problems. It focuses on the need to respect the potential worth of the individual. Without giving consideration to the speaker's rights and trusting his capacity for self-direction, we cannot begin to be effective listeners. Such active listening is an important way of bringing about changes in people. When listened to with this kind of sensitivity, people tend to be less defensive, more open to learning and hence more likely to convey clearly what they are feeling or thinking.

Individuals engaged in an interaction with another are often so busy thinking of the next point they are going to make that they fail to hear or see what a speaker is trying to say. Rogers and Farson (1986) describe a simple exercise which can be applied in testing for understanding:

'The next time you become involved in a lively or controversial discussion with another person, stop for a moment and suggest that you adopt this ground rule for continued discussion: Before either participant in the discussion can make a point or express an opinion of his own, he must restate aloud the previous point or position of the other person. This restatement must be accurate enough to satisfy the speaker before the listener can be allowed to speak for himself.'

Besides providing the listener with more information than any other activity, it helps to build positive relationships and tends to alter positively the attitudes of the listener. Listening, it is claimed, is a growth experience.

Examples in an organizational setting are given in Chapter 7. In Chapter 2 we have already seen the problems arising from the gap between the self-image and the feedback being received. These are avoided by creating a climate which is neither adversely critical nor evaluative. It has to be one of equality and acceptance.

Such a climate is assisted by knowing what to avoid and what to do. The principal blockage to communication lies in passing judgement, whether favourable or unfavourable. Unfavourable criticisms present a threat to the self-image while positive evaluations can sometimes make it difficult to voice troubling problems. On the positive side, a listener should be able to understand what the speaker is saying from his or her viewpoint. What is said may be less important than what is felt. It is these feelings to which the listener has to respond. The hesitancy of his speech, his tone and inflection, his facial expressions, his hand and eye movements all help to convey his total message.

The Role of Inference

Communication interactions involve not only what people say and do and what they hear and observe (smell, taste, etc.) but also the making of assumptions and the drawing of inferences. People very often do not distinguish between fact (what they have heard or seen) and inference (what they have concluded from, very often, incomplete data). When the inferences drawn are incorrect, the conditions exist for a breakdown in communication and the many consequences that can arise from that.

One authority in this difficult area has listed the factors which contribute to the confusion between what has actually been seen and what has been inferred. These include limited and impaired senses; physiological conditions such as those associated with hunger, thirst and fatigue and those incurred by the ingestation of alcohol or drugs; and many psychological factors, including emotion and stress, habit and set, values and needs, group and social influences and *our language* (Haney, 1986).

There are two kinds of declarative statements about what we observe or hear. We can walk along Princes Street, Edinburgh, Scotland, on a sunny spring or summer afternoon and look at a man wearing a cap with a button on top and say 'That man is wearing a cap with a button on top'. Or we can look at the same man and say 'That man is an American tourist'. The latter statement is an inference, because we have no evidence that he is an American tourist. We have *inferred* this because (1) he wears a cap of a kind worn by many American tourists and (2) he appears to walk from the knees like many Americans.

Statements of fact and inference are most difficult to distinguish. The structure of our language gives no indication of the difference between them in grammar, syntax, pronunciation or punctuation. In addition, the inflection with which such statements are made may have equal certainty. There is nothing in the nature of English or any other language which discriminates between fact and inference. Some people find it remarkably easy to utter inferential statements with the false assurance that they are dealing with facts.

Observation and inference confusion is frequently highlighted in dealing with an unfamiliar culture.

It was established before the advent of *perestroika* that to stand a chance of breaking into the East European market it was first necessary to demonstrate commitment to that group of markets. This may still be viewed as taking the form of exhibiting at the national industrial fair of the country concerned, usually on more than one occasion. It is not unusual for this to be followed by an invitation to give a paper at a technical symposium in the country.

One British engineer attending such a symposium for the first time was close to the point of delivering his paper when he deemed it advisable to make a prior visit to the lavatory. On being directed to it by his interpreter, he was confronted by two doors, one marked *Vijni* and the other marked *Vojni*. In desperation, he was about to toss a mental coin as to which was the appropriate door when a woman emerged through the door marked *Vojni*. With much relief he went in through the door marked *Vijni*.

continued

continued—

> While delivering his paper, the engineer had a great desire to show appreciation to his hosts for their not-inconsiderable hospitality. His urge was expressed in the use of the two words which had recently impinged on his awareness. At an appropriate point in his presentation he did his audience the honour of saying a few words to them in their own language. He addressed his listeners as *Vijni i Vojni* and continued to the end of his paper.
>
> On sitting down to a ripple of polite applause, he turned to his interpreter and enquired of her how she thought the paper had been received. 'They seemed to like the technical bits,' she said, 'but they are confused as to why you should address them as "water closets and urinals".'

Haney (1986) has developed a five-stage process by which the speaker can avoid the fact/inference confusion. To do so the procedure should be:

1 Detect the inference.
2 Calculate the risk.
3 Get more data.
4 Recalculate the risk.
5 Label your inferences.

By labelling your inferences you are in fact making sure that there is less likelihood of your own messages being misunderstood. When dealing with other people's inferences it is helpful to get them to label theirs, if necessary by insisting as subtly as possible that they should know the difference between what they really know and what they are only guessing.

There will always be occasions when it is necessary and even desirable to draw inferences. To be aware of this difficulty in communicating is very different from advocating slavish adherence to labelling all statements made and heard. The mark of an educated person is the ability to make a reasoned guess on the basis of insufficient information. If we were to insist on absolute clarity before making decisions we would be denying ourselves viable options and creative solutions.

SUMMARY OF NON-VERBAL COMMUNICATION AND COMPLETING THE COMMUNICATION LOOP

1 In interpreting emotions and interpersonal attitudes and feelings non-verbal cues are much better indicators than verbal ones. Good communicators address their questions and statements to these feelings and attitudes.
2 Sometimes feelings and attitudes are not what they seem because people send messages that are not genuine. When deception is practised, what people say and what their non-verbal behaviour implies become increasingly contradictory. When that happens the non-verbal signal is the one to rely on.

3   People often manipulate clues to project enhanced images of themselves. It is a bluff that should never be called. Central to good communication is a good relationship. If we indicate that we are aware of these little foibles we destroy that relationship.

4   The ambiguity of an oral message can be reduced by non-verbal communication which operates in parallel with the spoken word. These mediating body movements have been categorized as emblems, illustrators, regulators, affect displays and adaptors.

5   In order to communicate, people not only simultaneously speak, accompany their speech with non-verbal signals and hear and see what the other is conveying, they have also to make inferences, because language does not distinguish between fact and inference. Monitoring of one's understanding by labelling inferences can help in one's own communication and assist in understanding that of others by seeking further information.

REFERENCES

Argyle, M. *The Psychology of Interpersonal Behaviour*, Penguin Books, Harmondsworth (1983).

Birdwhistell, R. L. *Kinesics and Context*, Penguin University Books, Harmondsworth (1972).

de Bono, E. *Wordpower*, Penguin Books, Harmondsworth (1979).

Brown, G. *Listening to Spoken English*, Longman, Harlow (1977).

Eisenberg, G. Ambiguity as a strategy in organizational communication. *Communication Monographs*, **51** (1984).

Ekman, P. *Telling Lies*, Berkeley, (1986).

Ekman, P. and Friesen, W. V. Non-verbal leakage and clues to deception. *Psychiatry*, **32** (1969).

Gall, S. *Don't Worry About the Money Now*, Hamish Hamilton, London (1983).

Goffman, E. *Interaction Ritual*, Allen Lane, London (1972).

Hall, E. T. *The Dance of Life: The Other Dimension of Time*, Anchor Press/Doubleday, New York (1983).

Haney, W. C. *Communication and Interpersonal Relations*, Irwin, Homewood, Ill (1986).

Hofstede, G. *Culture's Consequences: International Differences in Work-Related Values* Sage, Beverly Hills, CA (1984).

Knapp, H. *Non-verbal Communication in Human Interaction* Holt Rinehart and Winston, New York (1978).

Koch, S. and Deetz, S. A. Metaphor analysis of social reality in organisations. Quoted in Daniels and Spiker *Perspectives on Organisational Communication*, William C. Brown, Dubuque, IA (1987).

Marshall, J. *Women Managers: Travellers in a Male World*, John Wiley, New York (1984).

Morris, D. *Manwatching*, Triad/Granada, St Albans (1977).

Pollio, H. R. *The Psychology of Symbolic Activity*, Addison-Wesley, Reading, MA (1974).

Rogers, C. R. and Farson, R. E. Active listening. In Haney (1986).

Spender, D. *Man Made Language*, Routledge & Kegan Paul, London (1980).

4
Effects of Situation on Communication

We know intuitively that different ways of communicating are necessary for different situations. A schoolmaster speaks in one way to his students in class, in another way on the sports field and in yet another during fire drill. Similarly, a manager speaks to his subordinates in one way in a business situation, in a different way in a social situation and in a different way again in an emergency.

If we can identify the situational factors in a way that assists us to explain and anticipate behaviour, then we are well on the road to communicating meaningfully.

This chapter addresses those situational aspects which mediate verbal and non-verbal behaviour, and which help perceptive communicators to bring together intention and utterance on the one hand, and the interpretation and felt meaning, on the other.

We have seen that oral and non-verbal communication operate in parallel to create meaning, despite the fact that under certain conditions, one may weigh more heavily. For example, in expressing attitudes, non-verbal elements are more significant as a pointer to what a person is feeling than the oral ones. There is, however, another factor which bears on the manner in which people convey and interpret meaning. That is the situation in which the communication takes place. While spoken and non-verbal communication originate within the person speaking or being addressed, and is expressed in the form of words, gestures and unconscious behaviours associated with speaking, we often have to know much more about the particular social situation in which people find themselves in order to understand more fully and to communicate meaningfully.

THE CONCEPT OF SITUATION

A situation is defined as the simultaneous occurrence of two or more people in dialogue talking about a particular topic in a particular setting

(Fishman, 1972). Thus a social network or community may define a beer and skittles evening for university members as a quite different situation from a lecture involving the same people. What is being talked about is likely to be different; the locale in which each takes place and the time at which it is held are likely to be different as well as the relationships of the interacting parties involved. Members of social networks who share a linguistic repertoire know when to shift from one variety of language to another, depending on the relationship concerned. So it can be seen that a shift in the situation in which the interaction takes place may require a corresponding shift in the language used. This, in turn, may signal a shift in relationships between members of a social network, in the topic or the purpose of their interaction, or in the privacy or locale of their actions.

Social Situations and Talk

Social situations have a structure of their own, different from the characteristics of the larger situation, although we shall see in Chapter 5 that the wider context frequently influences how people interact in a given situation. Since speech, and its parallel non-verbal manifestations, occurs in social situations, it is important to see how the underlying structure of situations determines how talk is organized. It has been pointed out by Goffman (1972a) that the social situation has been largely neglected in the study of what happens when people talk. A different form of language is used, depending on whether we are talking to someone of the same or opposite sex; whether the person being addressed is a superior, subordinate or peer; whether the situation is a face-to-face one or on the telephone; whether the conversation is formal or informal, routine or emergency, in the same language or through an interpreter.

The physical setting may require to be considered before a situation can be described or understood. A person justifying an action to a colleague in his or her own office will use language different from that in a board room. When a person of higher status is introduced to a small group involved in attempting to resolve some problem the style of language used will be one which is appropriate to the new situation created by the person's arrival.

Educational development

The following latter-day parable illustrates in a light-hearted way how different language is used when addressing people at different levels in a hierarchy. It also, incidentally, shows how a message can be distorted in transmission.

'In the beginning was the report and then came the assumptions.
The assumptions were without form and the report was completely without substance.

continued

---

continued

And the darkness was upon the faces of the workers and they spake unto
their seniors saying:
"It is a crock of shit and it stinketh."
And the seniors went to their Heads of Department and said:
"It is a pile of dung and none may abide the odour thereof."
And the Heads went to their Faculty Chairmen and said unto them:
"It is a vessel of fertilizer and none may abide its strength."
And the Chairmen went to their Deputy Director and said:
"It contains that which aids plant growth and is very strong."
And the Deputy went to the Director and said unto him:
"It promoteth growth and is very powerful."
And the Director went to the Minister and said unto him:
"This powerful new initiative will promote the development and efficiency
of lecturers and is strongly recommended."
And the Minister looked upon the report, and saw that it was good.
And the report became policy.'

Speaking occurs within the kinds of social situations drawn above.
Dialogue takes place through the participants taking turns at talking.
Through the statements they make, interacting parties provide each other
with information on intangible as well as tangible issues. They allow the
parties to the dialogue to gauge each other's attributes, preferences and
intentions, and in turn create the opportunity to present or misrepresent
information about their own. It has been shown by Goffman (1972b) that
people in interacting situations need this kind of information in order to
know how to deal with each other.

Attributes are not always directly evident, and one has often to rely on
non-verbal signals associated with these. It is possible for people in
communication to send information about themselves which is not wholly
accurate but which presents an enhanced version of the self. For example,
an individual in one organization meeting with someone from another might
convey the impression, consciously or unconsciously, perhaps by his style
of social behaviour or by the cut of his clothes, that he holds a higher position
in his organization than he does in reality.

Goffman maintains that the behaviour of people in a social situation is
designed to help everyone maintain the self they choose to project in that
particular situation. If contradictory signals suggest that the self being
presented is not the true one, a communicator has to refrain from making
and emphasizing points which make it clear that he knows this to be so.
If we destroy a person's 'face' we destroy the relationship with him. By
destroying the relationship it will become increasingly difficult to achieve
the instrumental purposes of the interaction, because the party alienated
will not be inclined to enter again into an open dialogue.

Situation and Turn Taking

Speech occurs within the kinds of social situations described above. Social exchange takes place through the interacting parties taking turns at talking. It has been strongly suggested that the act of speaking must always be referred to the state of talk that is sustained through the particular turn of talking, and that this state of talk involves a circle of others ratified as co-participants. Once a state of talk has been ratified, cues must be available for requesting the floor and giving it up. Collaboration between the parties has to be sustained to ensure that one turn of talking neither overlaps the other too much nor inhibits the exchange by failing to respond adequately.

Speaker gaze is an effective turn indicator only in the context of gaze aversion. In other words, one may suggest that any such gaze behaviour will only have importance in regulating turns of conversation where the background level of gaze is low, as with people who are unfamiliar with each other.

Verbal cues indicating that the speaker wishes the other person to take over the speaking role include drawl on the final or stressed syllable, pausing, the termination of any hand gesture or the relaxation of a tense hand position, and the use of phrases such as 'You know' and 'That's how I see it'. If the speaker wishes to continue talking, he or she may look away from the listener during a pause in speech, filling the pause with 'um' or 'er' and making a hand gesture which is not returned to rest during a pause.

If the listener wishes to say something, he or she may turn his head away from the speaker, start a hand gesture, or make a sharp, audible inhalation. Should the listener wish to indicate to the speaker that he or she should continue talking, this is usually done by head-nodding and saying such encouraging words as 'Yes', 'Mm' and 'I see'.

Beattie (1983) contends that in any dialogue the listener has to work hard in addition to timing his utterances carefully. He has to plan his utterances in advance of beginning to speak and has to ensure they are appropriate in context and cohesive with the preceding turn. Unlike the earlier frameworks for turn taking, which seemed to indicate switching on a signal at the end of a speaker turn after she has decided to stop speaking, Beattie's ideas suggest that she should vary her speech style, intonation and accompanying non-verbal signals in conversation, in order to involve a second person. Only by varying the patterns of one's speech and parallel non-verbal elements can interacting parties, it seems, fully weave the other into the fibre of their discourse.

Situations and Touch

Depending on a variety of facets of a situation, touch may be appropriate or completely inappropriate. Touch implies some kind of bond between the toucher and the touched. Much of the interest surrounding touch focuses on the variety of responses to it, particularly in its relation to the norms associated with it. The major response variance to touching is the degree to which it matches the intimacy of the relationship between the people concerned. This can vary with the environmental conditions in which the particular situation develops. To the extent that a person feels able to control interpersonal situations, he or she will be made less anxious by an unexpected bonding gesture such as touch.

Touching can influence people in different ways. In the right kind of setting touch can make people more positive about external stimuli and the toucher. Also, it can help people to comply with requests more frequently. It seems to assist in the creation of liking (Heslin and Alper, 1983).

Touching in communication situations is sometimes a sign that barriers have been broken. In negotiation situations, increase in touch or familiarity is a sign that agreement is about to be reached.

It would appear that there are constraints in interactions between higher- and lower-status persons in an organization in that the lower-status person finds it difficult to initiate touch. Therefore, people who initiate touch would be seen as having the status that gives permission to touch plus the warmth of personality or degree of social skills training that would motivate them to express a bonding feeling. A person who does not reciprocate touch would be low in either relative status or desire to bond with the toucher, or both.

DIFFERENTIAL RESPONSES IN SIMILAR SITUATIONS

We saw in Chapter 2 that when two individuals meet, the situation so created is one to which they bring their own perceptions. Everyone has experienced this, perhaps on holiday abroad or at home with tourists from overseas where the assumptions which they make are not shared by the locals. Often this can be ascribed to a different national culture, or where it occurs in organizations, a different organizational culture. However, even where the parties were brought up in the same national culture and worked in the same organization, the meaning that they impute to a given stimulus can differ.

Our organizations, due to task specialization and the different physical and social realities that can arise as a result, cause us to interpret stimuli in different ways. Additionally, what we perceive and create meaning from can be affected by whether we are in an optimistic or a pessimistic mood; whether we are stressed or relaxed, embarrassed, fearful, apathetic or angry; whether we are tired or fresh, are taking drink or drugs; whether the source of influence is credible or not, has influence over us or not, as when superiors are present or with colleagues whose respect is important for us; whether we have a stake in the outcome of an issue, be it material or moral—

for example, we may have a vested interest in it because we may make money from it or our values are involved, or some idea to which we have made a commitment is at stake.

The unique response which we make to different signals can be so affected by our conditioning, by the experiences that we have undergone, that it can be quite different from the conditioning and experience of another person. For example, superiors and subordinates in organizations usually learn to perceive themselves and each other quite differently. There are now many studies of the perceptions of a given event or events in which foremen and the workers responsible to them, heads of departments and subordinates, managing directors, accountants, engineers, sales managers and production managers all perceived the events in different ways.

We can all differ considerably from each other in the ways in which we respond to signals. Because much of our learning takes place out of awareness, we do not always fully realize the extent to which our perceptions differ.

The situation in which unique individuals meet and respond differently to that situation means that, until one or other is able to pass a message or messages in the other's terms, communication is unlikely to take place. For communication to happen a speaker's utterance and a listener's felt meaning have to coincide.

People who embrace the view that others inhabit the same mental world as themselves are making *projective cognitive similarities*. Most people can tolerate differences in judgements and opinions as long as they recognize them as such. No-one can tolerate differences that are capable of proof.

The Danger of Defensiveness

Our failure to acknowledge the differences between a reality and our perception of it, and the differences of perceptions from person to person, create a defensive mechanism in us. We then begin to find life threatening because those who have the idea that others share their world do not realize that this is not so. To cope with life, such people find it necessary all the time to defend their own world and to deny or attack the other person's (Haney, 1986). Most mature people are fairly tolerant of differences in values, judgements, attitudes and points of view, just as long as they realize that peoples' realities are not the same, and hence represent no threat.

Defensiveness is so pervasive and potentially so destructive to communication and any interpersonal relationships that exist that it merits further consideration. We saw in Chapter 2 that each person looks out on the world through a lens than provides a highly individualistic view of what and who is seen. This is what is called the person's frame of reference. At its centre is one's self-image—a complicated, multi-faceted, ambivalent, dynamic concept of self. This often operates out of consciousness. It acquires an importance which moves people to protect it at almost any cost.

Threats to the self-image can come from such things as failure, ridicule or rejection, especially if we have felt rather good about ourselves. But the greatest menace to the self-image is change. To be really threatening, change has to be large enough and quick enough and uncontrolled enough (by the possesser of the self-image). Just how large, quick and uncontrolled the change has to be to constitute a threat depends on how much an individual feels comfortable before moving into the *discrepant zone*. This is the area within which the margin of disparity between the self-image and the feedback concerning it is no longer tolerable.

Seeing Others and Ourselves

The images we form of others are usually made without their impinging on our consciousness. The reason for forming images of others is to predict their behaviour and to respond to them in whatever way is required by the situation. If a boss is a nasty piece of work, we usually know how to handle him. Problems arise when the nasty piece of work is inconsistent. We need consistency on the part of the people we regularly interact with to facilitate prediction and hence good communication. The basis of prediction is swept away if the image we have of someone does not hold up.

A significant behaviour change on the part of someone can destroy the image we have of that person, makes that person unpredictable and hence reduces the interaction capability with him or her. If we are in the place of that other and have our own self-image challenged, we run the risk of losing the ability to predict, control and know ourselves. People who have suffered a deeply traumatic experience, whether connected with a relative, husband or wife, drugs, unemployment, divorce, etc., will probably find on looking back that their self-image was being severely threatened. Under stress, people become separated from the real self and seek protection in an idealized self, usually founded on pride. Because of the felt necessity to maintain this false image, it becomes increasingly difficult to move out of the discrepant zone back into that more comfortable area where cues from feedback are not perceived as threats because they do not present too great a disparity from current images.

The Self-Image and Dealing with Others

True self-knowledge is the basis of a realistic self-image. The discrepancy arising from the image and the cues provided by feedback disappears and a valid self-concept emerges. Management writers claim that self-knowledge is self-development. Indeed, some go as far as to say they are one and the same thing.

Some people develop a strong self-concept unassisted. Those with problems of communication may need some training to assist them in the acquisition of the skills which promote this self-knowledge. The liberation of the energies which might otherwise be used to put a cocoon round the self-image creates the possibility to develop the skills to read others and hence communicate more effectively with them. The development of the self-concept is directly addressed in Chapter 11.

DIFFERENTIAL MOTIVATIONS IN SIMILAR SITUATIONS

While the various people who might be thrown together in different situations might respond in different ways to similar situations due to different perceptions, different earlier experiences, prior programming or differing self-images, they may also create a situational difference which will affect communications by the varying motivations they bring to an interaction.

It is not the purpose here to examine different theories of motivation. Most people are aware of Maslow's needs theory, Herzberg's two-factor theory and McClelland's learned needs theory. There are other theories of motivation. Suffice it to say that if we are to be capable of controlling or influencing behaviour, we must be capable of predicting reasonably accurately the responses of others and ourselves. It is only if we bring our own theory of motivation to the surface and examine its premises that we can avoid making decisions, taking action and communicating on the basis of unconscious, unexamined and untenable theory.

SUMMARY OF MAIN POINTS SO FAR

1 Situations affect the way people use language and related non-verbal movements in respect of who is talking to whom in what kind of physical environment and social setting.
2 Dialogue takes place through participants taking turns of talking. Taking the floor and giving it up are functions of gaze where the background level of gaze is low; of verbal cues including a drawl on the final or stressed syllable; of pause, termination of a hand gesture, relaxation of a tense hand position and terminal phrases such as 'That's how I see it'. A listener exhibits a desire to come into the dialogue by starting a hand gesture and to carry on talking by use of words like 'Yes' and 'Mm'.
3 Touch is a bonding gesture or measure of reassurance. It is a preliminary to one party indicating agreement. It usually is initiated by a higher-status person.

4 No two people have the same forces acting on them at one time or the same kinds of experiences, view a given situation in an identical way or react in the same way to the same stimulus.
5 If the margin of disparity between a person's self-image and the feedback provided by cues is too great it becomes intolerable and people become defensive. If our self-image is then challenged we run the risk of losing our ability to predict our own and another's behaviour and hence to respond in whatever way is required by the situation.

COMMUNICATION AND DISTRIBUTION OF POWER

Communication and Hierarchy

If activities require to be organized in order to be made efficient, we have to accept that some people will have responsibility for the work of others. Even groups which start out on the basis of egalitarian principles (for example, communes) find that an informal hierarchy develops in which natural leaders emerge. When the Israelites were making their long journey to the promised land from bondage in Egypt, Moses was their leader. So exhausted was he becoming in settling issues between people all day long that his father-in-law, Jethro, prevailed on him to save his energies by getting organized:

> Thou shalt provide out of all the people able men, such as fear God, men of truth, hating covetousness; and place such over them to be rulers of thousands, and rulers of hundreds; rulers of fifties and rulers of tens (Exodus 18.21).

In classical organization, things are not that much different from the time of Moses. People are arranged in different hierarchies by specialization to reduce costs by increased efficiency, and co-ordination of their efforts is necessary if the organization is to complete its mission satisfactorily. Certain individuals are put in charge of others to achieve the order required for ready achievement of objectives.

Some Approaches to Superior–Subordinate Relations

Given the existence of different statuses in organizations, formal or informal, it is not surprising that people put in authority very often use that authority to tell subordinates what to do. This is likely in organizations where the giving of orders is an accepted norm (for example, the emergency services) or where the culture is one which accepts or prefers an authoritarian style because of great difference in the power of individuals at different levels of hierarchy where the superior holds and exercises the power to reward or punish.

A second approach is the 'tell and sell' one, in which the superior tells his subordinate of a decision he has taken and tries to persuade the subordinate to accept it because of its advantages, either to the organization or to the subordinate, or both.

A third approach is 'tell and listen'. In this, the superior informs his subordinate of a decision made and asks his views about it.

A fourth approach is 'ask and tell'. Here the superior obtains information from his subordinate concerning some problem and then tells the subordinate what he has decided.

A fifth approach is the problem-solving one in which superior and subordinate together seek to identify the solution to a common problem.

The last approach is 'ask and listen'. It is one in which the superior asks his subordinate about some problem area and listens to the replies without advancing opinions of his own at this stage.

All these approaches require the use of appropriate language. For example, the 'tell' approach will incorporate language which uses orders, requests, suggestions and advice. On the other hand, the 'ask and tell' approach will utilize questioning language, comparisons, restatements and summaries before giving orders, requests and promises. These classifications from Wright and Taylor (1984) are ways of looking at how a leader relates to subordinates. The hierarchy inherent in structure and the styles or strategies used by superiors within that hierarchy are variants of the situational factors which mediate the oral and non-verbal language used.

Hierarchy and Structure

When hierarchies of specializations are put together in a relationship to meet the needs of what the organization is trying to achieve in terms of the control and the authority by which it is governed we call it organizational structure. One of the functions of bureaucratic organizational structure is to ensure that individuals do not attempt to use the organization to further their own interests but rather will be controlled and managed to work for the organization's purpose, particularly where there is legitimate disagreement concerning what the organization's purposes are and the way in which they should be achieved. In this perspective, organizations are not rational decision-making organisms but rather arenas in which various persons and groups compete. Many different interests participate. These interests usually want to take actions and make decisions that favour their own perspective and objectives, stated or implicit. Each group seeks the ability to affect organizational actions as it wishes. Such ability is in part created by the organization structure (Meyer *et al.*, 1978).

Control of information is a potent source of power. Thus, organization structures create power and authority by allocating certain persons to do certain tasks, and create informal power through the effect on information and communicative structures. Given the various interests in controlling the organization and the fact that preferences and beliefs conflict, it is clear that participants will be in contention over the allocation of resources and the control of information as they attempt to gain more influence.

In order to achieve organizational purposes, explicit rules are devised which seek to regulate the behaviour of participants. Communication is related to the interpretation and enforcement of rules. Yet action in accordance with the rules is problematic in social settings. There are high-level executives with decision-making discretion who are unobtrusively controlled by those who provide the information on which decisions are based. The now-classic work of Pettigrew (1987) in relation to the purchase by a British department store group of a second-generation computer indicates the importance of information control. The department head was able to influence the decision taken by the board of directors who had the formal authority to make the decision. He systematically filtered the information from computer manufacturers and his own personnel. The board making the decisions were never aware of the role of the department head as gatekeeper, who kept them apart from the information concerning the opposition to him within his own group. The board were of the belief that they were considering all the available information, but the structure and the central personality within it ensured that full communication did not take place.

Communication Across Hierarchies

Because of the interdependence between functions and hence of the personnel within them, people in modern organizations are required to take actions which impinge on the interests of people in other functions over whom they have no control. Different inputs have to be co-ordinated against a background of differences in the basic preferences of organizational participants, or because there are differences in beliefs about what actions are most likely to meet the various goals. Differences in preferences and beliefs about the consequences of their actions can arise from different socialization and training in a prior job, from the development of sub-unit identification and loyalty, from differences in information controlled and available, and from being embedded in different social networks both inside and outside the organization.

In consequence, conflict becomes an ever-present threat as individuals and groups attempt to impose their own solutions on issues. Because the actions of people in different functions require to be co-ordinated to meet the organizational purposes, it is necessary for the behaviour of people in various positions to be predictable, so that integration of the interdependent activities becomes possible. Lack of predictability is a barrier to good communication which is necessary for the handling of inherent conflict. In order to cross the functional barriers the interests of people in other functions have to be addressed, often in the language which each function uses and has developed.

The problem is compounded by the fact that in today's organizations, managers at different levels have responsibility for co-ordinating efforts of people over whom they have no direct authority, or for obtaining their co-operation across departmental boundaries.

Given the different perspectives from which issues are viewed from the various functional standpoints, there has to be some underlying explanation for the way in which people adjudge what is 'correct' communicative behaviour in a given situation. These are the largely *implicit rules* of communication that derive from the experience people have in a particular environment, which give them an instinctive understanding of what is appropriate (Shimanoff, 1980).

Communication and Role

The organization structure which we saw as being the source of group interest and conflict also occurs through the specification of roles which members are expected to play. Role is defined as 'the pattern of behaviour expected by others from a person occupying a certain position in an organizational hierarchy'. The behaviour expected of anyone occupying an office then becomes his role. Each individual has his own particular role among the group of people he interacts with—his role set. The pattern of interactions each member of the set has with the others in his own particular role is known as his role relationship. A significant function of this relationship is to reduce the areas of possible uncertainty to manageable proportions.

Regularity and predictability in social relationships are highly valued in individuals. They expect that the persons with whom they associate at work or in the family will behave in predictable ways. If they do not, the individual feels tense and uncomfortable and wants to do something to make life predictable. In all human groupings there are mechanisms for punishing people who do not behave in predictable ways and for rewarding those who do. Gradually, the norms of behaviour which emerge from the desire for predictability become part of the individual's personal make-up. He sometimes does not know how to explain why he behaves regularly in the way that he does. It is just 'the way we do things here'. In short, people cast other people in roles which are defined by their own expectations. These may be highly formal, as legal prescriptions and bureaucratic roles are, or they may be informal or implicit, as in custom.

(From Lupton, 1971, reproduced by permission)

People who represent a group in formal discussions have to bear in mind the expectations of that group. Negotiators, for example, may be constrained in their responses by their perceived obligation to their group, even though discussions elicit information which indicates that it is quite impossible for group expectations to be met. Those who are not party to discussions frequently have an influence on their outcome.

SOME INTER-ORGANIZATIONAL ASPECTS OF SITUATION

Face-to-face Situations

One of the assumptions underlying this book is that communication is instrumental. Because the outcomes which parties seek from their interaction may be a specific agreement, information or behaviour they are in doubt as to detail right to the end, for the very good reason that these are dependent on how the parties act and react towards each other. Since different people bring different perceptions to similar situations, the outcomes can be as variable as the people involved. No one has yet devised the bent measuring stick which allows us to compare the performance of different pairs in like situations. (See Figure 6.1 for a schematic representation of the diverse forces affecting people in communication.)

It is for these reasons that outcomes are said to be interaction dependent. This dependence is thrown into relief if the model of dyadic interaction is considered. In this model there is interplay of factors internal and external to the individuals concerned in the exchange. External influences show up in the relation between a person's actions and the previous actions of the other, while internal influences can be seen in the relation between an action and previous actions of the same person (Clarke, 1983).

Some Inter-organizational Situations

In commercial exchange activities the nature of the situation and the physical environment of the parties to a transaction help to determine how communication should be made. In selling/buying situations, for example, the distinction between the 'hard' and 'soft' sell is one which has often been made. A contingency model developed by Poppleton (1981) views the favourability of the situation for the salesman as being affected by three variables. These are the acceptability of the salesman to the potential buyer, the power of the salesman as reflected in his referent value and expertness, and the complexity of the task. Under clearly favourable or unfavourable conditions the more effective approach will be the hard sell. Under conditions of moderate favourability the soft sell will be more effective. In the hard sell the syllables are terse, dramatic and rapid. The soft sell, on the other hand, is characterized by gentle, melodious and leisurely tones.

In social exchanges between people of different cultures, whether or not representing organizations, communication is affected by the nature of the cultures involved. It is assisted if the exchange is a comfortable one for both parties. The man who holds the eye too long, as Westerners may believe of Arabs, or is over-familiar or personal, as Englishmen may believe of Americans or Indians, could well be behaving in accordance with the norms of his own culture. In the same way, the person who underplays the intensity of gaze, as a Japanese might do by the standards of American or West European communicators, may be regarded as deceitful, although that person could be behaving also in accordance with his own standards. Such reactions can be avoided if the situation can be anticipated by appropriate training.

Some Limitations

We have shown that the situation affects the communication between individuals talking about a particular topic. While there are certain rules we can follow to direct the way we address people in different situations, these can vary across cultures. The examples given just touched on the variety of situations which can arise. They are often unique and are ever changing. The atmosphere of a room consists of such fluctuating factors as temperature, colour and lighting, time of day and amount of background noise. Also, of course, a person's perception of even the stationary aspects of his or her surroundings is in a state of flux.

It has been claimed that the uniqueness of each communicative setting can be reduced to manageable proportions by looking at the dynamics of situations in abstract form (Mortensen, 1972). Every communicative situation can be analysed in terms of space, time and physical setting. Yet these categories are so broad that they do not possess the predictive quality to understand behaviour and respond in positive terms.

While some behaviours are predictable, so many remain unique that it is only cumulative experience and analysis of behaviours which permit a communicator to understand and be understood. Even that is generally dependent on the broader social context and structure within which an interaction takes place. This is addressed in the following chapter.

SUMMARY OF COMMUNICATION AND DISTRIBUTION OF POWER AND INTER-ORGANIZATIONAL ASPECTS OF SITUATION

1 Distribution of power within an organization is manifested in relations between bosses and subordinates. The relationship is reflected in the

language used, which differs depending on the relative status of the persons being addressed.

2 Organization structures and the specializations they embrace virtually guarantee that conflicting views will exist as to the organization's purposes and how they should be achieved. Different groups seek to impose their own solutions on issues. This is best achieved in part by addressing the interests of competing groups in the kinds of language they use.

3 The roles people play in organizations are the patterns of behaviour expected of persons occupying certain positions in organizational hierarchies. Regularity and predictability are highly valued in individuals and people are uncomfortable if others do not conform to role expectations. Roles vary from one organization to another.

4 People representing a group are constrained in their actions by the expectations of that group. One difficulty is that the representative is aware of issues and possible outcomes in the face-to-face situation which the group is not. An understanding of this aids communication.

5 Situational factors also affect communication between organizations. For example, the 'soft sell' and 'hard sell' are utilized under differing conditions.

6 Situational factors mediate oral and non-verbal communication. Situations have to be monitored and analysed continuously, as general abstractions are of limited use in predicting behaviour and communicating meaningfully, due to the uniqueness and ever-changing nature of situations.

REFERENCES

Beattie, G. *Talk: An Analysis of Speech and Non-Verbal Behaviour in Conversation*, Open University Press, Milton Keynes (1983).

Clarke, D. D. *Language and Action: A Structural Model of Behaviour*, Pergamon, Oxford (1983).

Fishman, J. A. The sociology of language. In Giglioli, P. P. (ed.), *Language and Social Context*, Penguin Books, Harmondsworth (1972).

Goffman, E. The neglected situation. *Ibid.* (1972a).

Goffman, E. *Interaction Ritual*, Allen Lane, London (1972b).

Heslin, R. and Alper, I. 'Touch: a bonding gesture. In Wiemann, J. N. and Harrison, R. P. (eds), *Non-Verbal Interaction*, Sage, Beverly Hills, CA (1983).

Haney, W. *Communication and Interpersonal Relations*, Irwin, Homewood, Ill (1986).

Lupton, T. *Management and the Social Sciences*, Penguin Books, Harmondsworth (1971).

Meyer, M. W. *et al. Environments and Organisations*, Jossey-Bass, San Francisco, CA (1978).

Mortensen, C. D. *Communication: The Study of Human Interaction*, McGraw-Hill, New York (1972).

Pettigrew, A. M. *The Politics of Organisational Decision-Making*, Blackwell, Oxford (1987).

Poppleton, S. E. The social skills of selling. In Argyle, M. (ed.), *Social Skills and Work*, Methuen, London (1981).

Shimanoff, N. *Communication Rules: Theory and Research*, Sage, Beverly Hills, CA (1980).

Wright, P. L. and Taylor, D. S. *Improving Leadership Performance: A Practical New Approach to Leadership*, Prentice-Hall, Hemel Hempstead (1984).

5
Contextual and Social Structural Determinants of Communication

When we live in a particular national or organizational culture we act in specific ways in particular situations. What often makes us do this is the social structure and context in which these situations develop.

If we can analyse the social structures in which dialogue takes place and fill out the social context within which it is played out; if we can put ourselves in a position to isolate the effect this has on the language we use and how it bears on our thoughts and actions; if we can do these things, we are more in a position to see how these factors further contribute to the meaning we take from messages. Also, we put ourselves in a better position to communicate meaningfully in the messages we ourselves convey.

This chapter examines how social structure and context mediate the oral, non-verbal and situational aspects of communication to complete a cluster of parallel communication activities without any one of which a message would lose meaning.

SPEECH COMMUNITIES AS COMMUNICATION CONTEXT

Communication as a verbal/non-verbal/situational phenomenon cannot be fully understood, explained or conveyed as meaningful unless it is also seen against the social context within which it is embedded. Language is used within a socially defined universe which reflects more general behaviour norms. This universe is the speech community. Any grouping of human beings characterized by regular and frequent interaction by means of a shared body of verbal signs and separated from similar groupings by significant differences in language usage constitutes such a community (Gumperz, 1968).

Groups with a degree of permanence, whether small bands bound together by regular face-to-face contact and a common overall purpose, modern nations with strong, readily identifiable regions or even occupational/ professional associations or neighbourhood gangs, may all be treated as speech communities. There is a presupposition that the verbal behaviour of such groups is based on certain grammatical rules to make any exchange intelligible.

Just as intelligibility presupposes underlying grammatical rules, so the communication of social information assumes the existence of regular relationships between language usage and social structures. Before we can decide what a person's social intent is we have to know something of the norms defining the appropriateness of acceptable language modes for different types of speaker. Some of the situational examples in Chapter 4 had an implicit social context which determined the way, for example, in which superiors addressed subordinates and vice versa, in different organizational roles.

Speech Community as a National Concept

Homogeneous cultures enjoy a speech community in which the context varies little from one area to another. In consequence, the language also varies little. Japan is one such country. Cut off from the mainstream of international relations for some 250 years during the Tokugawa period of its history, Japan developed and reinforced a strong national culture. It is just over 120 years since this period ended and Japan resumed its place in the comity of nations. As a result, there are powerful social structural factors which bear on Japanese values and group organization, on the modes of social relations and hence on individual behaviour, including language behaviour.

The way in which individuals in any society get together in groups is based on the concepts of *attribute* and *frame*. The concept of attribute applies to what an individual has in common with other individuals (for example, being a member of a professional association); the concept of frame may embrace an institution or a relationship binding a set of individuals into one group, as in being in a section or department in a particular company. The Japanese tend to see situations in terms of frame rather than universal attribute (Nakane, 1973).

Japanese social groups include people of differing attributes. As a consequence, any tendency to strengthen horizontal ties is weakened by the emotional involvement of the people concerned. This emotional contact is reinforced by the human relationships developed at the personal level in social circumstances. The effect of the group on the individual is to alter his or her ideas and ways of thinking. The sense of unity developed makes it difficult for people to leave the group.

Japanese group affiliations are one-to-one. For each Japanese there is one group which is paramount. There is an absolute loyalty, and no room to serve two masters. The cohesion among group members rests on the underlying relationship and social ties and obligations. Because of the almost total emphasis on the frame and vertical relationships, even individuals with identical qualifications tend to create differences between themselves. As this is reinforced, a subtle form of ranking emerges, based on relative age, date of joining the organization and length of service. While this must necessarily be adapted to changes, such adaptations are likely to be slow and made within the specific Japanese context.

The vertical ties in which firm personal links exist between superior and subordinate is expressed in terms of the *oyabun/kobun* relationship. Literally, this means parent/child. The *oyabun* may be someone in a senior position at work with whom a subordinate (*kobun*) has developed a close personal relationship. The *kobun* is helped by his *oyabun* in such matters as receiving advice when important decisions are made. The *kobun*, for his part, puts his own services at the disposal of the *oyabun* when he should need them. It is interesting to note in passing that the leader is an integral part of the group organization. He is expected to be involved in the group to the point where he has almost no personal identity. To convey the idea of leadership in Japan we have to have recourse to the *oyabun/kobun* relationship. There is no Japanese word which corresponds to the English word 'leadership'.

Central to this relationship is the concept of *amae*, which refers to the feelings normal infants harbour towards their mother—dependence, the desire to be passively loved and unwillingness to be separated from the warm mother/child relationship and cast into the world unsupported. Doi (1973) has maintained that such feelings are somehow prolonged into, and diffused throughout, the adult life of a Japanese so that they come to shape his whole attitude to other people and to reality. *Amae* is a word peculiar to the Japanese language, yet it describes a psychological phenomenon common to mankind. It shows not only how especially familiar is the psychology in question to the Japanese but also that the social structure is formed in such a way as to permit expression of that psychology. One might be justified in seeing the susceptibility to *amae* as the cause of the emphasis on vertical relationships.

These vertical relationships are supported by emotional ties and social obligations, and by the concepts of harmony and consensus which have arisen out of them. Consequently, open displays of power are seen as potential threats to harmony and 'face'. 'Face' is something people in all cultures like to maintain. In East Asia in general, this need is heightened by the fact that the house, family or clan and, by association, social needs are a greater motivating factor than the so-called self-actualizing needs. Social controls are external and are imposed by the sensitive feelings of pride engendered, and conformity is imposed by wounding, or the threat of wounding, this pride. This is the basis of 'face', which is a pervasive aspect of interpersonal relationships.

Avoidance of confrontation reflects these structures and customs. This can be seen in the use of affirmatives as negatives (Van Zandt, 1970). When a Japanese says 'Yes' he means 'No' or 'Maybe' at best. He will use the term '*Hai*' frequently, meaning literally 'Yes' but usually signifying understanding rather than agreement. If he draws breath through his teeth and says something like '*sah*' or 'It is very difficult' he means 'No'. To communicate effectively with a Japanese it is necessary to know how the social structure creates context which, in turn, bears on the situation. The verbal, non-verbal and situational elements are mediated by the context and social structure.

In the more familiar heterogeneous cultures such as those of the USA and Western Europe the context and social structure also give meaning to communication. West Germany is one such culture. It has a social structure characterized by low variations between the well-off and the not so well-off, and a correspondingly low power distance between levels in society. Social cohesion is assisted, among other things, by the concept of *Technik*. This refers to manufacture and the (engineering) knowledge and skills relevant to it (Lawrence, 1980). It reflects the different ways in which societies perceive and evaluate skill and knowledge and the differences in the way they group and label branches of knowledge. In English-speaking countries the distinction is drawn between arts and sciences, and engineering is seen as a branch of applied science with engineering a kind of junior partner. In West Germany, on the other hand, this distinction is not made. The output of most engineering is seen to be three-dimensional artefacts made by engineers who make things and seek workable solutions which do not cost too much. Much of it is carried out on site and is subject to environmental influences. Science output is knowledge, its work takes place in controlled conditions in a laboratory by scientists who seek ideal solutions and universal laws. Engineering therefore drives West German business, and the idea of *Technik* embodies this. Such an orientation requires to be addressed if effective communication is to take place. It is reflected in an emphasis on things practical, such as a commitment to doing things well, to the tasks in hand and the skills and knowledge to carry them out. The idea extends to all forms of activity.

An example of how communication might harness the idea of *Technik* would be where a new concept had been applied to the design of a product and it was being sold to a West German firm. The emphasis would need to be on the application of the product to the more efficient performance of the West German company and the enhancement of the skills of the personnel who would be using it. To be avoided would be the abstract notion of innovation, which is something likely to appeal in the USA.

Organizations as Speech Communities

It is only to be expected that there should be a strong relationship between what goes on in the wider culture and the way people behave in organizations. Social situations may have a structure of their own, but these can be influenced by the wider social context in which dialogue takes place. Hofstede (1984), in a large and sophisticated piece of research, identified the four cultural universals of 'power distance', 'uncertainty avoidance', 'individualism' and 'masculinity' (see Chapter 2). These represent different ways of viewing the world which interact to make people act and perceive as they do. They are developed in schools and organizations, and are reflected in them. For example, such national values as West German egalitarianism (low power distance) and *Technik* can be seen in West German organizations.

In US organizations we would expect to see American values emerge. For example, in the social structure imposed by organization the self-reliance of individuals is reflected in the idea of individual responsibility for a given position. In no way would we expect to see collegial management at the top of American organizations as we might have in West Germany. Because of the one-to-one relationships in Japan we would be surprised to see a form of matrix organization there even in multi-product, multi-market companies such as we might find in the United Kingdom.

In a study comparing English and Indian organizations, Tayeb (1988) found that national cultural attitudes were reflected in the organizational settings in the two countries. Indians, for example, were more obedient to their seniors than the English, were less able to cope with new and uncertain situations, more fatalistic and, when in a position of authority, less willing to take account of the opinions of others. These cultural characteristics appear to have been reflected in the Indian employees' lower perception of power, lower tolerance for ambiguity, higher satisfaction with the work organization and more directive attitudes to management practices than the English employees.

Yet, even within the framework of national cultures, organizations assume strong cultural dimensions of their own in which the organization, and perhaps more accurately, different parts of it (see Chapter 7) develop a form of company or departmental language which the members of that company or department have helped to create or perpetuate, and which evokes certain ways of thinking and excludes others.

The extent to which the national and social context are reflected in what people say and do depends on whether we are speaking of a low- or a high-context national culture. Hall (1976) first drew the distinction between the two. Communication in a high-context culture depends heavily on the context or non-verbal aspects of communication, whereas the low-context cultures depend more heavily on verbally expressed communication.

Low and high contexting correspond to 'elaborated' and 'restricted' speech codes as propounded by Bernstein (1972). In elaborated codes, meanings are explicit and individualized, as in the USA. The speaker differentiates himself from others as he individualizes his meanings. In restricted codes, speech often cannot be understood apart from the context, and the context cannot be read by those who do not share the history of the relationships or the assumptions which are made.

ORGANIZATIONAL LANGUAGE— COMMITMENT AND CONSTRAINT

The language used in organizations echoes that of the wider culture and, additionally, incorporates the specialized language that has evolved within the organization or specialized part of it. Japanese companies, with their emphasis on interpersonal relations, have a wide variety of words which are related to the concept of *amae* in social interactions. Equally, Americans have words that embody their own individuality, ruggedness, openness to innovation and the linearity and importance of time and other national attributes. West Germans have an abundance of words that underline their very positive attitudes to work and achievement and have a high incidence of use (Lawrence, 1980).

Just as the West German concept of *Technik* is the outcome of the way in which the German language classifies and labels knowledge, so does the language which develops in organizations, or significant parts of them, categorize the organization's experience in a way which evokes particular responses to issues that arise.

Existing organizations have an existing organizational language, either as entire organizations (and this is doubtful except in highly specific circumstances) or as parts of one. New entrants to the organization are introduced to the language associated with the jobs they are taking up. This sensitizes them to observe certain kinds of events and not others. It implicitly indicates how issues should be handled. Effective communicators have to be able to understand and use the language which is most appropriate in the circumstances.

Introducing the New Entrant to Roles and Rules

Accomplishment of Tasks

Socialization is usually acknowledged as the process by which people learn to be good organizational members and perform their tasks in a way that, as far as possible, meets objectives. Language serves the purpose of facilitating the performance of these tasks. It has two major dimensions which have been called 'technical' and 'relational'. Technical language makes possible detailed division of labour and talk about such tasks. In his study of a multinational soap company, Seaton (1976) gives examples of such language, as in 'heavy-duty powder', 'light-duty powder', 'mixed action', 'synthetic', 'enzyme' and so on. More importantly for us, relational language has two aspects which exist side by side, i.e. separation and integration. In other words, for work in an organization to be carried out, roles and responsibilities have to be separated but provision must be made for them to be co-ordinated and integrated back into the whole that is the company.

Entrants to the company studied by Seaton are trained for a particular role by a role maker or 'significant other'. By mastering the linguistic protocol the language of the role sensitizes the entrant to observing certain kinds of events and not others. The role occupant comes to accept and expect certain meanings and patternings of experience that stem from the language which 'goes with the job'. In this way, the role in the large organization inclines to the occupant existing in his or her own small world with its own rules, and so gives rise to the separation which is a condition and effect of specialization. At the same time, the process of linguistic naming re-integrates the new entrant into the entity that is the company.

Confusion is avoided because, in addition to internalizing the detailed requirements of his own role, the new entrant also partially absorbs the role demands of other performance areas in the organization insofar as they relate to him. His training is intended to bring this about. The firm's relational practices enable an executive to be switched from one country to another and make him feel at home quickly, due to the identical procedures and practices. In one sense this multinational company has created its own international occupational language. The individual is forged into the organizational community and all the members are integrated into the mechanism.

Organization of Thought

Language does more than facilitate the negotiation of tasks in an organization. As we have seen, it also serves to organize the way we think. Not only does the language suggest the habits and values of the organization or organizational unit, it also tends to mould how the individual sees himself or herself within the organization. This indicates that the particular multinational company studied by Seaton provides a culture, a way of life and a world-view for its employees. It meets the description of a sub-culture given by Turner (1971) as 'a distinctive set of meanings shared by a group of people whose forms of behaviour differ from these of the wider society'.

It is the mastery of the sub-cultural language that gives substance to the sub-culture. Members of the organization tend to become what they speak, although the views they develop may go well beyond corporate boundaries.

The Organizational Language

The 'universe of discourse' which comes to exist in a large organization implicitly designates how decisions should be taken and what the verbal basis of such decisions should be. It has been argued that there is no such thing as an abstract absolute form of logical reasoning which is applicable to all social contexts. As we have seen, what constitutes a 'reasonable' argument and what does not are products of specific social situational contexts in which different rationalities and logics can develop. The implication of this idea is that it is possible to gain insight into the particular language of an organization or group within it by noting preferred words and terms in contrast to those that are negatively valued.

In addition to suggesting the characteristic preoccupation and intentions of an organization or functional group, language acts as a major vehicle for a new entrant's socialization to the extent that it may affect how he sees not only the organization but also himself and the outside world. The very process of socialization, itself partly a function of language, ensures that organizational personnel adopt a corporate language which determines, to a large extent, members' ways of thinking and decision making. Where there is a strong functional or departmental culture with its own language, when decisions are taken across functions, as they increasingly are, then adjustment has to be made by personnel involved to 'tune in' to what the other groups are saying and to communicate with them in their terms if they wish to advance any project under consideration or make any decision which requires cross-functional communication.

Language, Symbolism and Metaphor

The 'real world', then, as perceived by regularly interacting groups of people sharing a common interest is, to a considerable extent, built up unconsciously through the group's language habits. We see and hear and otherwise experience very much as we do because the language habits of our speech community predispose certain choices of interpretation.

The following verbal concepts indicate the salience of language to the speech community, in this case the firm of Proctor and Gamble, as witnessed by the frequency of discussion about how discussion should be conducted.

———— *continued*

continued

'A *gloss* is a linguistic reformulation of an "event" which has previously been expressed in another way. To offer a gloss on something means to venture a way of classifying it in terms other than those by which it has been classified to date . . . A gloss affords a way of looking at an event from a verbal point of view which transforms its meaning without changing the referents which constitute the event. This is illustrated by the following story, which circulated in the company and almost became folklore. An advertising agency executive phones up a P and G brand manager after some poor sales figures have been announced.

Agency exec.:   "Joe, we've got these tough problems."
P and G exec.:   (always taught to think positively): "Hang on a minute, Jim. If I could put a gloss on what you've just said, I'd prefer to see not tough problems but exciting opportunities."
Agency exec.:   "That's what I said, Joe, we've got this insuperable opportunity."

The concept of gloss makes P and G executives very sensitive to the way in which things should be classified, and, on occasion, the alternative options open in classifying them. It makes P and G executives good debaters, because they have mastered the habit of "category switching" to score points, e.g. "I don't think I'm disagreeing with your analysis of the specific situation; but it is the specific situation we should be worrying about rather something much broader and fundamental."

Perspective in P and G means much as it does in common parlance: a point of view or an interpretation of a situation. To offer a perspective is to describe how an event should be seen. In practice, the more senior the manager, the more likely his perspective in a given situation to be accepted as the legitimate one.

Handling is one of the commonest words. In theory, the way one "handles" a situation means how one deals with it, the style with which one "does" things. In practice, because so much of executive life revolves around verbal symbols, handling comes to mean how one communicates about a situation, what one says about it, to whom one says it, and in what order verbal interaction occurs. "Handling" of a situation frequently means the ability selectively to structure language content in line with what one knows of the specific audiences whose co-operation one must seek to affect the situation. This may include deciding what media to use (X may be mobilized with a formal written request for assistance, Y with a chatty phone call and Z with a personal visit), as well as what to say and how to say it. An executive's ability to "handle" situations is central to his success in the firm.

'Handling' involves a complex repertoire of integrated responses focused round a problem or issue. It involves knowing what formal procedures have to be operated in different contexts, what informal sources to take into account, knowing where the points of resistance and co-operation are likely to be strongest (and what you plan to do about it). But most of all, it involves corporate linguistic competence—understanding the firm's "universe of discourse" knowing what constitutes a valid argument, how it should be

---

continued

continued ——————

expressed to be most effective, and in what order people should be exposed to it. "Good handling" by an executive means more than competence in coping with any one problem; it suggests an all-pervasive kind of socialization based on an understanding of implicit and explicit norms, role demands and communication methods . . . all these things in fact, which make an executive a "good operator".

Positioning, in Procter and Gamble, is a linguistic concept normally encountered when a more powerful individual has to "steer" or direct a less powerful individual. To be "positioned" is to be confronted with a pre-planned, highly deliberate analysis of one's performance either over a period or in dealing with a particular project. All six-monthly assessments constitute a "positioning". In some cases, it may be an itemization of one's strengths and weaknesses, carefully structured so that the salient criticisms are delivered clearly but diplomatically, in such a way that one will be motivated to improve. In other cases the "positioning" may be more blunt, and amount to a threat of dismissal if corrective action is not taken. The interest of the concept in relation to a linguistic study is that it suggests the firm's emphasis on the verbal manner appropriate to particular situations. There are linguistic practices or "vocabularies of action" that all company members must learn.'

(From Seaton, 1976, reproduced by permission)

If language tends to form viewpoints as to what choices are available and organizations or parts of them organize experience in different ways through language, then the notion of a consensual context within which people communicate is one in which different perspectives exist. How can we arrive at solutions when our different 'groupspeaks' may have left us with no agreement as to what our problems are? The danger lies in thinking that because we all speak English or German or French, problems are defined or resolved by plain words, when this is patently not so in very many instances. It is only where there is a speech community with shared perspectives that plain words assist communication.

If we relate our communications to the kinds of problems which managers in organizations face and the decisions they have to make, there are further complications. Managers do not often find their problems straightforward. More often, they have a mess, with a significant history entangled in past mistakes and cover-ups, confounded by power struggles, questionable motives and conflicting agendas (McCaskey, 1988). The significance of the information available is problematical; defining the problem is the problem; key players have different value orientations that lead to political and emotional clashes; contradictions and paradoxes appear. In such circumstances, symbols and metaphors rather than logical arguments are used to advance a position. McCaskey claims from his research that in the early stages of poorly constructed problems metaphors can be more important than logic.

In ambiguous situations, into which category most problems fall, a frequent response is to draw an analogy between one object that is familiar and another that is much less so. The ability to see one object A as another B in the process of making B meaningful is the symbolic function. Symbolism and metaphor are inextricably linked.

Following earlier works suggesting strongly that the symbolic function is not just something human beings possess but a fundamental determinant of the reality we experience from art, science, religion and everyday life, Morgan (1980) has argued that any paradigm (an alternative view of reality which different disciplines may possess) is characterized by metaphors (shared ways or a 'school of thought'). These suggest specific puzzle-solving techniques which are appropriate to the metaphor. This original work identified the machine and the organism as the metaphors most frequently used in organizations. More recently, Morgan has gone beyond these and has convincingly shown how different metaphors illuminate different aspects of an organization and mask others (Morgan, 1986).

These metaphors suggest clearly according to Schön (1979), in his study of policy analysis, that it is problem definition and not problem solving that is crucial, and that this is mediated by stories analysts recount when they talk about a particular issue. In an exploratory study of ambiguity with an induced metaphorical framework, Boland and Greenberg (1988) concluded that organistic metaphors appear to focus attention on the environment, growth and decentralized structures. Mechanistic metaphors focus attention on internal, centralized processes that carefully control the rate of change. Their work, as well as that of Schön, suggests that the development of organizational myths and stories can have an important influence on the kind of problem an organizational member will formulate in a given situation and on the solution that will be proposed for it. It indicates that the management of ambiguity is dependent to an important extent on metaphor and the symbolic function.

The root metaphor originally propounded by Pepper (1954) goes well beyond what we have examined thus far in terms of thought, action and perception. It provides a strong philosophical basis for the necessity of a root metaphor in any attempt to claim reliable knowledge based on theory. This view in defining problems does not ask whether we should use metaphor or not. Instead, it asks which metaphors we are using, if they are selected responsibly, which elements of the situation we are putting into relief and which we are hiding. Boland and Greenberg maintain that as our understanding of problem definition and the management of ambiguity improves, the root metaphor will become increasingly dominant.

Stories, Myths and Ceremonies

The stories told by organizational members often originate, like root metaphor, in attempts of dominant groups to create and perpetuate powerful symbols, with the help of which they can control or manipulate the organization or the context in which it exists. This control can be achieved through language or classifications.

Associated with stories are other symbolic expressions such as myths, ceremonies, heroes and villains. The reality in an organization, as it appears to its members, is essentially a symbolic construction which will last as long as it is enacted by them. These stories and myths give them symbolically loaded points of reference. They are not the same as the objective history of the organization. As such, they often have some factual data in common with the historical event but the meaning assigned to these points of reference may be quite different. These clusters of symbolic representations which are used to guide actions are often referred to as habits, customs, traditions or values.

A myth to guide actions

Marks and Spencer, the UK retailer of a selective range of good-quality, well-designed and attractive merchandise at a price representing value for money, have a special relationship with their suppliers. In return for a guaranteed outlet for their products these suppliers require to be efficient to provide Marks and Spencer's customers with this value for money. Efficiency means producing to tight specifications at an acceptable cost. Efficient producers are rewarded by long-term contracts, but must be prepared to change a poorly selling line at short notice.

Marks and Sparks, as the organization is familiarly known by generations of its customers, provide support services which help supplying companies to maintain and improve their efficiency and increase their profitability. It is only through an adequate profit that suppliers can continue to thrive and keep ahead of the game in which the relationship is seen as crucial.

The company welcomes the attention its suppliers pay not only to themselves as customer but also to the buying public. Indeed, it would be critical of suppliers who did not see this kind of activity as an important aspect of their business. One story quoted by Tse (1985) which has wide currency among the company's personnel is communicated by them, in terms of an expectation to suppliers. Peter Wolff is managing director of S. R. Gent, a company supplying Marks and Spencer with women's blouses, skirts, dressing gowns and nightwear. One Saturday Wolff was patrolling as usual around the women's counters in the Marks and Spencer Marble Arch store in London, assessing the acceptability of the goods his company had supplied, when a customer, suspecting his motives, turned round and slapped his face. Wolff was not so much interested in the woman as in what she was buying. But

continued

---

continued ────────

such is the stuff of which myth is created that the story has been taken into company lore. It is certainly in the interest of Marks and Spencer to perpetuate the story. Wolff is the hero character who, by his attention to the needs of the Marks and Spencer customers, has increased the turnover of S. R. Gent from £170 000 in 1966 to £74 million in 1983, when it went public.

In order to communicate effectively with people in organizations it is first necessary to understand the symbolic representations that organizational members make and which reflect the way in which they see and do things in the organization. Good communication uses this knowledge to make language meaningful in terms of the hearers.

SOME FURTHER CONSIDERATIONS ON LANGUAGE AND THOUGHT

The Sapir–Whorf Hypothesis

Much of what we have already examined is based on the assumption of a link between the language of the group and its ways of thinking, which go beyond seeing language merely as a means of expressing ideas. The main argument over the years has been whether the functions of one's mind are determined by the nature of the language we use or whether it suggests selective ways of categorizing and perceiving it. Current evaluations come down on the side of the latter.

The notion of language as a guide to the reality of organizations as perceived by its members is a theme which has been dominated by Sapir (1929) and Whorf (1941). The central notion of that hypothesis is that language operates not simply as a device for reporting experience but, more significantly, as a way of defining and classifying experience for its speakers. It is a way of ordering experience. Because different languages have their own peculiar and favourite lexical and grammatical devices which are employed in the reporting, analysis and categorizing of experience their users tend to think in different ways. As a result, people using one language may classify and label experiences in a particular way which results in their viewing a problem differently from someone using another language which is divergent and unrelated.

On Identifying Key Organizational Orientations

From his research conducted in the advertising department of a multinational soap company, Seaton (1976) considers organizations as linguistic *domains* with their own 'vocabularies of motive', images and systems of naming and labelling.

In order to recognize a domain, and hence to be in a position to communicate meaningfully with members of it, Seaton suggests three criteria:

1 The significant occurrence of language: these are the metaphors, idioms, imagery, vocabulary, etc. which are not found elsewhere outside the social context within which it occurs. Therefore if an organization uses words which are rare in the wider national/regional culture, or habitually employs language which exists in the wider culture but with a different meaning, then it will tend towards being a domain. By noting preferred words and terms in contrast to those that are negatively valued it is possible to gain insights into the 'universe of discourse' of a particular group.

2 The significant quantitative non-occurrence of language: the names, idioms, metaphors, imagery, vocabulary, etc. which is found elsewhere in the wider culture outside the social context of the organization. Exclusions from a particular social vocabulary are significant when the words excluded are relatively common outside the social context which excludes them. In Seaton's research, for example, there was a low incidence of words expressing uncertainty and doubt. The implication of this was that when communicating with members of the soap company, words suggesting ambiguity, ignorance and hesitation were to be avoided.

3 The subjective assessment of individual members of an organization or an important part of one. When a new entrant to an organization or group forms the impression that it has its own language that has to be consciously mastered then a domain is likely to exist.

Note that the concepts of speech community and linguistic domain are very similar. They are also very similar to the linguistic expression of micro- and pico-cultures addressed in Chapter 6.

A TOTAL COMMUNICATION SYSTEM

As we have seen, communication is an activity which takes place at the verbal, non-verbal, situational, contextual and social–structural levels. These are interrelated and lose meaning in isolation. Together they can be described as a multi-channel or total communication system which Birdwhistell (1973) has called the 'integrational aspect of the communication process'. In the broadest sense the integrational aspect includes all behavioural operations which:

1 Keep the system in operation;
2 Regulate the interaction process;
3 Cross-reference particular messages to comprehensibility in a particular context;
4 Relate the particular context to the larger contexts of which the interaction is but a special situation.

Whether we are speaking about the language that people use as inhabitants of a particular country or region or as members of a particular organization or a department within one, these parallel channels constitute a sound means of making communication meaningful. They require to be mastered by communicators who aim to convey a message in which the interpretation matches the speaker's intention. If a hearer understands and accepts a message, then he has been influenced (Hovland *et al.*, 1953).

It is easy to assume that the use of plain words will avoid the kinds of blocks that prevent genuine communication. This may well be so in a speech community where the language is highly technical as in an information systems group or on a flight deck of an aircraft. It is not enough where dialogue is across nations or across different parts of organizations which can, with justification, be called speech communities.

SUMMARY

1 People brought up in a national culture unconsciously absorb the strictures and commitments which the social structure imposes on them. This was demonstrated in terms of the vertical principle and the one-to-one relationships which form the basis of group organization in Japan and contrasted with West Germany. Each requires a different communication approach.

2 Equally, people who have been absorbed into a public or private organization live with similar strictures and commitments stemming from the structure which has evolved in the organization. They have ranks or positions, symbols of relative power, customs and traditions. Each organization has a unique structure and particular ways of viewing and doing things which have to be addressed if communication is to be effective.

3 Whether we are talking of national or organizational cultures, there is something these have in common. This is a capacity to handle a problem or issue by classifying it in a particular way which might be classified otherwise in another national or organizational culture. When a person from one culture meets a person from another there are likely to be different viewpoints on the same issue. To understand the other viewpoint is the basis for good communication.

4 An organizational language or 'universe of discourse' develops in an organization which implicitly designates how decisions should be taken. An understanding of this organizational language is necessary to communicate both with and within the organization. To effect this understanding, it is necessary to identify (a) preferred words not found outside the social context, (b) words found outside in the wider culture which do not occur inside the organization and (c) the subjective view of new entrants as to the language they have had to learn.

5 Communication is a parallel activity involving oral, non-verbal, situational, contextual and social structural elements which together provide meaning. So interrelated are they that if one is used in isolation, or even if one element is omitted, much of the meaning is lost.

REFERENCES

Bernstein, B. Social class, language and socialization. In Giglioli, P. P. (ed.), *Language and Social Context*, Penguin Books, Harmondsworth (1972).

Birdwhistell, R. L. *Kinesics and Context*, Penguin University Books, Harmondsworth (1973).

Boland, R. J. and Greenberg, R. R. Metaphorical structuring of organizational ambiguity. In Pondy, L. R., Boland, R. J. and Thomas, H. (eds.), *Managing Ambiguity and Change*, John Wiley, New York (1988).

Doi, L. T. *The Anatomy of Dependence*, Kodansha International, Tokyo (1973).

Gumperz, J. J. *Language in Social Groups: The Speech Community*, Stanford University Press, CA (1971).

Hall, E. T. *Beyond Culture*, Anchor Press/Doubleday, New York (1976).

Hofstede, G. *Culture's Consequences: International Differences in Work-related Values*, Sage, Beverly Hills, CA (1984).

Hovland, C. L., Janis, I. L. and Kelley H. H. *Communication and Persuasion*, Yale University Press, CT (1953).

Lawrence, P. A. *Management in West Germany*, Croom Helm, London (1980).

McCaskey, M. B. The challenge of managing ambiguity and change. In Pondy *et al.* (1988).

Morgan, G. Paradigms, metaphors and puzzle-solving. *Administrative Science Quarterly*, **25** (1980).

Morgan, G. *Images of Organisation*, Sage, Beverly Hills, CA (1986).

Nakane, C. *Japanese Society*, Penguin Books, Harmondsworth (1973).

Pepper, S. C. *World Hypotheses*, University of California Press, CA (1954).

Sapir, E. The status of linguistics as a science. In Mandelbaum, D. G. (ed.), *Culture, Language and Personality*, University of California Press, CA (1929).

Schön, D. Generative metaphor: a perspective in problem setting in social policy. In Ortony, A. (ed.), *Metaphor and Thought*, Cambridge University Press, Cambridge (1979).

Seaton, A. V. Language and the secondary socialisation of employees in the multinational corporation: the occupational world-picture of the marketing executive. In Baker, M. J. (ed.), *Buyer Behaviour*, Proceedings of the Marketing Education Group Conference, University of Strathclyde (1976).

Tayeb, M. H. *Organisations and National Culture: A Comparative Analysis*, Sage, London (1988).

Tse, K. K. *Marks and Spencer: anatomy of Britain's most efficiently managed company*, Pergamon, Oxford (1985).

Turner, B. *Exploring the Industrial Sub-Culture*, Macmillan, London (1971).

Van Zandt, H. F. How to negotiate with the Japanese. *Harvard Business Review*, November/December (1970).

Whorf, B. L. The relation of habitual thought and behaviour to language. In *Language, Culture and Personality: Essays in Memory of Edward Sapir*, Sapir Memorial Publication Fund (1941).

Part 2
Communication and Action

Part 2

Communication and Action

Part 2
Communication and Action

6
Influence, Persuasion and Negotiation

As organizations have grown larger, more diversified in products and markets and more technically sophisticated, so they have become more complex. They are characterized by interdependence, in which managers, professionals and technical staff at most levels find that whenever they want to get something done many people can block or delay their actions because they have some power over the situation. They are also characterized by difference, in which diverse goals, values and outlooks lead different people to different conclusions on issues.

What can people do when they try to meet their work targets in these conditions of complexity? What can they do to get their way when they want a particular outcome in face of people who are in a position to block them, wanting different outcomes? When people act in a way which tries to influence something in favour of their group or individual goals their actions and communication behaviours can be said to be political.

Politics is about the use of influence and power. Power in the guise of formal authority, can be used to achieve one's ends by means of the giving of orders. In Western society this is increasingly likely to be achieved by the processes of persuasion and negotiation. Some frameworks for enabling us to understand and address these problems are given in what follows.

INTRODUCTION

Individuals in their interactions with others often seek to influence them because they have some goal they wish to achieve. In organizational and inter-organizational settings these goals usually relate to organizational matters. Sometimes personal interests are aligned with the interests of the organization, but there are occasions on which the temptation to pursue personal goals is too much. This pursuit of personal goals can take place consciously or unconsciously, as we shall see. People's actions and communication behaviours are aimed at influencing an outcome on any issue in favour of their goals, organizational or personal. Recognition of this implies that their actions are political.

THE PERSUASION PROCESS

The Influence Process Continuum

Influence is exercised by leaders at all levels of organizations, both in organizational hierarchies and with peers and others not in an authority relationship. The range of the influence process is shown in Figure 6.1.

Asking for help or *entreating* is the most passive type of influence since the influencer is largely helpless in a given situation. At the opposite end of the continuum is *commanding*, where the influencer enjoys great power. The acceptability of a command can depend on the relative positions of the person giving it and the person receiving it, and the degree of such acceptability may be culturally determined; it can also be affected by particular situations, as where decisive and immediate action is required. Nevertheless, it is maintained that the great majority of influence situations fall within the area B to C in Figure 6.1, that is, *persuading* and *negotiating* (Tarver, 1986).

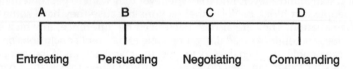

Figure 6.1 *The influence process continuum*

Persuasive Message Strategies

The idea of persuasive message strategies is not new. As pointed out by Miller (1983), the bases of social power identified by French and Raven (1959) each implies a corresponding persuasive strategy.

Six bases of individual and organizational power

Reward power is based on the belief by one individual or organization X that another individual or organization Y has the ability to mediate rewards for him or it and will actually deliver such rewards if X co-operates.

Coercive power is similar to reward power in that it is based on an individual's or organization's control of resources or ability to facilitate another individual's or organization's goal achievement. It relies, however, on the belief that punishments will be forthcoming or rewards withheld unless the requested behaviour is exhibited.

Legitimate power rests on the belief by one individual or organization that another individual or organization has the right to prescribe behaviour.

continued

---

continued ────────────────────────────

Traditional legitimate power stems from the values internalized by an individual or organization that another person or firm has the right to exert influence and that behaviour should be changed to accord with that influence. It is granted informally and is based on an individual's or organization's reputation, position and role.

Referent power results from the willingness or desire of one individual or organization to be associated with another and to maintain such an association. Such a desire may result from the demonstration of desirable behaviour on the part of the second individual or organization, from similarities in characteristics of the two, or merely from the fact that they have been closely associated over time.

Expert power is based on the belief that an individual or organization has special knowledge or expertise within a given area, and that it can confer advantages on a second individual or organization which sees these advantages as significant for its operations.

*Information power** draws on the special information an individual or organization holds as a result of the operations he or it performs and his or its special relationship with sources of information which are of significance for the performance of another individual or organization.

(Adapted from French and Raven, 1959)

*Information power was added by Raven at a later date.

For example, successful use of reward power depends on the persuader's ability to cause the person to be persuaded to perceive that the persuader has the power to control rewards and confer them on the persuadee in return for the latter's compliant behaviour.

Similarly, Kelman's (1961) three processes of social influence are grounded in differing sources of the persuader's power. The potential for compliance, for example, exists when the persuader is perceived as having the means to control rewards and punishments. This potential is usually realized by the persuader translating the ability to reward or punish into symbolic carrots and sticks by subtly or directly drawing the attention of the person to be persuaded to specific rewards resulting from compliance or specific punishments for failure to comply. Both French and Raven's and Kelman's means of influence centre on characteristics of the potential persuader or on persuadee outcomes resulting from compliance rather than on the content of messages in themselves. They imply but do not spell out types of symbolic inducements. Therefore to translate a specific basis of power into a specific package or message content is a necessary further step for developing sets of persuasive message strategies.

Table 6.1. Compliance-gaining message strategies. The examples are drawn from a situation in which a manufacturer, because of appreciation of his country's currency in relation to that of the agent's country, is seeking to become more price competitive there. He is asking the agent to accept a reduced commission in line with his own reduction in margin in the belief that his business will be increased and that the agent will obtain a greater aggregate commission than under the previously agreed rate. The agent feels that there is a matter of principle involved and that his rate of commission should remain inviolate. (Adapted from Marwell and Schmitt, 1967)

Message strategy	What the strategy implies	Manufacturer	Agent
(1) Promise	If you comply, I will reward you	'If you agree to reduce your rate of commission, we will revoke the annual renewal of the agreement and replace it with one for five years.'	
(2) Threat	If you do not comply, I will punish you	'If you feel you can't reduce your rate of commission, we feel the market demand will be negligible and perhaps we should discontinue our relationship with immediate effect.'	
(3) Positive expertise	If you comply, you will be rewarded because of the order of things	'If you reduce your rate of commission, the stimulation of demand will result in a greater aggregate commission.'	
(4) Negative expertise	If you do not comply, you will be punished because of the nature of things	'If you don't reduce your rate of commission, our market share will fall even further and so will your annual commission.'	
(5) Pre-giving	You reward target before requesting compliance		
(6) Aversive stimulation	You continuously punish target to obtain compliance by making cessation contingent on compliance	'We would certainly consider some way of speeding up commission payments on extended credit contracts if you were to reduce your rate of commission.'	
(7) Debt	You owe me compliance because of past favours I have done you	'We have regularly reduced our price under pressure from you, but have paid you full commission. We would hope that you will now reduce your	'We have built up your business here as a result of our hard work and expertise. Surely you're not going to

	Description	Example
(8) Liking	You are friendly and helpful to get target in good frame of mind so that compliance will be achieved	'It's important for you and us that our relationship is maintained. I need your help and I'm asking for . . .'
(9) Moral appeal	A moral person would comply	'You must agree, a principle is a principle and not for negotiation.'
(10) Positive self-feeling	You will feel better about yourself if you comply	'If you accede to our request, you will live in the realization you have acted in an honourable way.'
(11) Negative	You will feel worse about yourself if you do not comply	'If you were to insist on going back on your word, do you think you could live with yourself?'
(12) Positive altercasting	A person with 'good' qualities would comply	'You are experienced and professional businessmen who, I'm sure will agree to the proposal in our mutual interest.'
(13) Negative altercasting	Only a person with 'bad' qualities would not comply	'We know that when the chips are down your commercial judgement wouldn't let you make an ill-advised decision.'
(14) Altruism	I need your compliance very badly, so do it for me	'It's important for you and us that we get the price down. I need your help and I'm asking for . . .'
(15) Positive esteem	People will think highly of you if you comply	'If you agree to this reduction in commission, your associates will respect your judgement in the light of subsequent events.'
(16) Negative esteem	People you value will think worse of you if you don't comply	'If you don't agree to this reduction events may well lose you the professional respect of your associates.'

Three processes of individual and organizational influence

1 *Compliance* occurs where a person or organization accepts an influence
attempt because the person or organization being influenced expects to
elicit a favourable reaction from the influencing individual or organization.
The behaviour will only be maintained in special public situations and the
personal or organizational values and beliefs may be quite different.

2 *Identification* occurs where a person or organization identifies with another
and attempts to establish or maintain a desired association with the
influencing person or organization. It involves a belief that the behaviour
is maintained privately but only in the appropriate role, (for example, shop
steward, boss or supplier or customer firm).

3 *Internalization*—influence is accepted because the influencing individual's
or organization's demands are consonant with the individual's or
organization's values. The content of the behaviour is intrinsically
rewarding. The behaviour becomes part of a personal or organizational
system and is exhibited independently of any external source.

(Adapted from Kelman, 1961)

Using such an approach, Marwell and Schmitt (1967) developed a list of the
compliance-gaining strategies shown in Table 6.1. These, with the exception
of liking and pre-giving, are readily translatable into specific symbolic
inducements. Additionally, the implication of the strategy and examples of
use in relation to each are given. Because the parties to an issue in conflict
both use persuasive message strategies, the examples include two parties.
Some of the strategies are more relevant for one party than the other. In
the promise strategy, for example, rewards are more likely to be offered by
the manufacturer seeking the reduction in agent's commission than the agent
himself. The agent, in the circumstances, is more likely to use the moral
appeal, which can encompass appeal to principle, sense of fair play, legal
basis and precedence.

As indicated, there can be degrees of emphasis in applying the strategy.
Under 'threat' the use of the word 'perhaps' moderates the likelihood of
punishment and finality in that it leaves the door open for the agent to come
back with an accommodating response. It also illustrates that there can be
overlap of the categories, as where the threat also contains an element of
negative expertise.

A Persuasive Message Strategy Model

Attempts to reduce by cluster analysis those sixteen compliance-gaining
strategies to obtain a smaller number of variables showed that this was

difficult because the clusters were highly situationally bound. However, Miller and Parks (1982) have sought to classify these message strategies on the reward/punishment and persuader/persuadee dimensions, giving the following four types of strategies:

1 *Persuader-onus/reward-oriented strategies*: the persuader specifies the rewards that will be forthcoming to the persuadee if the persuadee complies with the message recommendations.
2 *Persuader-onus/punishment-oriented strategies*: the persuader specifies the punishments that will be forthcoming to the persuadee if the persuadee fails to comply with the message recommendations.
3 *Persuadee-onus/reward-oriented strategies*: the persuader specifies the positive self-reinforcing contingencies that will accrue for the persuadee if the persuadee complies with the message recommendations.
4 *Persuadee-onus/punishment-oriented strategies*: the persuader specifies the negative self-reinforcing contingencies that will accrue for the persuadee if the persuadee fails to comply with the message recommendations.

Figure 6.2 depicts this four-part classification. It can be seen that a wide variety of compliance-gaining strategies fit neatly into one of the four general types. In the process they have eliminated 'liking', a strategy not readily translatable into a specific message. In its place they have added 'negative moral appeal' to provide a greater balance to the strategies.

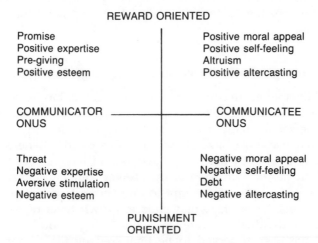

Figure 6.2. *Four categories of persuasive message strategies. (From Miller and Parks, 1982, reproduced by permission of Academic Press)*

Factors Affecting Message Strategy Selection

Research has shown that situational differences have an impact on strategy choice. For example, in intimate interpersonal relationships punishment-oriented strategies are more likely to engender hostility, resentment or insecurity on the part of the intended persuadee than in low-intimate interactions. Equally, individual differences of persuaders can be expected to influence the symbolic inducements they choose to employ. To some, almost any strategy is ethically acceptable, regardless of the reaction it triggers on the part of the persuasive target; for others, anti-social, punishment-oriented strategies are judged to be unethical and are thus unlikely to be used. Cultural factors have also been shown to affect strategy choice: for example, Asians have a higher likelihood of using virtually all the persuasive strategies, particularly those with a positive orientation, than North Americans (Burgoon *et al.*, 1982). Situational factors have also been highlighted in that which individual or group benefits is seen to affect that choice.

Regardless of message strategies selected, good communicators have certain behaviours in support. Every individual in a conflict situation seeking to persuade another to his or her viewpoint is both a proponent seeking to convince and an opponent who must be persuaded if agreement of any kind is to be reached. To be persuasive a good communicator 'should speak like an advocate who is seeking to convince an able and honest arbitrator and should listen like such an arbitrator, always being open to being persuaded by reason. Being open to persuasion is itself persuasive' (Fisher, 1983). By being attentive to what the other party is saying, a communicator is in a better position to select the most appropriate strategy in the circumstances.

Strategies to Resist Persuasive Message Strategies

To date, all the interest in compliance-gaining activity has been one-sided, focusing only on the potential persuader (the agent) as an active element in the interpersonal attempt to induce the recipient (the target) to behave in a preferred way. We have shown in Table 6.1 that where there are opposing interests, both parties are agents and targets. The persuasive message strategies of each were of themselves compliance-resisting.

Where there is a one-way attempt to influence a target the recipient of a persuasive message strategy may choose, for whatever reason, to resist compliance. Individual preferences concerning compliance-resisting strategies have been observed to be tempered by the demands of the particular situation. Situational dimensions relevant to varying kinds of interpersonal persuasive situations have been identified. These include *intimacy* (the degree to which parties to a compliance-gaining transaction are 'close' or 'distant' relationally; *consequences* (the extent to which the outcome of the interaction has short- or long-term consequences); and *rights* (the extent to which the initiator of the compliance-gaining strategy is justified in doing so).

Research has suggested that there is a number of strategies that can be adopted within these categories (McLaughlin *et al.*, 1980). Identity-managing resistance strategies such as comparing the other (unfavourably) to oneself, acting hurt and pretending astonishment so that the other will feel guilty can be expected to occur most frequently in intimate situations. Identity managing should be less effective with non-intimates because there is no feeling of relational commitment to exploit. A justifying strategy is more likely to be used where consequences are more likely to be short term rather than long term. A negotiation compliance-resisting strategy is most likely to be used in situations in which resistance is believed to pose a threat to an intimate relationship. A non-negotiation compliance-resisting strategy, while it may facilitate the achievement of the target's meeting instrumental objectives, suffers from the drawback that it can potentially threaten relational goals. These risks may be modified if the intimacy level is low and/or the relational consequences of resisting compliance are short term and/or the target's rights to resist are high.

ORGANIZATIONS AND THE EXERCISE OF INFLUENCE

When the communication process is related to organizations its nature becomes more complex. People in their various capacities and roles develop ways of thinking which are partly shaped by communication and are linked to the organization or the part of it in which they work. These different ways of thinking often result in conflict. This subject is developed later.

Power and Politics in Organization

Organizational perspectives have been developed to explain what actually goes on in organizations as distinct from what the normative literature says should happen. This reflects a shift from firms as consensual environments where techniques are applied irrespective of the people involved to considering them as political environments. In a significant work, Pfeffer (1981) makes the point of the omnipresence of power and its importance for understanding what goes on in organizations. Power affects decisions in relation to such processes as the allocation of resources and development of strategies. It has an effect on the structure that evolves or is created in organizations and is reflected in that structure.

Where functions and individuals in them perform boundary-spanning roles power accrues to it or them from coping with critical uncertainties in the environment. According to Piercy (1985), this coping is accompanied by the assumption of the information-processing burdens to absorb these uncertainties for the core of the organization. Such departments, functions or individuals create dependencies in other parts of the organization. They may therefore have the potential to exercise their resultant political strength in the manipulation of information important to decision-making processes and on which others in the organization rely.

The idea that better decisions will follow the development of information systems and that information is essentially neutral has been challenged at a number of points. In successful companies informal practices seem to be preferred to formal systems. This is not to say that information is not important. On the contrary, the more important the problem, the more important it is to have relevant information about it. It has been shown that sub-units operating and controlling information systems tend to gain status and influence as a result. Resistance to such systems arises from the fact that change and sophisticated information handling imply a redistribution of power.

Studies have shown that people in their sub-units react to these perceived threats to this status or reputation by political behaviour in relation to information. This is evident in such fields as marketing research (to justify decisions already taken), sales forecasting (to create organizational slack and hence flexibility in handling uncertainty), setting of targets (either to benefit from exceeding a target or quota or to avoid the penalties of not reaching it) and budgets (to advance the interests of their own group, section or department).

Where dependency exists and one party to a relationship is relatively more powerful, conflict is inevitable, even where they are working towards corporate ends. The boundary spanners have the capacity to resolve such conflicts through either the use of influence strategies or the exercise of that power.

Pfeffer maintains that this use of political behaviour to resolve issues is only likely under certain conditions. He sees these conditions as related to interdependence and specialization, disagreement about uncertainty or goals, resource scarcity, conflict and where the issue concerned is perceived to be of prime importance. These contingencies are ever present in organizations. Given that the use of power and politics is dependent on the occurrence of a variety of contingencies, then processual and resource outcomes may be analysed as political outcomes. Piercy (1985) puts these together in an information–structure–power model. This was originally derived for the marketing function but can just as easily be related to other boundary-spanning functions (for example, R&D in a high-technology

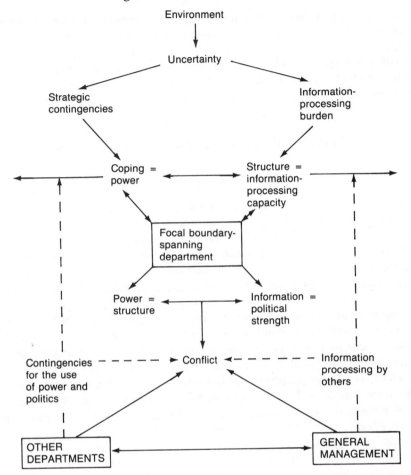

Figure 6.3. *A model of information processing, power, politics and a boundary-spanning department. (Adapted from Piercy, 1985)*

market or production in a stable, cost-conscious one). The ISP model is shown in Figure 6.3.

The ISP Model

The model, adapted for a chosen boundary-spanning department, views that department as a participant in competition with others to cope with the strategic contingencies facing the organization in which structure is an information-processing capacity that confers power. Information is a resource capable of being used politically rather than simply as a component of a 'rational' approach to problem solving. In the ensuing conflicts which will inevitably arise with other departments and with general management, that boundary-spanning department which controls key information in a given situation will tend to be the department whose views will prevail. A mastery of the conflict resolution skills is likely to ensure this is so just as similar skills in another competing department will tend to counter that power.

POWER BETWEEN ORGANIZATIONS

Power Bases and Their Effects

In considering persuasive message strategies it was noted that the bases of social power (French and Raven, 1959) was relevant to such considerations. Although originally developed in relation to interpersonal relations, they have been widely used in the inter-organizational context. Together with the Kelman (1961) studies, these underline that a firm's total power is a combination of several power bases and that these studies supplement more widespread focus on the economic aspects of power. The need to distinguish among the various power bases has been cogently argued by Kasulis and Spekman (1980). They maintain that the use of different power sources has different consequences in terms of understanding on the part of the organization receiving the influence attempt, which, in turn, results in different levels of long-run co-operation. They demonstrate this by combining French and Raven's classification of power sources with Kelman's three consequences of influence attempts as in Table 6.2. They break down French and Raven's 'legitimate' point into 'legal–legitimate' and 'traditional–legitimate'.

The importance of this typology lies in the fact that it establishes the power sources best used where a high level of long-term co-operation is desired. This is particularly so today, when the notion of a 'preferred supplier' is

Table 6.2. *Sources and consequences of power in relation to long-run co-operation. (Based on Kasulis and Spekman, 1980)*

Power base	Likely consequence of an influence attempt	Expected level of long-run co-operation
Coercive	Compliance	Low
Reward	Compliance	Moderate
Legal–legitimate	Compliance	High
Referent	Identification	Low
Expert	Identification	High
Traditional–legitimate	Internalization	Low
Informational	Internalization	High

gaining increasing support and buyers seek to establish associative relationships in which suppliers' needs are considered at appropriate decision points. A buyer's commitment to his sellers is seen to be as important as the seller's commitment to the buyer. It also has significant implication for those long-term arrangements between organizations such as distributorship, licence and joint-venture agreements.

Dependence and Conflict

Where organizations align themselves in a voluntary business relationship, that relationship exists because the organizations see benefits in it. Thus they have a mutual dependence, but this dependence is rarely equal. Inter-organizational relations are more likely to be characterized by unequal than by equal power. One party to that relationship will therefore enjoy a *relative* power advantage.

By aligning themselves with other organizations in a relationship of dependence, organizations commit themselves to co-operative activities. These activities can be simple episodes within a limited relationship, such as a one-off, where a buying firm can freely choose among available alternatives. Within the need to co-operate to meet each other's needs, as in sales/purchase transactions, behaviour can be highly competitive. As relationships become more extensive, as in long-term contractual arrangements such as distributorship or in quasi-vertically integrated organizations (Blois, 1980), the general tenor is much more co-operative. Within such a relationship conflicts may arise between individuals who have to operate the agreements on a continuing basis. Long-term conflicts cannot be sustained when alternatives exist to provide partners with a more acceptable working atmosphere. When organizations reach an impasse on an issue, it can sometimes only be resolved by the party possessing the relative power exercising that power in the knowledge that, for example, other potential distributors exist or that the other party will acquiesce because they perceive the costs of giving in as being less than the benefits of holding out.

In such circumstances the resolution of conflict, which is very much a matter of communication, becomes central to the effective integration of activities between organizations. The interrelationships affecting the outcomes of interacting negotiators of differing organizations have been shown by McCall and Warrington (1989). In their model, environmental influences, influence strategies and skills, behavioural predispositions of the people involved and situational influences all interact to make the parties behave in a particular way. The interaction of the parties themselves also affects outcomes. The model provides a reference point for communicators who can relate it to

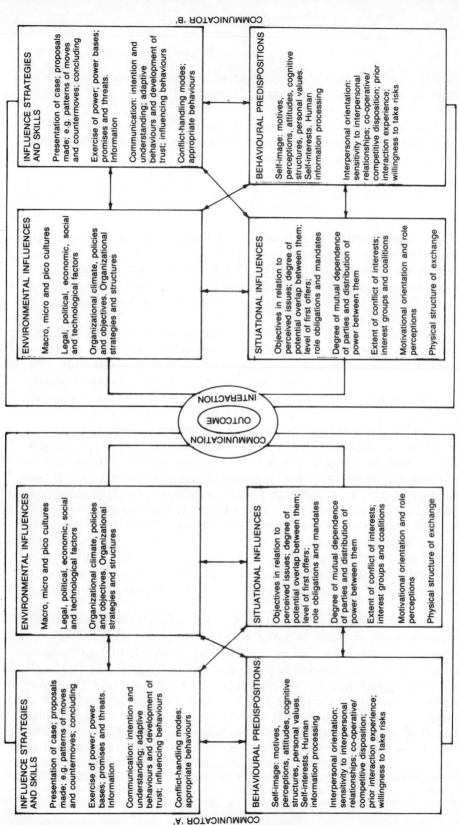

Figure 6.4. Factors influencing communication interactions and their outcomes both inside and between organizations. (Adapted from a paper by Gallwey and Wainwright, 1980)

particular issues on which they seek to resolve some conflict. This provides the basis for the communication model shown in Figure 6.4.

A COMMUNICATION MODEL FOR ORGANIZATIONS

Because people are normally recruited to fill job descriptions, it is important that they should have perspectives which relate what they do in their specialized functions to the wider organization. Only by doing this is it possible for managers at different levels below general management to foresee and predict those factors which bear on what they are seeking to do when more than one viewpoint exists. It is also a step in the direction of creating awareness of what others in an organization are trying to do, either in their own or in an organization with which they do business. It helps people in organizations to see their own behaviour from the viewpoint of others and so assist them in choosing the behaviour most likely to have acceptable outcomes.

Figure 6.4 seeks to encapsulate this in the interaction of organizational structures and processes, individual behavioural traits and concepts of objective and subjective power with influence strategies and communication skills. It also illustrates how different factors in interacting organizations can result in differing viewpoints being brought to the communication exchange.

The model accommodates the persuasive message strategy model (Miller and Parks, 1982) and the situational, cultural and individual factors seen to affect message strategy choice. Equally, it encompasses the Piercy information–structure–power model and allows consideration of environmental uncertainty and of the coping/information-processing behaviour of boundary-spanning departments which possess the political power to influence the outcomes of conflict situations involving other departments or sub-units. It draws on and incorporates the inter-organizational perspective of McCall and Warrington (1989), in which the implementation of plans is viewed as negotiated, agreed instruments and where the focus is on the influences and skills in the face-to-face interaction. Equally, it takes account of the Kasulis and Spekman (1980) synthesis of power bases and their effects in relation to the level of long-run co-operation.

SUMMARY OF MAIN POINTS SO FAR

1 Managers and professional and technical personnel at most levels pursue organizational and personal goals and seek to influence outcomes in a way that enhances these goals, i.e. their actions are political. Such political

actions are usually by means of persuasion and negotiation. Sometimes it is necessary to give orders to achieve these political ends.

2 Different forms of persuasive message strategies have been described with examples of usage. These were grouped into a four-category model. Such message strategies are necessary in organizations, which have come to be regarded as political environments. A persuasive message strategy rests on sources of power and the needs and feelings of individuals.

3 Boundary-spanning functions and personnel help their organizations to cope with environmental uncertainties. They create dependencies in other parts of the organization by virtue of the information they gather and hold. They use this information, consciously and unconsciously, to further departmental, functional, factional, sectional or individual interests.

4 A department exercising a boundary-spanning function is in competition with others to cope with strategic contingencies facing the organization in which structure is an information-processing capacity capable of being used politically (for example, to obtain advantageous outcomes in conflict with other departments and general management in relation to such issues as allocation of resources). An information–structure–power model was described.

5 Power and politics are central to inter-organizational relations. Organizations see benefits in aligning themselves with other organizations and therefore have a relationship of mutual dependence with them. As this relationship is rarely equal, conflicts inevitably arise. In such circumstances communication lies at the heart of conflict resolution and the integration of activities between organizations.

6 A communication model has been derived which encompasses the persuasive message strategies model, the information–structure–power model and the inter-organizational perspective in which implementation of strategies and plans are viewed as negotiated, agreed instruments. This model assists people to view their own behaviour from the viewpoint of others. It emphasizes all the factors affecting communication inter-actions and outcomes.

NEGOTIATION PROCESSES

When negotiation as a conflict-resolving process is addressed it is useful to view it against the background of the communication model shown in Figure 6.4. This highlights these factors bearing on outcomes and acts as a checklist to remind interactors of what they may wish to take into account in relation to the issues for resolution as they affect both parties. It is also a timely reminder that what goes on within organizations (for example, in relation to values, assumptions, objectives and expectations) has implications for the interests of the parties and for the positions they take up. This will affect outcomes of inter-organizational disagreements.

Formal Negotiations

Attempts have been made to simplify analysis of the negotiation process by reducing it to sub-processes or stages (see Figure 6.6). The first of these stages in the face-to-face situation is *distributive bargaining*. In formal negotiations this stage is characterized by the assumption of extreme positions by both parties as a means of exploring the likely range of negotiations and as a starting point for the evaluation of the acceptability of the demand being made.

There is some evidence to indicate that early co-operative behaviour tends to promote the development of trust and a mutually beneficial co-operative relationship. Early competitive behaviour tends to cause suspicion and a competitive response. At this stage, competitive behaviour is usually quite acceptable where parties are meeting for the first time. First, it is often expected and assumes a ritual character. Second, no commitments have been made, with the result that competitive behaviour is less likely to receive a retaliatory response than one taken at a later stage when positional lines have been drawn. Research indicates that the higher the initial demands, the more advantageous the agreed outcome. There is also the cautionary corollary that the higher the demand, the less likelihood there is of settlement.

Extreme demands in initial proposals largely determine the course of negotiation. It is here that rules and norms are first established if there has been no previous interaction between the parties. Earlier negotiations will have set the benchmarks against which decisions will be measured and where issues such as trust and toughness in bargaining are considered. Opening moves are generally used to convey information not only about how each party is disposed to the other in terms of co-operativeness or competitiveness but also about what the other party is aspiring to, both for the organization and self.

A useful representation of this has been developed on the assertive/ unassertive and unco-operative/co-operative dimensions of behaviour (Thomas, 1976) (see Figure 6.5). The assertive/unassertive dimension measures how a negotiating individual seeks to satisfy his or her own objectives and the unco-operative/co-operative dimension how far the negotiator tries to satisfy the objectives of the other. Avoiding behaviour is only likely to be used in negotiation where the negotiator employing it is in a strong position and wishes to further weaken the stance of an opponent. Compromising is a strategy which is directed at resolving conflict

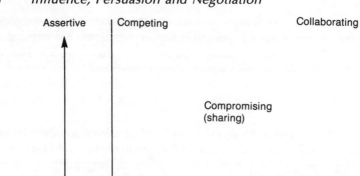

Figure 6.5. *Conflict-handling behaviours open to negotiators. (From Thomas, 1976, reproduced by permission)*

by means of deals and trade-offs. A competing approach attempts to create win/lose situations and employ the exercise of power to achieve one's ends. Collaborating behaviour seeks solutions acceptable to both parties as a result of confronting differences and sharing ideas and information. If both negotiators have this approach, integrative and elegant solutions can often be found. If, however, one of the parties adopts a competitive approach, then the other party has to adopt that approach also and compromise is likely to be the order of the day, as where two competitive opponents meet and hope to reach agreement. Good negotiators must therefore have the skills to be co-operative or competitive as the situation warrants.

When extreme positions are taken up, the behaviour and the language used by the participants reflects this stance, i.e. hard and uncompromising (see Figure 6.6). If such positions are repeatedly reinforced in proposals it becomes progressively more difficult for each party to move in the direction of the other. Fears of position loss ('If I concede, she might not respond') and image loss ('if I concede now, she'll think I'm giving in') make such moves difficult.

Getting Movement

To escape from the position where he has become increasingly committed to an original position, making retraction difficult, the negotiator has a way out. It is encapsulated in the phrase 'to convey without commitment' (Morley and Stephenson, 1977). Skilled negotiators use signalling behaviour to break out of such non-conclusive argument. By verbal and non-verbal clues they make a proposal in such a way that the possibility of agreement is created.

Consider the statement 'These are our standard conditions'. If the statement is made in a neutral way it will merely indicate the existence of standard conditions and imply that these represent the bottom line. If, however, the accent is placed on the word 'standard', a more subtle emphasis with a shift of meaning is being made. There is a suggestion that conditions may be up for negotiation. A skilled negotiator will be sensitive to the clue being given and will make an appropriate response. He might say 'We can't really accept your conditions *as they stand*'. A further sensitive enquiry might elicit a further proposal: 'If you were *prepared* to reduce the rate of liquidated damages from 10% to 5% we *might consider* . . .' The possibility of agreement has been created without the negotiators yet committing themselves. A promise message strategy is being signalled subject to a sensitive response.

Integrative Bargaining

Once movement has been initiated, the negotiators can apply themselves to their interests in the issues that separate them. To this extent, they are progressively more open and frank and can be said to be entering a phase characterized by movement towards agreement. The more sure a negotiator is of the other's commitment and the less uncertainty there is for him, the more he can react rationally to the other's moves.

Where there is a number of issues on which the sides have differing interests, one side may sometimes try to deal with the issues one by one. This should be seen for what it is, and that is an attempt to steal a march on the other party. Wise negotiators reserve their position by keeping issues linked, and never agree to anything until they know the full extent of the demands being made. By maintaining this kind of flexibility a negotiator is more likely to reach a mutually favourable agreement. All issues are juggled simultaneously, so presenting to the other side a complete package which that side can then evaluate.

The exchange of information that takes place during this stage sees the negotiators using the range of their persuasive message strategies and skills to convince their opponents that they should move more towards the negotiator's point of view. In the process they test the commitment of the other side to the positions they have taken up and seek to uncover information which they can use for mutual influence. If a financial manager in the opponent's organization reveals that the offer of the negotiator's organization is the lowest, or an engineer indicates that his tender is the only one to meet specification, or the organization's bank manager divulges that a very favourable view of the company is taken by the bank, that is

SKILLS PREDOMINANTLY REQUIRED WITHIN EACH STAGE OF THE NEGOTIATION PROCESS	SKILLS PREDOMINANTLY REQUIRED TO EFFECT MOVEMENT FROM ONE STAGE TO THE NEXT IN NEGOTIATION PROCESS	NATURE OF REQUIRED BEHAVIOUR AND LANGUAGE	EXAMPLES OF LANGUAGE USAGE
① PRE-NEGOTIATION STAGE To determine objectives in relation to environmental and known or likely situational factors: to establish best level of first offer where appropriate To identify where possible nature of issues to be resolved. If necessary by the interactive process: to identify possible intangible issues To plan the negotiation, e.g. by identifying or building in trade-offs; to prepare alternative courses of action to meet different contingencies; to establish authority limits	**② A** To make, where necessary, written and/or oral presentations, e.g. propositions for mutually dependent activity, of such a quality as to elicit a positive response to open negotiations		
③ DISTRIBUTIVE BARGAINING STAGE To test limits and further isolate issues; to identify factors in the situation which affect relative power To identify whether basically co-operative or competitive strategies should be used To establish preferences and needs of opposing party To push for most advantageous outcome	**④ B** To convey without commitment, by use of indicating behaviour, implying willingness to move from an entrenched position provided some movement is made in return by opposer. To achieve a positive response by appropriate verbal and non-verbal skills	③ Reflects this stage i.e. 'hard', uncompromising ④ Provision of signals by words, by pitch and stress and by body language and other actions	③ 'My members will settle for no less than a 10% increase, with no strings attached' 'We couldn't possibly agree to such a low price. On the contrary, such is the demand for our product that ...' 'Do you mean to say you cannot supply for less than ...?' ④ 'We might consider such a step should you find it possible to ...' 'These are our standard conditions' 'Perhaps we could take a break to see how we might find a solution to this'
⑤ INTEGRATIVE BARGAINING STAGE To be aware of own and other party's style of behaviour; to adopt appropriate conflict-handling mode(s) To exercise the range of interpersonal skills, especially those concerned with communicating and influencing		⑤ Reflects the need to identify common ground by addressing interests and by non-confrontive behaviour	⑤ 'Perhaps we could defer discussion on that point until we know the extent of ...' 'That is a principle at the heart of our company policy and is not open to negotiation' 'Can you clarify ...?'

INTERACTION

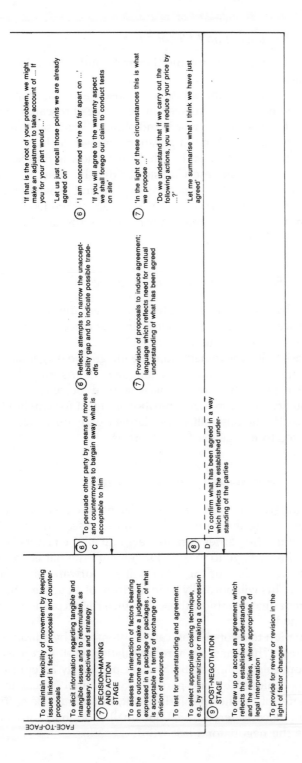

Figure 6.6. *A negotiation skills model. The cycle of negotiation shows the skills required within each stage and for progression between stages. This includes examples of the language used in support of the behaviours at each stage and between stages involving face-to-face interaction. 1. The same individual(s) would not necessarily be involved at the pre- and post-negotiation stages but would need to be party to the continuity. 2 These stages are a conceptualization of the real thing. In practice, negotiations do not always fall into such neat categories. For example, where the number of issues is small and negotiators know each other's style the participants may move almost directly to stage 5. Where a negotiator attempts to tie in 'extraneous' issues, the process may be gone through again. In international negotiations cultural issues can de-emphasize certain stages*

a cue for the negotiator to increase his demands and so obtain a more favourable outcome.

The language used reflects the strategies chosen and the behaviours preferred. The skilled negotiator was seen in one piece of research to make fewer proposals and to avoid certain words and phrases which say favourable things about the negotiator and, by implication, unfavourable ones about his opponent. He is more likely to let the other party know in the exchanges what his feelings are (Rackham and Carlisle, 1978). This may or may not be genuine, but it has the effect of appearing explicit and above board (I'm very concerned we're so far apart on . . .'). He is also more likely to give advance indication of the kind of behaviour he is about to use ('Can I ask you a question . . .? What . . .?').

Bargaining Away the Unacceptable

Once commitments have been demonstrated and tested, the gap separating the parties is narrowed. Further movement can take place only when the parties identify the ultimate bargain.

At this point of facilitating movement from the integrative bargaining stage to the concluding one the precision of the language in ensuring that each party has a similar perception on what is agreed becomes of prime importance. The ability to summarize a position and test for ambiguity are the skills which provide the possibility of isolating clearly only these issues which the parties see to be against their interests.

Decision-making and Action Stage

The moves and countermoves of the parties have now reduced the area of conflict to the stage where they are in a position to assess the possibility of reaching agreement. The parties seek to weigh up all the factors bearing on the outcome and now have to make a judgement on what is and what is not acceptable to both. One or the other will put forward his proposal for the final bargain. This will normally be in the form of a package, because issues have been kept linked until all those in which there could be conflict have been established.

Bringing a negotiation to a conclusion can be attempted by summarizing the position reached. This may be a recapitulation of the concessions exchanged and proposals made which a weaker party may accept in their totality. Often, it is achieved by one party making a final concession. Its magnitude is a matter of on-the-spot judgement, but should be sufficient in that it should not be considered trivial but small enough to convince an opponent that it is the negotiator's last word.

Neither of the parties knows exactly how much he can maximize his advantages. A negotiator can only make assumptions about an opponent's preferences, expectations and goals. It is the testing of these assumptions which is a prime function of negotiators, and the interpretation made will vary with the experience and perception of the tester.

There are two forces at work on the parties. One is the esteem motivation that drives them to strike the best possible bargain and provide the satisfaction of a job well done. It is this knowledge which provides the personal satisfaction. The other is the security motivation to settle when a reasonable bargain is identified, rather than seek a more advantageous outcome at the possible risk of no agreement.

The language at this time has to ensure that an agreement will be made that will stick. There is always a temptation to agree, leaving certain points unclear. An efficient agreement can never be guaranteed, but can be greatly assisted by summarizing and testing of understanding. While both these behaviours can be used at all stages, they take on a greater significance as agreement is approached. If the parties go away with different perceptions of what has been agreed that is a recipe for future conflict and further negotiations.

The nature of the negotiation will determine what takes place next. In commercial negotiations it is not unusual to confirm in writing what has been agreed, to avoid misunderstanding. This is followed by the post-negotiation stage, in which the understanding is given expression in contractual and legal form. In industrial relations bargaining, the legitimacy of the agreement is seen in its operation from the perceptions of the participants.

The Informal Negotiation Process

There is much more to negotiations than winning contracts or getting the advantage for management or unions, or creating and sustaining agreements that advance an organization's goals. Such negotiations are often characterized by formalized relations.

There are also less formal negotiations, which take place all the time, in which the principles of persuasion and exchange apply. These are not sustained by legal sanctions as in commercial agreements, which often hold organizations to agreements after one or other of the parties sees the costs of maintaining the agreement as exceeding the advantages stemming from it. They do not involve adherence to ritual, as often witnessed in formal negotiations.

Typically, a manager, whether concerned with strategic directions, technical operations or a professional service, will wish to get something done or embark on a course of action that requires the support of others. The authority that a subordinate has had delegated to him or is tacitly implied as his responsibility in given situations depends on the views of others, including that of his immediate boss, of what he is seeking to do. It is not surprising that managers concern themselves with ensuring and maintaining authorization to get things done themselves and with having access to, and influence on, the resources through which their ideas can be implemented. A viable strategy for whatever purpose should embody a 'good goal' and is both 'authorizable' and 'producible' (Lax and Sebenius, 1986).

An individual with any authority in an organization therefore has at one and the same time a series of agreements, explicit or implicit, by which he carries out what he feels he has to do to meet his task objectives. He has to produce the goods, whether tangible products or services, or more elusive ends such as co-ordination or safety. In the process he must keep his mandate agreements (his purposes, authority and resources) in good shape. At the same time, he must also maintain his production agreements (the means and people through which he gets results). Ideally, these should be kept in alignment. When managers do this they are in the middle of linked negotiations. They face a similar form of negotiation when representing their organizations in negotiations with external parties.

Such agreements are subject to change. Inside organizations they are often not recorded and so are subject to reinterpretation. Because there is no mechanism for enforcing them, special care has to be exercised, particularly where they may be unstable. The sustainability of such agreements depends on how binding a commitment the parties make to them and what advantages are seen to stem from adherence to them. It is therefore up to the parties to anticipate likely problems. They should carefully examine the possible future problems in terms of later unfairness, new information and changed alternatives.

Linked Bargaining

Managers negotiate with those people reporting directly to them over issues which are of concern to their own bosses. Also, managers deal with their own bosses in relation to questions that concern their dealings with their subordinates. To this extent, the manager is in the middle of a network of linked agreements.

In internal dealings a manager can build a coalition in support of his desired position. He can also 'buy off' potential opponents by structuring his proposals to their relative advantage. When internal parties' interests on various issues are not in direct conflict, consensus is sometimes reached only on the basis of a minimally acceptable agreement but results in a proposal unacceptable to an external party.

It is possible to use external negotiations to achieve a preferred internal decision. By controlling the information available to him, the 'in-between' manager is in a position to affect the outcome of internal issues, such as where a firm close to bankruptcy was involved in linked agreements with their unions (internal negotiations) and their creditors (external negotiations). The managers so misrepresented the creditors' minimal conditions as to obtain penal wage concessions from the unions. In other circumstances it is not unusual for someone within an organization to enlist the assistance of some respected external authority to add his support to achieve a preferred solution where disagreement exists. Similarly, it is possible to use internal negotiations to achieve a desired decision externally by filtering information, acting as if the positions of others were fixed, manipulating demands and deadlines, altering agendas and changing mandates.

A number of factors have to be taken into account in these interactions between internal and external negotiations (for example, the effects of different cultures and styles within and between organizations, the roles of misperception and irrational behaviour). These are addressed in the following chapters.

When Informal Becomes Formal

So far we have emphasized the persuasion and negotiation elements in the influence process continuum (Figure 6.1). However, any consideration of influence and persuasion is not complete without an examination of *commanding*. In bureaucratic structures where decisions are taken under conditions of urgency (for example, army, emergency services) there is little time to indulge in negotiation or other conflict-solving behaviour and orders have to be obeyed; where rules determine how people behave, this lends itself to the giving of orders.

In other situations, even in organizations which view a certain amount of conflict as productive, negotiation and persuasion may be followed up to the point where a manager uses his formal authority to decide an issue on which resolution of the conflict does not appear to be emerging, when quick, decisive action is vital on important issues, when unpopular actions need to be implemented and on issues vital to organizational interests where the superior knows he is right. Just when and how such interventions will be made in what is becoming increasingly a two-way process depends on a number of variables, including the culture of the organization or department, management style—often seen as an analogue of culture, the personality of the manager himself and the nature of the business.

SUMMARY OF NEGOTIATION PROCESSES

1 A representation has been given of how parties to a negotiation are disposed to each other in terms of co-operativeness and competitiveness

and also of what each party is aspiring to for the organization and for involved individuals.

2 Against the background of the model explaining communication interactions and outcomes a negotiation skills model was illustrated. This highlights the skills required at different stages of negotiation and those needed to proceed from one stage to another.

3 A less formal negotiation process was described in which people at different managerial levels bargain explicitly or implicitly with their bosses for the authority and resources they need to meet their task objectives. At the same time, they also have explicit or implicit agreements with the people through whom they get results. To that extent, they are involved in a network of linked negotiations. They face a similar series of linked negotiations internally and with external parties.

4 There are situations in which a manager requires to exercise his formal authority by 'commanding' (for example, when subordinates cannot agree on joint action, or on issues vital to the organization's interests).

REFERENCES

Blois, K. Quasi-integration as a mechanism for controlling external dependencies. *Management Decision*, **18**, No. 1 (1980).

Burgoon, M., Dillar, J. P., Doran, N. E. and Miller, M. D. Cultural and situational influences on the process of persuasive strategy selection. *International Journal of Intercultural Relations*, **6** (1982).

Fisher, R. Negotiation power. *American Behavioural Scientist*, **27**, No. 2 (1983).

French, J. R. and Raven, B. H. The bases of social power. In Cartwright, D. (ed.), *Studies in Social Power*, University of Michigan Press, Ann Arbor (1959).

Kasulis, J. T. and Spekman, R. E. A framework for the use of power. *European Journal of Marketing*, **14**, No. 4 (1980).

Kelman, H. C. Processes of opinion change. *Public Opinion Quarterly*, **25** (1961).

Lax, D. A. and Sebenius, J. K. *The Manager as Negotiator: Bargaining for Cooperation and Competitive Gain*, The Free Press, New York (1986).

Marwell, G. and Schmitt, D. R. Dimensions of compliance-gaining behaviour. *Sociometry*, **30** (1967).

McCall, J. B. and Warrington, M. B. *Marketing by Agreement: A Cross-Cultural Approach to Business Negotiations* John Wiley, Chichester (1989).

McLaughlin, M. L., Cody, M. J. and Robey, C. S. Situational influences on the selection of strategies to resist compliance gaining attempts. *Human Communication Research*, **7**, No. 1 (1980).

Miller, G. R. On various ways of skinning symbolic cats: recent research on persuasive message strategies. *Journal of Language and Social Psychology*, **2**, Nos 2–4 (1983).

Miller, G. R. and Parks, M. R. Communicating in dissolving relationships. In Duck, S., *Personal Relationships: Dissolving Personal Relationships*, Academic Press, London (1982).

Morley, I. E. and Stephenson, G. M. *The Social Psychology of Bargaining*, Allen and Unwin, London (1977).

Pfeffer, J. *Power in Organisations*, Pitman, London (1981).

Piercy, N. *Marketing Organisation: An Analysis of Information Processing, Power and Politics* Allen and Unwin, London (1985).

Rackham, N. and Carlisle, J. The effective negotiator: the behaviour of successful negotiators. *Journal of European Industrial Training*, **2**, No. 6 (1978).

Tarver, J. L. A case for teaching persuasion and negotiation in the business school. *Business Education*, **7**, No. 3 (1986).

Thomas, K. W. Conflict and conflict management. In Dunette, M. D. (ed.), *Handbook of Organizational and Industrial Psychology*, McNally, Santa Barbara (1976).

7
Communication Problem Solving Within Organizations (1)

Rational decision making is very much a Western tradition. Yet decisions are often taken on a non-rational basis. Organizations consist of groups of people who themselves develop a particular way of viewing things which appears to them as objective. In larger organizations different groups or functions evolve different outlooks and indulge in political activity in support of the positions they take up. Individuals often try to influence such positions in their own perceived interests. Senior managers seek to curb individual interests and to exercise control by encouraging the development of views consistent with their aims for the organization or for themselves.

All groups and individuals within them use communication to achieve group and individual ends in either their capacities of leaders or as subordinates. Managers with corporate responsibility employ communication skills as a means of integrating highly specialized groups and departments for the purpose of achieving organizational goals.

INTRODUCTION

What we usually understand by organization is the reduction of uncertainty and the creation of order and stability. One manifestation of this creation of stability is organization structure. The necessity for the specialization of tasks and the placing of people in authority over others eventually to meet the organization's goals are reflected in these structures. It is also reflected in the roles and rules which emerge or are prescribed for people working in an organization. These represent some of the means by which influence is exercised by senior managers. Others are the processes of induction into the organization's procedures and the motivational and control activities which result in outcomes which the top management of an organization seeks to bring about.

The behaviour of subordinates is thus largely specified and circumscribed. At the same time, managers who feel constrained by these controls will normally try to negotiate some area of discretion, of creativity, of self-expression and hence of uncertainty. The power wielded by virtue of the role that top managers fulfil in their attempts to exercise influence and control is, to a certain extent, countered by subordinate managers' ability to cope with the uncertainty they themselves help to create.

For example, a sales manager with a knowledge of overseas markets from an earlier job might have prevailed on his general management to enter those markets as a preferred solution to a problem of peaks and troughs in demand. As a result, production is exposed to uncertainty in making minor modifications to products to meet the needs of particular markets; R&D requires to take the new markets into account in the design of new products; accounts need to take notice of variable costs resulting from modifications and the allocation of appropriate overheads to the new activities. The sales manager's ability to smooth out demand by entering markets where demand takes up the slack in the troughs facilitates efficient production; the identification of specific factors of different markets on the product clarifies the position for R&D, who will want sales to monitor the markets; and determining the relevant proportion of sales staff to export activities helps to derive the appropriate allocation of fixed costs. All these factors give the sales manager power, since his superiors, as well as peers, come to rely on him to carry out his tasks well.

DECISION MAKING AND PROBLEM SOLVING IN ORGANIZATIONS

The Myth of Rationality

Management decision making is what constitutes much of management activity and has, for a long time, been a focus for writers on management in organizations. Classical thinking about decision making has sought to lay down a decision-making sequence which includes careful definition of the problem, establishment of decision criteria, an exhaustive search for information, generation of numerous alternatives and a calculated choice among these alternatives. It has been seen as an orderly and rational process.

In our Western tradition those things which are regarded as determinable by objective or 'scientific' tests constitute a universal, objective or *external physical reality* (Schein, 1985, p. 89). For example, if two managers are arguing about which product to launch on the market they can agree to define a test market and establish criteria by which to resolve the issue.

However, the rational model of decision making has been strongly challenged on a number of counts. For most people the human brain can only retain about seven pieces of information in the short-term memory (Miller, 1968; Simon, 1979). The implications of this for decision makers is that managers cope with the provision of stimuli by employing strategies which make the task more manageable, e.g. by 'lumping' events together in order to retain greater amounts of information. Thus managers do not deal with new information piecemeal but tend to force it into pre-existing mind sets even if it does not really fit.

The rational model has been further challenged on the grounds that decision making is characterized by 'bounded rationality'. Decisions are made not on the basis of all reasonably available information but as soon as there is sufficient information.

Table 7.1. Apart from the limited ability of individuals to process information, research has shown many information-processing biases. (Based on Hogarth and Makridakis, 1981, as adapted by McCall and Kaplan, 1985, reproduced by permission)

Bias/source of bias	Description/example
Availability	If a person can easily recall specific instances of an event, he or she may overestimate how frequently the event occurs (and vice versa)
	Chance events or cues can hinder or help by pointing a person in a particular direction
Selective perception	What one expects to see biases what one does see
	People seek information consistent with their own views
	People downplay information that conflicts with a consistent profile
Concrete information	Vivid, direct experience dominates abstract information; a single personal experience can outweigh more valid statistical information
Data presentation	The items presented first (primacy) or last (recency) in a series assume undue importance
	Whether information is collected sequentially or all at once affects what is processed
Inconsistency	People have trouble applying a consistent judgemental strategy across similar cases, even though they believe they are consistent
Law of small numbers	Small samples are deemed representative of the larger population (a few cases 'prove the rule'), even when they are not
Complexity	Under time pressure, processing of complex information may be quite superficial
Gambler's fallacy	Seeing an unexpected number of similar chance events leads to belief that an event not seen will occur (e.g. after observing nine successive reds in roulette, believing chances for a black on the next roll are greater than 50/50)

The whole field of information, while becoming increasingly sophisticated with rapid developments in information technology, is subject to all sorts of conscious or unconscious manipulation or interpretation. The various biases identified in human information processing is shown in Table 7.1.

Another reason for questioning the primacy of the rational model is that different functional managers will tend to view a problem in relation to their own mental sets unless they have worked in other functions and have an awareness of how these functions view the issue.

Because of differing time horizons, R&D and sales staff can have difficulty in communicating. In a study of different types of organizations, Lawrence and Lorsch (1967) noted that the length of the time horizon depended on the kind of work being done. For salesmen the completion of a sale could take minutes, days, weeks or even months. However, even their longer time horizons were much shorter than those of research staff, for whom a one-

---

A study of two radiology departments during the year that each began to operate its first body scanner gives a good example of latent collision between sub-cultures.

'Prior to the arrival of the body scanners, technologists in both hospitals made clear occupational distinctions among themselves. Some X-ray technologists even resented the sonographers and the 'specials' techs, not simply because their pay was higher, but because theirs was not 'dirty work', and because radiologists accorded the latter groups higher prestige. However, before the arrival of the scanners, conflict between the various technologists remained mute, since all technologists were required to pull duty assignments in the main department.

Once the body scanners arrived, the specials techs (for different reasons in the two hospitals) were assigned less frequently to the main department, and the CT techs were absolved of X-ray responsibilities. Moreover, the scanner operations began to preoccupy the radiologists' attention, and the technologists perceived that the radiologists were no longer interested in the older technologies. As a result of these events, the boundaries between the various technological sub-units quickly solidified and sub-cultural identities became apparent. X-ray techs began to complain more frequently about their work, while sonographers and specials techs deplored the privileged treatment given CT techs and began to protest loudly about being assigned to X-ray. CT techs began to derogate X-ray work as well as the lofty attitudes of the sonographers and special techs, who in turn concluded that CT work was mere 'button-pushing.' Seemingly, the only common ground was that members of each technological sub-culture blamed the 'bosses' and the radiologists for the perceived inequities of their respective situations, and each therefore began to press hard their individual claims with whomever would listen. In response, administrators haphazardly attempted to respond to sub-cultural pressures; but since honoring one group's claims involved affronting another, administration actions only amplified the conflict.'

(From Van Maanen and Barley, 1985, reproduced by permission of Sage Publications, Inc.)

or two-year horizon was normal to meet their objectives. When a salesman says he needs a product 'soon' and the researcher promises one 'soon' they may be talking about completely different periods of time and not realize it.

Buyers are often surrounded by sets of contradictory expectations. They themselves like room for manoeuvre in the deployment of their talents and specialist skills. They are often specialists in negotiation and shop around for the best available terms. However, the finance department may want the product to be cheap, the engineers want it perfect (and therefore are reluctant to change from known suppliers), production wants it now and the salesman wants some tactical advantage where he can use reciprocal purchases as a lever.

As they think about information and talk things through, managers become emotionally involved with the problems raised. How a problem is defined can affect choice, and this has been shown to be influenced by historical solutions, the power attributed to the source of the problem statements, previous decisions and by perceived discrepancies between an existing state of affairs and a desired one (McCall and Kaplan, 1985). This raises the question of whether it makes sense to focus exclusively on a choice when the definition of a situation can easily predetermine choice.

Where definitions of the situation arise out of group action, this is where certain people in the organization or group are in agreement as a matter of consensus. Other groups may seek to define the problem differently; and it can become a political issue, as where production sees a fall-off in sales as reflecting insufficient effort on the part of marketing and marketing sees it as production's failure to deliver on time.

When opinions about suppliers, customers, the organization or how a problem in relation to any of these should be approached are matters of consensus not externally testable, these are what Schein (1985) calls *social reality*. It is sometimes referred to by other authors as 'intersubjective reality'. In such circumstances the group shares assumptions about which decisions are based on consensual criteria (for example, 'Let's decide by majority vote'). If an organization is to act coherently it must also share assumptions on which of its decisions are scientifically resolvable and which are based on consensual criteria. Thereupon it can be said that decisions can be rational or irrational. The acceptance of irrational decision criteria may seem rational in the circumstances.

Very often an individual's judgement is coloured by his or her own experience, a perception that may not be shared by everyone else. A young chemical factory engineer had his leg damaged when a revolving drum exploded as a result of chloride stress corrosion. Consequently, when it came to placing an order for replacement equipment he, now chief engineer, insisted on drums being reinforced by forged high-tensile hoops. This was despite technological advances which included corrosion-proof metal, centrifugally cast drums with circumferential welds which eliminated the need for vertical stress welds, and more than generous safety margins. He resisted the rational argument, although annual energy savings would have run into thousands of dollars. This captures what Schein calls subjective or *individual reality*. It could equally relate to an individual's desire to act in a way which meets his or her own needs for elbow room and self-expression, or a desire to nurture a particular self-image or to adhere to a particular value.

What is defined as physical, social and individual reality is itself the product of social learning and, by definition, part of a given culture. However, culture norms have less importance in the area of physical reality, which operates by natural laws as discovered by the scientific method. Cultural assumptions are crucial in the area of social reality as distinct from the physical or individual reality. The fact that codes are shared does not mean agreement of opinion. The same codes can accommodate the varying opinions of individual reality.

Decision Making and Communication

Problem solving and decision making are the stuff of management. Managerial decision making and problem solving are processes which, drawing on McCall and Kaplan (1985, p. 116), are so much part of the same thing that what is needed is a new term to encompass both. In default of such a term both processes will be used here interchangeably.

An indication has already been given that decision making is not the rational process which management literature has addressed in the past and, to a certain extent, is still doing. It is not the result of a dispassionate, almost mechanistic process in which problems are perceived, alternative solutions weighed and rational decisions made. Research into managerial behaviour has completely reversed this traditional picture of managerial work. In place of a view of managerial activities in which planning, organizing, co-ordinating, motivating and controlling take place through established relationships in a hierarchical structure using formal information systems to meet organizational objectives we have a new perspective (Table 7.2).

This is a view of managers working in a swirl of activity in which decisions are made in fits and starts. It is also a picture in which managers are dependent on many people other than subordinates, with whom reciprocal relationships should be created. In studies of American and British managers the time that managers spend with others ranges from about half to 90% of that available to them (Stewart, 1982). It is a picture of managers who live in a political world in which an ability to make a point cogently, to trade-off and to compromise are paramount. People feature more importantly than is usually suggested in many textbooks on management. Because people are up front, they can be educated and trained to become more effective. The more the 'why's' and 'how's' of managerial behaviour are understood, the better will people be able to respond as events unfold, induced, as they

Table 7.2. *The changes of our understanding of managerial work and behaviour (From Stewart, 1983, reproduced by permission)*

From viewing managerial behaviour as primarily

Orderly	*to*	Disjointed, characterized by brevity, variety and fragmentation
Planned	*to*	Reactive and instinctive
Working with subordinates and boss	*to*	Recognizing the importance of lateral relationships
Having established relationships	*to*	Developing and maintaining reciprocal relationships
Using formal information	*to*	Also using informal, speculative information
Non-political: focused on organizational objectives	*to*	Political, pursuing own and own group's objectives

From emphasizing

The managerial job	*to*	Recognizing differences between managerial jobs
Common behaviour	*to*	Recognizing wide differences in behaviour

often are, by chance, ignorance, recklessness and confusion. The better the skills they can apply in the process, the more efficiently is the organization likely to perform.

In a situation where interpersonal interactions constitute such a large part of the daily managerial task, communication takes on a significant role. If decisions are taken on a basis of limited information, or limited ability to handle it; if irrational behaviour can impact on organizational decisions; if people seek to influence decisions by acting in their own interests and/or in the interests of groups with which they identify at a given time; if they find themselves entering into coalitions with other interest groups over a particular issue or issues; if all these things happen then how people communicate and construe meaning in an organization is central to such interactive activities.

THE SOCIAL CONSTRUCTION OF ORGANIZATIONAL REALITY

Rationalities, Logics and Symbols

To understand how meaning is communicated and interpreted in organizations it is first necessary to look at how an organization's activities create meaning for people, that is, how it makes its *social reality*. In a seminal work (Berger and Luckman, 1971) the process is investigated by which people construct social order and yet regard it as reality with an existence independent of themselves.

Thompson (1980) pursues this theme by analysing the social construction of reality in organizations with different types of rationalities or logics favoured by various groups. He sees the process of socialization into an organization as involving the internalization, on the part of the new entrant, of the various patterns and symbolic meanings that have become dominant in that organization. The more this socialization is effective, the more predictable and controllable the new entrant's conduct will be. The new entrant learns which rationalities or logics are important in the organization

Table 7.3. *Some logics and the characteristic viewpoints they impart. (Adapted by permission from Spillard, 1985)*

Logic	Characteristics
1 Raw material logic	Sees itself as exploiting particular raw materials. Their processes, technologies, rules, values, expectations and structures are all dictated by its orientation to the raw materials
2 Process logic	May be bound as above but to a processing function. Retailing, advertising, assembling typical. It is the processing that comprises the organization's unique competence
3 Technological logic	Technology provides the organization's strength and focus as in electronics, metallurgy, processed food
4 Product logic	Product is central, as in cars, computers, carpets, insurance policies. All characterized by concept of product and product range for which firm is recognized
5 Market logic	Defined in terms of market they serve. This can be a market segment. May consider making and marketing any product needed by segment
6 Product/market logic	Defined in terms of a product and a market. Firm involved in assembling and selling a system does this, as do package-tour operators
7 Marketing task logic	Introduces a classification of possible operational stances, i.e. analytic/exploratory/reactive/risk averse or defensive/aggressive/passive or welfare/revenue earning. These mutually exclusive
8 Personality logic	Firm's actions are dictated by significant powerholder(s). Usually only used as veto or when culture built up over time. Small/medium firms in this category
9 Philosophical logic	Difficult to define. May be determined primarily by values usually described in bi-polar terms, e.g. team orientated/individual orientated, risk taking/mechanistic

and which represent basic and often long-standing assumptions that people in an organization or an organization unit share, to bring meaning to their interactions. Spillard (1985), in his examination of organization and marketing, lists nine different logics, for each of which he has shown the characteristic viewpoint it imparts (Table 7.3). This should be enough to indicate that there is more than one system of meaning in an organization; there is also more than one interpretation of such meanings. No firm possesses only one of these logics, but there is likely to be one or two which are dominant and which underpin the organization's whole existence.

Managerial ideology has been described as a symbolic meaning system. In it, certain rationalities or logics dominate in an organization and the words that are used, the actions which symbolize these logics, what is considered right or wrong, fair or unfair, all operate to maintain a shared perception of the social reality. They all happen in face of the threat of discrepancies arising from individual or group perceptions or from developments taking place in the environment.

In view of the fact that functions, departments or sections in an organization are likely to have different value scales and symbol preferences it is easy to see how an overarching ideology that spans a complete organization can be extremely useful for maintaining social order if it can succeed in masking or eliminating such differences. To function as a group, either as a department or a total organization, the individuals who come together must establish a system of communication and language that permits interpretation of what is going on. Because human beings cannot stand too much uncertainty, categories of meaning that filter out what is unimportant, while focusing on what is important, become a major means of reducing uncertainty and overload and a precondition for co-ordinated actions. Language is the principal mechanism by which people make assertions, have social intercourse, name things and, to a degree, understand each other.

Creating and Imposing Definitions of Reality

While ideologies play an important part in the social construction of reality and its maintenance in organizations they are supported by tacit agreements and understandings of a less formal kind. The 'knowledge' we have about our world, and have consequently taken for granted because of its reality, is created, passed on to others and maintained in social situations. Much of what we 'know', what we understand as the way things are, both about the world at large and about our membership of organizations, is derived from organizations. It is therefore necessary in strong organizational cultures to share the assumptions of those colleagues with whom organizational members have to interact.

Organizations cannot take for granted the commitment of members to their particular viewpoints. In order to develop and sustain consensus and co-operation as well as to legitimize hierarchic arrangements, senior managers attempt to manipulate or select suitable attitudes, values and knowledge (Salaman, 1980).

Motivation and Performance

Management-level members of an enterprise are often exposed to rewards to motivate them to commitment to organizational objectives. Short-term rewards may include such items as bonuses based on performance to induce high effort. Exposure to training schemes is intended to increase on-the-job effectiveness. These schemes will obviously vary in style and content with differing levels of management. Longer-term factors include support for higher qualification in business management subjects, promotion structures to enhance career advancement and implied provision for stability in life plan, style and cycle, engendering and perpetuating their motivation.

Presentation of Favourable Definitions of the Organizations

While reward systems assist in determining the orientation and commitment of managers, the creation of definitions and assumptions is greatly assisted by emphasis on individual qualities, strengths and failings. The aspiring manager must change his or her behaviour in the interest of improved performance. Management development and appraisal schemes attempt to evaluate individual performance, usually highlighted in the annual appraisal interview. This implies a rationality that individual performance is measurable. Such programmes do not yet take account of performance in relation to group or social processes as indicated by research (for example, the work of Belbin, 1981). People are becoming more interdependent in organizations, with the result that individual performance becomes increasingly difficult to evaluate.

Recruitment and Selection Processes

Organizations are continually seeking personnel with appropriate knowledge, skills, attitudes and motivations. By that we mean that they are searching all the time for people who will be amenable to methods of organizational control and likely to have commitment to organizational goals and culture. It is fairly clear that, as so often with organizational rationalities, what is seen as logical is eventually based on value premises.

SUMMARY OF MAIN POINTS SO FAR

1   Information is necessary to decision making. Yet conscious or unconscious bias means it can be manipulated for a particular purpose or interpreted in favourable ways. Often decisions are taken on minimal information as if they were based on certainty.

2   People can only handle a limited amount of information. After that they store it in ways that bias it.

3   Managers in different functions and at different levels will view situations and problems in different ways, using information selectively to reinforce their viewpoints.

4   Definition of a situation can predetermine choice, rendering irrelevant the rational approach.

5   Whether a rational or non-rational approach is followed in a particular situation is determined by the organizational culture.

6   People in organizations view situations in the light of their own precedential experience or their aspirations.

7   Managerial work is *not* orderly, planned, contained within a boss/subordinate structure where relationships are established, decisions are based on support systems, founded on organizational objectives and guided by managers who act in a common managerial way.

8   Managerial work *is* characterized by brevity, instinctive reactions, relationships across functions with decision making supported by informal information in addition to what the information system produces, by political action in pursuit of group or personal objectives and is witnessed by wide differences in management behaviour.

9   People in organizations construct their own reality and yet see it as something external to themselves. In the process they embrace different logics or rationalities. As a result, they use criteria to decide issues that they have come to accept as definitive.

10 People are recruited to organizations, are trained, rewarded and evaluated in accordance with criteria which suit organizationally determined ends.

MANAGING MEANING

Communication and Organizational Culture

So far, it has been indicated that irrationality has as much effect on decisions as rationality, that organizational culture can explain much of what is considered irrational in terms of social reality and that the values of different groups can, in a number of cases, be given a common frame of reference by an overarching ideology or value system which is largely dependent on language to provide a common code to align meanings and action. Carbaugh (1985) places organizational culture firmly in the communication arena. Communication, he argues, is an intersubjectively generated and regulated symbolic activity that is largely oral and which constitutes a degree of shared meaning and a sense of community. These shared symbols and meanings, created communicatively, may be called a culture. It is built up over time and is an essential element in any organizing activity.

Management as an Oral Tradition

Using as justification research on managerial roles and work which has repeatedly shown that managerial activity has a high oral communication content, Gowler and Legge (1983) draw on perspectives from social anthropology to make the proposition that management may be viewed essentially as an oral tradition. Their contention rests on the idea examined above that managers at all levels share a set of implicit and explicit meanings acquired through innumerable interactions, and that these shared meanings can only be demonstrated in communication. It is within this framework that Gowler and Legge have developed a model of the process by which control is exercised in organizations. This model predicates two components of oral management, (1) what they call a techno-social order, characterized as 'plain speaking', and (2) a moral–aesthetic order, characterized as 'rhetoric' or what has been described by them as the use of a form of word delivery which is lavish in symbolism and, as such, involves several layers or textures of meanings (Figure 7.1).

The techno-social order includes those meanings which invoke ideas about achievement, as in the references and admonitions by managers and traditional management theorists to policies, objectives, goals, plans, outcomes and effectiveness. The moral–aesthetic order includes the implicational meanings which enrich and embellish the intentional means of the techno-social order and which arise within the assumptions that emerge in the social reality of organizations.

The power of the model resides in the way in which the plain speaking and rhetoric can be intermingled and still be given the *appearance* of plain speaking. The implications are immense in terms of management as a political activity concerned with the creation, maintenance and manipulation of power. It is argued that while managers often espouse and proclaim the virtues of plain speaking, they frequently adopt a type of speech that is highly ambiguous, namely rhetoric.

It can be seen by reference to Figure 7.1 that plain speaking and rhetoric are represented as the opposite ends of a continuum. When the symbolic content of a statement is increased, the emphasis moves from plain speaking

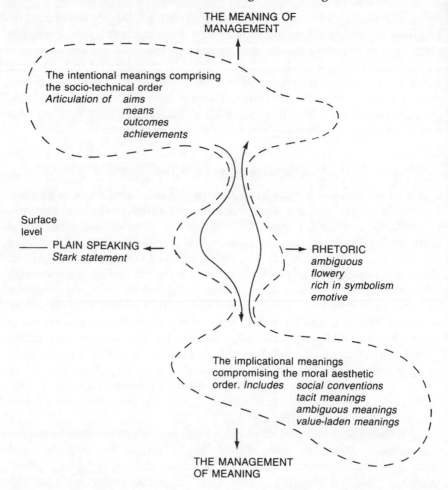

Figure 7.1. *The rhetoric of bureaucratic control. (Adapted from Gower and Legge, 1983: the words in italic have been added by the authors)*

to rhetoric. Rhetoric has been described as a type of ritual; it says something about the speaker, the spoken-to and the situation which goes beyond what is contained in the surface message.

No language is so flexible that it can dispense with rhetoric. Words, after all, are only symbols of thought and language is inadequate to convey its complexities of meaning without it.

Since rhetoric is lavish in symbolism it has the power to engage attention and arouse emotion, and to increase the degree and variety of ambiguity in any act of communication. Because sets of rules are metaphorically connected with one another and allow meaning to leak from one level to

'. . . Because written and official Arabic is divorced from the language of everyday life, it has a particular influence on the literate Arab. This manifests itself in general vagueness of thought and in over-emphasis on the psychological significance of linguistic symbols at the expense of their meaning by fitting the thought to the word rather than the word to the thought . . . Over-exaggeration and over-assertion become material means of communication, with the result that a simple statement in English cannot be translated into Arabic literally without losing part of its meaning. Within their own countries Arabs are compelled to over-assert and to over-exaggerate, otherwise there is a good chance other Arabs will misunderstand them. If an Arab says what he means without exaggeration, other Arabs might think he means the opposite. This can lead to misunderstanding in negotiation by non-Arabs who do not realize the Arab speaker is following a linguistic tradition. In the same way, Arabs often fail to realize that others mean exactly what they say if it is put in a simple, unelaborated manner. To many Arabs, a simple "no" may be perceived as a sign to continue rather than a direct negative.'

(Adapted from Shouby, 1951)

another (Douglas, 1973), people are often unable to distinguish between the two. It is from the ability to stimulate flows from one order to another that rhetoric derives its evocative and directive powers. This interpenetration of the orders or levels is shown in Figure 7.1.

SOCIALIZATION INTO ORGANIZATIONS

Filling the Role

Analogous to the rational and irrational/political approaches to decision making are the structuralist and social interaction perspective on role. Role is the concept which is typically used to connect the individual member to the organization's requirements, often laid down in definitions, regulations or instructions. The structuralist perspective argues that the nature of organizations can be described in factual and quantitative terms. The activities, intentions and viewpoints of people who work in the organizations need to be taken into account. Certain behaviours are expected of those who fill organizational positions; their actions are interpreted in the light of these expectations, shaped as they are around the pursuit of some goal. The individual complies because he or she comes to consider such behaviour as proper, or because of the pressure to conform to the expectations which are often backed up by sanctions. A formal, rationally organized company structure involves clearly defined patterns of activity, functionally related to the purpose and objectives of the organization with no great scope for any discretionary activity.

An alternative conception of role to the one which defines it in terms of the expectations of others, and the one to which we subscribe, is the social interaction approach. In this there is emphasis on the ongoing processes of negotiation, diplomacy and trading-off which characterize organizational life (Strauss, 1978). Role is a constantly changing negotiated product of the interactions of different purposes and priorities between different and conflicting interests and capacities.

This difference between role as organizational office and that as the personal identities of organizational personnel as identified by Strauss can be seen, according to Salaman (1980, p. 134):

> as reflecting on one hand a view of organizations as essentially consensual phenomena arising from internalization of individual members' prescribed roles where, if expectations are known and consistent, conflict should be minimal; and on the other hand, a view of organizations as arenas of constant conflict, negotiation and compromise where individuals attempt, with greater or lesser success depending on their power in the organization and their location within a hierarchy, to achieve their own ends and priorities which derive from their extra-organizational identities.

The essence of organizational roles is captured in the conception of role as involving creativity rather than just conformity. The actions which organizational members take depend on the interpretations made by them in their organizational world, influenced by the symbols and assumptions which have evolved in the organization. Such a view does not deny the importance of organizational rules and the demands of others, but neither does it ignore the processes of interpretation, negotiation and compromise that underline the production of actions and behaviours within a framework of rules and constraints (Salaman, 1980). Such actions reveal these demands and rules and reconstitute them.

Working Within Rules

A role tends to draw attention to a certain level of consensus and focuses on the processes by which people want to meet the expectations of certain others or negotiate new expectations, therefore rules in organizations are used to overcome poor motivation and members' reluctance to act in accordance with corporate ambitions. Thus order and predictability are achieved when commitment and motivation cannot be assumed. They allow for certain discretion in their use.

Again it is useful to consider structuralist and interaction approaches. The structuralist view of rules defines norms and expectations, irrespective of who the organization's personnel happen to be, and continues to exist, despite the turnover in personnel. Such an approach is not concerned with the meaning of organizational roles or the process involved in their interpretation and application.

The interactionist approach attempts to describe the relationship between rules and behaviour. Research has indicated that rules are an element in the constant conflict at managerial levels between members of organizations. This conflict is typically where subordinate members attempt to increase their areas of discretion to reflect their self-interests and values.

Senior members endeavour to reduce the uncertainty caused by this discretion through the creation and imposition of rules. These represent the bottom line in terms of performance. Except where they are devised for such purposes as safe or orderly operation, the rules are negotiable, i.e. they are political in their nature and at managerial level are abstract in their definition to permit variations of interpretation.

In terms of groups or functions within an organization, rules are used not to determine their behaviour but to achieve their particular priorities or to obstruct other groups. Thus we have a situation in which individuals and groups bargain with or about the interpretation of rules, to achieve purposes about which they have strong views or gut feelings. In responding to rules, people act as if they determined behaviour and interpret them through the rationalities and logics important to them and the social reality they share.

Induction of New Entrants

As we saw in Chapter 5, the new entrant to a multinational soap company was trained for a particular job by a role model or 'significant other'. As he absorbs the language of the role, this sensitizes him to observing certain kinds of events and not others. Thus he comes to accept certain patternings of experience through the language that goes with the job. The rules which accompany the job are related to the language of the role which provides their justification. The mode of thinking which the language evokes implicitly, indicates how decisions should be taken.

SUMMARY OF MANAGING MEANING AND SOCIALIZATION INTO ORGANIZATIONS

1 Management can be viewed as an oral tradition. Managers can best achieve the outcomes they want by mixing plain speaking or factual statement with rhetoric which appeals to values and conventions that have come to be accepted. By giving this the *appearance* of plain speaking, managers at higher levels are able to create and manipulate power.

2 The concept of an individual's role in an organization was at one time seen as carrying out the behaviours expected of those who fill organizational positions. A more modern conception of role is one of diplomacy and trading-off in relation to the different purposes and priorities between different and conflicting interests.

3 The interests of individuals are reflected in their own value preferences and motivation. Where this is likely to conflict with corporate ambitions, rules are imposed to try to ensure bottom-line performance. The discretion which junior members of an organization exercise creates uncertainties for senior managers, and these uncertainties are reduced by the imposition of rules. People act as if rules determined behaviour, and they interpret them through the logics and rationalities which have evolved.

4 New entrants to an organization are introduced to the language associated with their role. This sensitizes them to observing certain kinds of events and not others. It evokes a certain mode of thinking and implicitly indicates how decisions should be taken.

COMMUNICATING VERTICALLY IN ORGANIZATIONS

Roles, Tasks and Individual Reality

Even where roles are relatively negotiable and rules relatively flexible or even negotiable over time, the subjective reality perceived by individual managers in an organization, particularly those below top management level, can be such that they wish to express their individuality in the work situation. They fight to get valued what they produce from their efforts.

The organizational world adopts a rationality which does not allow people to admit the extent to which self-convenience, temperament and personal values play a part in determining how they and others see their jobs and how they decide to do them. Wise people in the system keep their interests hidden. As a result, covert battles take place in organizations as people pursue self-interests in the name of organizational effectiveness. Success in pursuing what is personally important is not revealing that self-interests are involved. These self-interests are at the heart of what brings meaning to a person's life at work. They make the direct connection between an aspiring manager's ambitions and his or her skills in constructing a social reality that allows his or her accomplishments to be seen and valued (Culbert and McDonough, 1982). It is this sense of receiving recognition of one's worth which is central to people's self-esteem.

Senior managers seek to exercise control against excesses in the expression of self-interest which, if unchecked, would operate against the interests of the organization by creating the conditions for self-indulgence to flourish. They do this by trying to specify the types of commitment and responsibility needed to make their organizations work in the direction of corporate or their own goals. To ensure accountability they look for standards. Some of these emphasize *inputs*, in which attempts are made to measure the efforts exerted and the extent to which rules and procedures have been followed; others emphasize *outputs*, in which bottom lines such as profitability, contribution and quotas are agreed, as in systems of control such as management by objectives; yet others emphasize *impact*, in which the effects of the individual on the wider world are assessed. Because these cannot eliminate self-interests and because self-interests are not voiced, the attempts to ensure accountability becomes a direct managerial challenge. Senior managers self-conveniently resort to treating their input, output and impact proposals as absolutes, regardless of what is at stake personally for those involved in a situation as it unfolds. Such absolute statements put people in binds where, in order to do what is personally important, they comply with all the stipulated procedures and fail to produce satisfactory results. This approach does not take into account that when people embark on a new task or assignment they engage in the implicit process of aligning personal values with what they perceive to be the task requirements. It is these systematic biases which permeate their view of the organizational world. Such biases play a major role in making organizations effective. Culbert and McDonough have explanations for both the individual seeking to create a positive image for himself within an organization and one who sees himself threatened by a reality constructed without his best interests in mind. These are 'framing' and 'fragmentation'.

Managing the Image

People have to *frame* situations to create self-convenient organizational reality. They have to begin by constructing and marketing a reality that allows others to value both this orientation and the contribution that orientation produces.

Framing has three basic components:

1 A simple story that links an individual's commitment to a highly principled logic connected to
2 The practical consequences flowing from such a commitment backed up by
3 The legitimacy base underlying this position.

Framing fixes one's position and/or contribution within a reality construction where details can be disputed but where one's basic stand is reinforced by multiple levels of impact and appears more or less unassailable.

Handling Unrelated Definitions of Commitment

Where framing is the tactic employed in actively getting a contribution valued, *fragmenting* is the tactic used by people when they are on the receiving end of a reality that was constructed without their own interests in mind. What does a person do when held to an absolute definition of commitment which bears little relation to his own contributions or overall goals? It is as if the 'framer' assumes that his own interests will be at the centre of things for him at all times, and that there are not other people and matters of concern, other perspectives and survival needs.

People can deal with such situations in different ways. The person at the receiving end can split the truth into fragments which he or she reveals at self-convenient times. Its cogency lies in the fact that although every fragment is more or less true, the totality is misleading. To the manager whose immediate interests involve a cutting back of the cost budget and who protests about overtime payments, a subordinate fragments by responding, 'I assume that your recent directive urging preferential treatment for our large customers implied a variance in my overtime budget'. Fragmenters, however, tend to be inconsistent in their behaviour. Different stories are told to different listeners; they define roles and responsibilities differently at different times. Much of what they do is without the conscious intention to deceive. Nevertheless, there is deception. Subtleties are added, emphases and details omitted. It seems to be the only way to cope where more and more people see themselves as having a stake in what we do.

Another survival tactic is that in which individuals give the illusion that their own commitments are sufficiently broad to take in those embraced by others. This tactic pays lip service to what others are about while the individual carries on the pursuit of his or her own reality, as before. It is a response which acknowledges that there is no pay-off for confronting others on their undervaluing of the individual's reality. It recognizes that it is impossible to please everyone. Thus it allows individuals to protect themselves by keeping different concepts of output and different and limited areas of commitment from public recognition.

Tasks and Self-Interests of Groups

Since no organizational reality fits everyone, people bargain and negotiate on their interpretation of events to find an interpretation that best serves a critical mass of self-interests, including their own. Departments, functions, sections and factions negotiate their own reality. It provides each group with a common frame of reference and identity which prompts members to adopt positions on organizational issues which suit their group purpose. Top managers, in seeking to overcome this functional or sectional viewpoint and to promote the viewpoint of the overall organization, adopt such means in pursuit of this end as task forces, project groups and rotation of staff in different departments. These means, however, will not entirely eliminate these different perspectives. The reason is that unless there is an overarching ideology or organizational culture which values this viewpoint, and hence promotes the resolution of conflicts, the pull of the social reality in the section, function or department may be too great.

The self-interest of groups is perhaps seen at its most extreme and most visible in relations between management and workforce representatives. In the post-Bhopal/Chernobyl era considerable focus has been directed to occupational risk. In fact, occupational risk and its concomitants of health and safety have been a contentious issue between many unions and managements for years, if not at the megalevel of these catastrophes.

It has been claimed that risk perception is a cultural concept and that concerns about risk depend less on the nature of the danger than on the observer's political and cultural biases. It is the world view and the ideological premises of a group that shapes perceptions of risk. The concepts of accountability, responsibility and liability that pervade debates about risk are, in effect, political statements expressing points of tension and value conflicts in a given organization or society. This whole question of risk is inexorably drawn in to the deep-rooted adversarial stances that characterize industrial relations in much of Western society (Nelkin, 1985).

The language used by different groups to describe risk and suggest remedies for it is judgemental. The terms used to describe an issue in conflict can direct blame and imply responsibility for remedial action. Some words imply order or chaos, others certainty and scientific precision. By the selective use of words or phrases an event can be trivialized or rendered important, can define an issue as a problem or reduce it to a routine; it can indicate fear of risk as a phobia or as a genuine concern.

Language can be used as a political tool by interest groups to gain tactical advantage. Such groups strive to impose their definitions of reality on the other side and use euphemism or vagueness to obscure issues. They conceal judgements that are problematic or subjective behind words of certitude. They use metaphor and imagery to express their ideologies and to dramatize issues and evoke support. In the management–union conflict situation the language used by both parties in their efforts to impress, assuage and persuade the other side, and indeed to win wider support, will reflect their values and beliefs. If the issue is of sufficient seriousness, a social debate will be created and the same kind of language and symbols used in the wider setting.

Examples are given in Table 7.4, drawing on the useful work of Hilgartner (1985). This is an exploration of the political language used by labour and management as they struggle to control the definition of the occupational

Table 7.4. The political language of risk. How management and unions use language in their interactions. (Adapted and tabulated from Hilgartner, 1985)

	Management language	Union language
Theories of society	Emphasizes consensus, common goals and common interests of management and unions in their concern for workers' health and safety. Condemns illegal, unethical or careless practices. Denies profit motive can lead to neglect of safety and health. Some key words and phrases are we, our, us best interests, mutual advantage our environment unproductive conflict reasonable solutions based on fact defend our trade secrets	Emphasizes conflict and the need for protection against injustice. Sees organizational relationships as adversarial and the economic system as exploitative. Believes firms provide only legal minimum of information on risk and seeks greater access to it. Some key words and phrases are costs are the enemy of employee protection invisible hazards insidious occupational disease the leading form of violence unfair battle for workplace safety right to know
Health risks	Emphasizes that all life involves risk on or off the job. Underlines the need to adhere to safety rules. Belittles people who fear chemicals. Deprecates the irrationality of people expressing such views. Key words and phrases are misinformed, unscientific, emotional phobia no evidence vital nutrients, necessary long-established practice minute quantities, low doses, traces, acceptable levels hypothetical normal	Emphasizes threat to the workers, their helplessness in the situation and the pain and devastation they experience. Challenges the adequacy of what is being done. Key words and phrases are real people severity preventable, life-saving silent killer, time bomb, toxic substances, harmful powerlessness progressive deterioration, expendable need for information
Economic risks	Emphasizes the danger of high prices to the firms's future brought about by the increased costs of implementing further health and safety measures. Stresses the benefits of low costs. Key words and phrases are marginal improvements, diminishing returns mutual benefits costs and benefits pricing out of markets, reduced competitiveness standards of living efficiency, effective use of limited resources	Emphasizes worker health and sees the threat to profits as the reason for failure to develop further health and safety measures. Claims management exaggerates costs of improvements. Key words and phrases are profits versus health inadequate information cost–benefit analysis a moral outrage adequate compensation justice

health problem and thereby structure the policy agenda. Much of this is transferable to the more closely defined organizational situation. Examples relate to what is broadly described as the chemical industry.

In the examples given under 'Health risks' in Table 7.4 the expressions 'vital nutrients' and 'long-established practice' underline the futility of trying to eliminate exposure to such risks as these may contain. Vital nutrients cannot be avoided, the implication being that they are necessary to life itself. Long-established practices imply that these have been culturally sanctioned as safe. 'Traces' implies that if a dose is so small then so is the risk. The expression 'silent killer', when related to a particular chemical, is a metaphor which stresses the idea that chemicals are foreign, that they invade the body and contaminate people. The 'time bomb' image connotes the hazard as a presence that is quietly ticking away, waiting to strike with devastating force at some time in the future. Metaphor and rhetoric are used to convey the idea of a reality. The political language used evokes and reinforces stock explanations for the problems posed by organizational life. These opposing explanations or political myths depend on unprovable premises about society, the organization and the individual. The contradictory views of management and union advocates constitute two opposing clusters of political myths.

Despite their sharp ideological differences, management and unions according to Hilgartner, use similar tactics to impose their will or enlist public support:

1 Each group uses emotional imagery to dramatize its version of risks.
2 Each uses images that emphasize its lack of control over the risks and situations that threaten it.
3 Each accuses the other of exaggerating.
4 Each presents itself in a favourable light, while calling its opponents irrational or immoral and identifying them as a source of problems in the organization.
5 Each evokes widely shared values, such as prosperity, health, justice, efficiency and equity to position itself on the 'right' side of the controversy.
6 Each group argues that its viewpoint is based on careful analysis of 'facts'. As a corollary to this assertion, both groups treat science and expertise as political resources, invoking the conclusions and opinions of specialists as tools for persuasion.

In this way each group builds up a dramatic picture of the occupational health and risk controversy, presenting an image of organizations, naming heroes and villains, identifying certain 'problems' as urgent and others as less urgent, and proposing 'solutions' to the problems it defines. Resolution of the problems arising from such opposing ideologies is a continuing difficulty. The deep conflicts between organized labour and management limit the prospects for negotiation. Outcomes depend primarily on the ability of each group to impose its will. Using language, the proponents on each side evoke familiar myths and construct emotional dramas to achieve a favourable political outcome.

Manager–Subordinate Interactions

So far we have seen how individuals and groups can influence and be influenced by the behaviour of others in an organizational hierarchy. However, organizations exist to carry out a function in society. The activity of influencing the behaviour, beliefs and feelings of other group members of an organization in an intended direction is vested in and carried out by leaders. Much of the literature on leadership focuses on manager–subordinate relations and a large amount of research has gone into studying management styles in the search for what determines leadership success.

One approach to leadership maintains that, irrespective of managerial style, it is the interpersonal skills which can be applied in face-to-face situations that determine success. How well the styles are applied in different situations is more important than what style a leader should use (Wright and Taylor, 1984). This assumes in the first place the manager's capability of analysing the work performance of subordinates and identifying the room for improvement. This rests on the questions of how serious the problem is, why it has occurred and what can be done about it. Given this, a manager's behaviour in interaction with his or her subordinates can be viewed as being made up of a number of elements of two primary components. These can be verbal or non-verbal. The range of verbal behaviours is perceived, if erroneously in certain situations, to be much wider than the non-verbal components and, as such, merit that much more attention.

The principal purposes for which a manager may wish to interact with a subordinate are gathering information, influencing behaviour and handling emotion.

Obtaining Information

The ability to *elicit precise and relevant information* is a useful skill in the manager's repertoire. By means of carefully phrased questions and statements, the manager can better get to the heart of a problem. Questions and statements used for this purpose include the following.

Open Questions

These ask for general information concerning some topic or issue, and as such are posed in such a way that the subordinate has to give some form of information. A simple 'yes' or 'no' is inappropriate:

'What do you think of the new continuous centrifuges?'

Probes

These are helpful in obtaining more detailed information. They often follow open questions and are usually aimed at focusing more closely on what has been described:

'How do the maintenance engineers view the new continuous centrifuges?'

Closed Questions

These are useful for establishing points of fact, e.g. answers which can be made by 'yes' or 'no' or by numbers, data, etc.:

'Does the crystal damage on the new continuous centrifuge affect minimum quality standards?'

Comparisons

These are used to get subordinates to explore facts in a new light or to reveal their own needs, values and opinions:

'How does the quality compare with the output of the batch centrifuges?'

Hypotheticals

These questions are another way of encouraging the subordinate to explore his or her own ideas or feelings:

'If we could get a budget allocation to replace the batch centrifuges with another battery of continuous machines, would you be in favour?'

A further group of information-gathering components are those concerned with *managing the flow of information*. These include the following.

Lubricators

These embrace such expressions as 'Yes', 'Uh-huh', 'I'm with you' and 'Mmm' which, if accompanied by appropriate paralinguistic emphasis or non-verbal cues denoting interest such as head-nodding, invite subordinates to continue talking.

Inhibitors

These are words or phrases which, if accompanied by the appropriate inflexions or non-verbal cues, indicate disinterest. They include such expressions as 'I see', 'Yes, but' and 'Oh', which are signs that the manager is seeking to take over the speaking role or an indication that the subordinate has said enough on a particular topic.

Bridges

These are phrases which provide a smooth transition from one topic to the next in longer interactions, as in 'That seems to exhaust . . . Can we turn now to . . . ?'

A third group of information-gathering components comprise those activities involved in checking out ambiguities in relation to what has been agreed. These include the following.

Testing Understanding

This usually involves paraphrasing a subordinate's comments and seeking his agreement. If he does not agree, a further explanation on his part may be required and that may also be paraphrased. Any area of misunderstanding can thus be progressively eliminated. This avoids agreement at the expense of understanding and prevents future misunderstandings on the issue:

'What you seem to be telling me is that the continuous centrifuge cannot always produce the minimum required purity on refined sugars as the batch machine, but that the savings achieved exceed the costs of remelting.'

Summaries

These draw a thread through the main parts of a discussion and ensure that there is agreement before proceeding to the next point:

'What we have agreed is that you will let me have a comparison of the performance of the continuous and batch machines on white sugars on the basis of a week's operation showing kilowatt hours per ton of sugar produced, the cost of remelting rejected product on the basis of the operation of each of the last three weeks, and that you will obtain from costing the projected profit-abilities for each type of centrifuge based on the week with the lowest remelt.'

Influencing Behaviour

With able subordinates, similar question and statement types can also be used to move them to analyse their own performance, problems and development needs, and indeed to make proposals for their own development. It therefore serves to develop high levels of commitment because of the subordinates' involvement in the solutions and also to give practice generally in diagnosing and solving performance problems.

Behavioural influence components can be classified within the two main categories of *direction* and *inducement*. Components which provide direction include orders, requests, advice and suggestions. Inducements, on the other hand, give the subordinate reasons for complying. These can include promises, threats and explanations which appeal to some form of legitimate power or moral rules such as precedent, equitability, needs and opportunities. Table 7.5 shows the components for influencing behaviour developed by Wright and Taylor (1984).

Handling Emotion

The skilful use of questions and statements can also have an application in influencing a subordinate's emotional reactions. Emotions such as anger, frustration, anxiety, fear, resentment and so on are easily aroused and can get in the way of a subordinate coming to a well-considered solution to a problem. This can be avoided, generally, by the avoidance of insensitive words and by the use of neutral statements which provide no further incentive to the emotion and so allow it to burn itself out.

The two main techniques for dealing with high emotion are apologies and reflectives.

Apologies

These are used where the manager has some responsibility for his subordinate's adverse emotional reaction. A sincere apology can sometimes alleviate the situation.

Reflectives

These return to the speaker the emotional content of what he has said in a concerned way:

'You feel it would be unfair to . . .'

Table 7.5. *Components for getting the subordinate to maintain a satisfactory level of performance or to do something differently to improve it. (Reproduced by permission from Wright and Taylor, 1984)*

Component	Appropriate use	Inappropriate use
Orders		
e.g. 'Do it now' 'This is the way it will be done'	With staff who need or prefer clear, precise instructions. Where compliance is vital due to special circumstances (e.g. time constraint, emergencies etc.)	Where the benefits do not justify any resentment or stifling of ideas which may result
Requests		
e.g. 'I have a problem' 'Could you next time then please . . .'	With subordinates who are more motivated by being asked or may contribute useful ideas to the problem	With subordinates who need or prefer clear, precise instructions
Advice suggestions		
e.g. 'You could improve on that by . . .' 'The disadvantage of that is . . .' 'But this way . . .'	With staff who prefer guidance and may be influenced in the desired direction by the logic of the situation (e.g. those lacking experience)	Where compliance is essential and advice may be ignored
Promises		
e.g. '. . . then I'll give you the opportunity to tackle bigger projects'	Where the task may lack intrinsic reward and extrinsic reward must be introduced for motivational purposes	Where the promises cannot be fulfilled. When the subordinate will perform the task effectively anyway
Threats		
e.g. 'I will make you regret it' '. . . and I shall begin formal disciplinary proceedings'	Where compliance is essential and cannot otherwise be achieved (e.g. advice ignored, no available rewards, etc.	When more positive methods are available. Where threats cannot be fulfilling. When the subordinate would perform adequately anyway
Explanations		
e.g. '. . . because the reason is that . . .'	With those subordinates who are more motivated by understanding the reasons for doing something	When the explanation will be rejected leading to unproductive argument

continued

Table 7.5. *continued*

Component	Appropriate use	Inappropriate use
Praise		
e.g. 'I think that was well done because . . .'	To provide immediate feed-back about the subordinate's standard of performance in a specific area and appreciation of it	If too general, imprecise or late. When used in a patronizing way without conviction
Criticism		
e.g. 'Where you went wrong was . . .' 'But this could be overcome by . . .'	To provide feedback on sub-standard performance in a particular area with emphasis on how to do it better next time	When used negatively without emphasis on how to do it better. When it is likely to impair performance further due to resentment aroused
Leading questions		
e.g. 'You must agree that . . .' 'Don't you think that . . .?' 'You do see the point why . . .?'	To gain compliance or accept-ance by signalling the expected answer. Can be used to emphasize or check on a point made	For encouraging a sub-ordinate to express his or her views, feelings, etc. With reticent staff. For gaining commitment

Review of the Question and Statement Approach

The approach adopted by Wright and Taylor in relation to managing manager–subordinate interactions has a number of limitations. Such control by means of questions and statements takes no account of the image the subordinate seeks to maintain and the individual's need for meaning. It takes little account of the need of individuals as subordinates to express themselves and exercise their own decision making in exchanges with their manager; it does not address the amount of authority mandated to subordinates by managers and the reliance managers place on subordinates with their own sources of influence.

It does, however, provide a useful framework where the context is low and meaning is largely conveyed via the technology, e.g. in the finance office, the air-traffic control tower or the data-processing department. It can apply in relation to specific shopfloor issues. In other words, it is of use where the language used is itself highly specific and its meaning unambiguous. The leadership levels addressed are likely to be in the lower echelons or in highly specialized technologies where job specifications are tight and the actions of individuals are highly circumscribed.

Negotiating in Hierarchies

Seeking information, directly influencing behaviour by questions and statements and handling emotion are far from being the only way in which subordinates can be controlled. Orders, even when softened by the manner of their delivery, may be inappropriate for middle managers. While managers at all levels, by virtue of their formal authority, have the final say in their exchanges with subordinates, much direct managerial action still involves negotiation. Even where orders, however expressed, are an option, that option may be ineffective (Lax and Sebenius, 1986).

Because, typically, a manager delegates part of his mandate to a subordinate, the latter has a certain discretion and autonomy, some of which he is likely to have negotiated during the course of his relationship with his manager. As a result of such precedents, expectations are developed which, if perceived to be violated, would be interpreted as a breach of trust. Add to this the fact that the manager comes to rely on a subordinate who may have his own sources of information and influence. In order to maximize on the subordinate's resources the manager encourages or, at worst, tolerates disagreement on various proposals for action. Because the subordinate has a vested interest in favourable outcomes he backs his own judgement, and will only hold his critical faculties in abeyance if he perceives the issue to be outside his mandate. Interdependence brings conflict in its train, and negotiation is the most effective means of resolving it. In the process the manager is constrained in the extent to which he can give direct orders. Any specific proposals or issue has to be seen in the context of this wider negotiation.

It has been argued by Lax and Sebenius that an order is a bargaining tactic, that authority generally derives from agreement and that it is often changed by renegotiation. In the bargaining range between superior and subordinate an order is a take-it-or-leave-it offer, a commitment to a position: like a take-it-or-leave-it offer, an order is sometimes accepted. This acceptance increases the credibility of subsequent orders. Equally, it can be ignored or rejected. The wise manager may handle such situations by giving orders that are of little intrinsic importance for him because they will be accepted and are likely to improve his subsequent credibility. He may avoid giving commands which he sees as likely to be rejected, i.e. subject to counterproposals.

The language used in such circumstances requires to be appropriate to the situation. The language of suggestion is different from the language of request and that of command different from both.

Reducing the Incidence of Explicit Negotiation

To avoid explicit bargaining on frequent occasions, perhaps with a number of subordinates, a manager seeks to reduce its incidence. He may develop particular expertise to which others defer, or he may strike a broad-ranging agreement with a subordinate whereby he grants the subordinate permission to make a range of decisions affecting him. This agreement establishes a number of acceptable orders which are sometimes loosely defined. Within the range an order is likely to be accepted and negotiations can be concluded by exception and at small cost to the manager.

By this sort of agreement the subordinate gives his superior the authority to decide or command. Yet the range of decisions over which formal rights are given in authority relations is rarely clear. It is often tested and tacitly renegotiated by the parties.

Hierarchies and Integration

The ultimate aim of the management of these behaviours in an organizational hierarchy is the performance of tasks at a level which contributes acceptably to the achievement of organizational objectives. The role of the manager in any line-management situation is to ensure the adequate performance of his subordinates. As we have seen, it is not just a question of giving orders, which at certain levels may not be the appropriate approach. The relationship with each subordinate is, to a greater or lesser extent, a negotiated one, the nature of which is determined not only by the actions of the manager but also by the inputs of each individual subordinate.

Hierarchies define clearly who is responsible to or for whom. Managers at different levels know that, in addition to their responsibility for the performance of subordinates, they have to bring together the work of each subordinate to ensure the integration and co-ordination of their activities. Where subordinates disagree or pursue conflicting courses of action such discord may be resolved by direct intervention. In many situations (for example, those involving subordinates who are relatively senior in the hierarchy) such direct intervention is inappropriate. When this is the case, the manager may invite those in disagreement to come to him with a solution. Failing that, he can act as facilitator, mediator or chairman, and his communication skills require to be directed to this end (Mastenbroek, 1987).

The fact remains, however, that while most of the literature and research on leadership usefully examines manager–subordinate relations, significant current problems, at least in large organizations, lie along another dimension. Co-ordination of activities is not the clear-cut process where the manager's ultimate authority can be called on to resolve a contentious issue. Functional interdependence and responsibility often without the authority to get things done in modern organizational structures, require skills of a different order. These involve communicating laterally with peers and others, a subject addressed in the next chapter. In order to achieve this a manager has to negotiate the necessary enabling resources through his boss.

SUMMARY OF COMMUNICATING VERTICALLY IN ORGANIZATIONS

1   Self-interests at work are what bring meaning to an individual's organizational life. He seeks to get valued what he produces from his own efforts. To prevent self-indulgence on the part of subordinates, senior managers look for standards in terms of what subordinates do and how they perform.

2   Framing is the tactic people use to create an organizational reality which suits their personal convenience and preferences. Fragmenting is what they do when superiors construct a reality which does not permit the expression of the subordinate's interests.

3   Groups negotiate on the interpretation of events which best serves a critical mass of self-interests. It was seen in confrontations between management and union groups on issues of occupational risk that each group uses specific language as a political tool to gain tactical advantage. Judgements that are subjective or problematic are concealed by statements of certitude. Vagueness is used to obscure issues.

4   The activity of influencing the behaviour of other organizational members in an intended direction is carried out by leaders. One approach to leadership, irrespective of managerial style, is the interactive skills approach where, by question or statement, a manager is able to elicit information, encourage its flow and test for understanding as well as handle emotion. It is particularly useful where the context is low, the language highly specific and the meaning unambiguous, as where job descriptions are tightly written and the actions of individuals closely controlled.

5   Much managerial action, even within boss/subordinate relationships, involves negotiation. This is the most effective means of resolving conflict arising from the interdependence of those managing and those managed. This interdependence arises from the fact that a manager delegates part of his own mandate to a subordinate and comes to rely on him.

6   Hierarchies define clearly who is responsible to or for whom. Managers oversee the performance of subordinates and integrate their work towards

organizational goals. However, modern organizations are characterized by responsibility without formal authority to match. In these circumstances lateral communications assume salience.

REFERENCES

Belbin, R. *Management Teams: Why They Succeed or Fail*, Heinemann, London (1981).

Berger, P. L. and Luckman, T. *The Social Construction of Reality*, Penguin Books, Harmondsworth (1971).

Carbaugh, D. Cultural communication and organising. In Gudyburst, W. B., Stewart, L. P. and Ting-Toomey, S., *Communication, Culture and Organizational Processes*, Sage, Beverly Hills (1988).

Culbert, S. A. and McDonough, J. J. *The Invisible War: Self Interests at Work*, John Wiley, New York (1982).

Douglas, M. Introductory chapter to Douglas, M. (ed.), *Rules and Meanings*, Penguin Books, Harmondsworth (1973).

Gowler, D. and Legge, K. (1983) The meaning of management and the management of meaning. In Earl, M. J. (ed.), *Perspectives on Management: A Multi-Disciplinary Analysis*, Oxford University Press, Oxford (1983).

Hilgartner, S. (1985) The political language of risk: defining occupational health. In Nelkin (1985).

Hogarth, R. M. and Makridakis, S. Forecasting and planning: an evaluation. *Management Science*, 27 No. 2 (1981).

Lax, D. A. and Sebenius, J. K. (1986) *The Manager as Negotiator: Bargaining for Co-operation and Competitive Gain*, The Free Press, New York (1986).

Lawrence, P. R. and Lorsch, J. W. *Organisation and Environment*, Harvard University Press, Boston, MA (1967).

Mastenbroek, W. F. G. Chairmanship at negotiations in organisations: a model to facilitate decision-making. *Journal of European Industrial Training*, 11, No. 6 (1987).

McCall, M. W. and Kaplan, T. E. *Whatever It Takes: Decision Makers at Work*, Prentice-Hall, Englewood Cliffs, NJ (1985).

Miller, G. A. The magical number seven, plus or minus two: some limits on our capacity for processing information. In Miller, G. A., *The Psychology of Communication*, Penguin Books, Harmondsworth (1968).

Nelkin, D. *The Language of Risk: Conflicting Perspectives on Occupational Health*, Sage, Beverly Hills, CA (1985).

Salaman, G. Organisations as constructors of Social reality II. In Salaman, G. and Thompson, K. (eds), *Control and Ideology in Organisations*, Open University Press, Milton Keynes, (1980).

Schein, E. *Organisational Culture and Leadership*, Jossey-Bass, San Francisco, CA (1985).

Seaton, A. V. Language and the secondary socialisation of employees in the multinational corporation: the occupational world picture of the marketing executive. In Baker, M. J. (ed.), *Buyer Behaviour*, Proceedings of the Marketing Education Group Conference, University of Strathclyde (1976).

Shouby, E. The influence of the Arabic language on the psychology of the Arabs. *Middle East Journal*, 5 (1951).

Simon, H. Information processing models of cognition. *Annual Review of Psychology* (1979).

Spillard, P. *Organisation and Marketing*, Croom Helm, London (1985).
Stewart, R. *Choices for the Manager: A Guide to Managerial Work*, McGraw-Hill, Maidenhead (1982).
Stewart, R. Managerial behaviour: how research has changed the traditional picture. In Earl, M. J. (ed.), *Perspectives on Management*, Oxford University Press, Oxford (1983).
Strauss, A. *Negotiations: Varieties, Contexts, Processes and Social Order*, Jossey-Bass, San Francisco, CA (1978).
Thompson, K. Organisations as constructors of social reality I. In Salaman, G. and Thompson, K. (eds), *Control and Ideology in Organisations*, Open University Press, Milton Keynes (1980).
Van Maanen, J. and Barley, S. R. Cultural organization: fragments of a theory. In Frost, P. J., Moore, L. F., Louis, M. R., Lundberg, C. C. and Martin, J. (eds), *Organizational Culture*, Sage, Beverly Hills, CA (1985).
Wright, P. L. and Taylor, D. S. *Improving Leadership Performance: A Practical New Approach to Leadership*, Prentice-Hall, Hemel Hempstead (1984).

8
Communication Problem Solving Within Organizations (2)

Communication is far from being confined to leaders and subordinates in an organizational hierarchy. Much of what managers do involves communicating with each other across functions. This is often aimed at competing for scarce resources or co-ordinating the efforts of groups over which a manager has no direct authority but for which he or she retains accountability. Effectiveness in these situations is largely a function of informal networks, the maintenance of which demand particular communication skills. Where interests and outlooks differ, there is always the likelihood of conflict for which alternative communication strategies are available, including that of conflict prevention. Major changes enforced by environmental circumstances disrupt established communication patterns and interests and require a combination of motivation, expectation and commitment to succeed.

LATERAL COMMUNICATIONS

The way organizations are structured means that people, to differing degrees, are dependent on one another to get things done, both for themselves and for the organization. It has long been realized that in industrial markets, decision making takes place across the functions, and considerable responsibility for promoting and integrating these activities resides with general management. This diffusion of the decision-making process throughout the organization was confused at one time by the rise of the brand/product manager.

The product manager's job was and remains typical of the now-acknowledged much broader responsibility of managers in general. Where such a product management structure exists, as in some large food-manufacturing organizations, the job of the product manager involves a wide range of relationships outside the line management chain of command.

To ensure that all efforts are productively co-ordinated, he has direct profit responsibility for a particular product line. However, he has to depend on many others over whom he has no, or little, formal authority. The product may be made in an entirely separate firm; advertising may be carried out in a separate division; the sales force is another chain of command. In the same way, distributors are independent. In addition, these functions or organizations deal with many individual products and product lines.

The brand/product management concept places resource integration within the marketing function. With the development of divisional and complex multilateral structures, integration has largely moved out of the marketing function to division and general management (Doyle, 1979). This has resulted in a greater proliferation of interactions between people working in different functions of the organization. It has also resulted in the placing on division/general management the responsibility of ensuring that functions other than marketing are oriented towards target customer groups and that their activities are co-ordinated towards company goals. Spillard (1985) and others claim that it is the responsibility of marketing management to ensure that this company-wide orientation and co-ordination does, in fact, take place. This, together with a number of other factors, accounts for the growth in importance of communication skills. These other factors include the increasing size and complexity of organizations and of the processes of making and distributing products or of performing services. Technological progress increases reliance on those with specialized skills and highlights the need to harness their skills by interacting with them.

The fact that functions as well as people are interdependent when it is a matter of getting things done means that the social realities and rationalities that exist in different departments, sections or groups come, of necessity, into conflict. Basically, differing viewpoints are reinforced by the conflicts that specialization reveals. Much focus on conflict has arisen from the elevation of the importance of marketing. Attempts to introduce the marketing concept have generated within organizations a new sub-culture often in conflict with more traditional tasks and viewpoints in organizations. Table 8.1 shows the typical conflicts identified between marketing and other departments of an organization.

Whereas conflicts in the vertical dimensions of hierarchy stem from attempts of managers to exercise control, those in the lateral relationship arise either from conflict among groups in competition for scarce resources or that among groups in functional relations in which co-ordination is a primary concern. Exercising influence and control outside the line management function has been referred to as 'indirect management' (Lax and Sebenius, 1986).

Table 8.1. Summary of organizational conflicts between marketing and other departments. (From Kotler, 1985, reproduced by permission)

Department	Their emphasis	Marketing's emphasis
R&D	Basic research	Applied research
	Intrinsic quality	Perceived quality
Engineering	Long design lead time	Short design lead time
	Few models	Many models
	Standard components	Custom components
Purchasing	Narrow product line	Broad product line
	Standard parts	Non-standard parts
	Price of material	Quality of material
	Economical lot sizes	Large lot sizes to avoid stockouts
	Purchasing at infrequent intervals	Immediate purchasing for customer needs
Manufacturing	Long production lead time	Short production lead time
	Long runs with few models	Short runs with many models
	No model changes	Frequent model changes
	Standard orders	Custom orders
	Ease of fabrication	Aesthetic appearance
	Average quality control	Tight quality control
Finance	Strict rationales for spending	Intuitive arguments for spending
	Fixed budgets	Flexible budgets to meet changing needs
	Pricing to cover costs	Pricing to further market development
Accounting	Standard transactions	Special terms and discounts
	Few reports	Many reports
Credit	Full financial disclosures by customers	Minimum credit examination of customers
	Low credit terms	Easy credit terms
	Tough collection procedures	Easy collection procedures

Competing for Scarce Resources

Interest Groups

The question of interest groups was raised earlier to introduce notions that people seek to have valued what is important to them in their work, and that differing perceptions of risk arising from opposing ideologies lead to the use of language that reflects these perceptions. We shall now look more closely at interest groups in the context of lateral relationships.

The formal allocation of task responsibilities creates power and the 'ownership' of certain activities which are concentrated in sub-units in an organization. They have been shown to be concerned with their own survival and power. To achieve this end, key people in the sub-unit collect and filter information in a way which enhances the sub-unit's value in organizational decision making; or they seek to convince others that they have information needed for organizational purposes (Pfeffer and Salancik, 1978).

Other interest groups arise across functions. Professional accountants retain an allegiance to their associations as well as to organizations for whom they work. Trades unions represent the interests of their members, often across functions or departments. In both examples it is possible to envisage a culture with differing degrees of congruence with the corporate cultures. Strong overarching cultures permeating the entire organization have been observed in non-union companies such as IBM, Hewlett Packard and 3M (Peters and Waterman, 1982). Within these organizations, the pattern of labour–management relations appears to be one of harmony. This could be because of full goal congruence in which there is unlikely to be need of the counter-pressure of a union sub-culture. At the other end of the spectrum, opposing cultural values of the union call in to question the dominant corporate values. In these circumstances conflict is inevitable and ongoing.

Even between functions which are intended to work towards corporate ends, cultures are just as likely, if not more so to work in a way that encourages the disintegration of the very unity the organization tries to engender (Van Maanen and Barley, 1985). Corporate plans which describe the strategies and prescribe the action to be taken in their implementation often assume a unity of values, attitudes, perceptions and language that does not exist. It is only in the founding phases of organizations that little or no sub-cultural differentiation develops. Organizations which remain small and local may also maintain close social ties and a unitary system of values. Professionalized occupations such as medicine, law and accounting have a similar collective understanding.

Interest Groups in Competition

If organizational politics are manifested in actions to promote the self-interests of groups, then the critical issue would appear to be the identification of the sources of power. These can be harnessed and used for the generation and use of information useful to the group concerned. Information is a political resource. It is characterized by selective use to further a group's interest in the power stakes. This bias is further seen in influencing the underlying premises on which a decision is modelled or the criteria of choice used.

When a Scottish polytechnic ran both undergraduate and postgraduate business programmes the acceptance of a given staff/student ratio as the basis for allocating staff to departments starved the postgraduate programme of resources. Because it was more resource demanding by the nature of its work, it therefore had to teach more hours per number of staff than the number teaching on the undergraduate programme. Inexperienced top managers like easy and quantitative decision criteria because they can be defended on the basis of mathematical fairness, although it may be found to be grossly unfair qualitatively and undesirable in terms of output.

It is no secret that marketing departments, because of their boundary-spanning role, frequently hold or acquire information which allows them to reduce the uncertainty of the environment for other groups. For example, the most cost-efficient production is obtained where throughput is stable. Marketing is in a position to reduce production uncertainties by use of sales force activities or by negotiation of a given level of stocks to stabilize orders in a volatile market. Similarly, R&D holds an important position in high-tech markets; production and marketing uncertainties are reduced by R&D's ability to continue to design appropriate new products within production's ability to make at a competitive price and marketing's need for products with a competitive edge. Finance departments, by introducing company-wide accounting systems, define the accounting conventions to be used (and, by implication, those not to be used), thereby reducing ambiguity by the provision of readily understood and regularly repeated performance measures.

This ability to cope with others' uncertainty creates dependencies which can be controlled through this power. Only if alternatives exist which could be substituted could these dependencies be removed. If an acceptable sales agency could carry out the work of the sales force or contract research be substituted for R&D then the power of these functions would be diminished. Examples of increasing power and reducing substitutability can be seen in the growing dependence of management on computer systems and personnel (for example, in banks and insurance companies). The pressure on prices in the 1960s and 1970s in high labour cost sugar-producing countries resulted in considerable automation and continuous processing to contain direct costs. As a result, skilled maintenance engineers can command a premium for their services arising from the power which they possess.

Interest Groups and Budgets

Nowhere is the battle for resources more visible than in the budgeting process. In a classic study of public service budgeting in the USA, Wildavsky (1979) established that the greatest determining factor of the size of this year's budget is last year's budget. Most of the budget is a function of previous decisions. It is an incremental process informed by such notions as fair shares. To maintain or increase their budgets people use deliberate political behaviour in terms of budgeting strategies. They protect the optimal long-term interests of the function to which they belong by pressing for the financial and other resources necessary to protect and further these interests. Not only do the different functions in an organization vie for control of resources through their top managers, there is also contention within the functions. They seek to obtain for the different sections or sub-units of which they are members a share of the allocated budget. Managers and representatives of these sub-units within functions pursue ends in relation to the budget which meet their perceived needs or aspirations. Such ends are more likely to be achieved if the individuals concerned, as well as using a system which provides procedures for the 'rational' analysis of budget proposals, have an understanding of the power structure and mastery of the political skills which can influence outcomes (Piercy, 1986). Communication competence is central to these outcomes.

Interest Groups and Coalitions

In order to meet better what they seek to achieve, interest groups, through their leaders or representatives, look around to see what support they can muster for their ends. They need support to achieve outcomes which they could not obtain without that support. Other groups identify their own interest from time to time in the achievement of that interest group's aims. We therefore find coalitions of two or more interest groups which may last only as long as the issue involved is of importance to one of the parties. Support by one group builds up 'credits' with the interest group given the support. These credits may be called on to enlist support when another issue arises in which that interest group has a neutral position: 'We would like your backing on this one. Hopefully, we'll have as successful a result as when *we* supported *you* on . . .'

Co-ordination and Indirect Management

If the ongoing struggle to increase or maintain resources is a function of managerial actions outside the normal line management structures it is equally true that the integration of specialized activities relies to a large extent on similar actions. Despite the fact that many management textbooks urge a careful match of responsibility and authority, control and accountability do not come together so easily. Not only do divisional and matrix organization structures make decision making a cross-functional concern but also managers are seen increasingly to bear responsibility for tasks carried out through units, organizations and individuals not reporting directly to them. In these circumstances the skills of a manager as persuader, politicker and negotiator are called on in considerable measure.

Product managers right through to most line managers need these skills pinpointed by analysis of the increased complexity and interdependence reflected in new organizational forms; skills that have been identified from the increasing specialization and professionalization, with the increased emphasis on information and how it is used; skills which are more necessary than ever in societies that increasingly refuse to accept formal authority.

It is not only in private organizations that indirect management skills apply. Public managers have traditionally confronted indirect management situations.

'Take the case of Tom Sullivan, a regional official of the Department of Health, Education and Welfare (HEW). One day Sullivan received a directive from then HEW Secretary Caspar Weinberger in Washington. In effect, Sullivan was ordered to expedite the inspections for fire safety of nursing homes in Massachusetts, where many of these homes were old, many-storied, made of wood, and scandalously under-inspected. Federal funds supported many of these homes and could have been withdrawn without inspection and firecode compliance. But this would have 'thrown many old people on the streets', given the acute shortage of any such facilities. Though several state agencies had to co-ordinate and actually carry out the inspections, Sullivan has no formal power over any of them. Further, the Massachusetts legislature was reluctant to approve money for additional inspectors required to meet the deadlines.

Sullivan was facing a classic indirect management situation. Long experience had taught him that a 'hard approach', adverse publicity and withholding funds, would almost surely boomerang, with the feds taking intense press and congressional heat for being highhanded and insensitive. So he would have to arrange a 'deal' across government boundaries that would cause these inspections to be carried out. For example, he might secure compliance in return for modifying federal standards to apply more directly to Massachusett's situation as well as offering federal personnel and money. Such aid might, incidentally, further state goals apart from the inspections. Sullivan could also appeal to shared interests in protecting old people from fire while holding the (undesirable and none-too-credible) shutdown option as an alternative. If successful, he would have crafted a series of understandings to get the inspections underway, arrived at through an overt and covert process of persuasion, inducement, and threat.'

(Reprinted by permission of The Free Press, a Division of Macmillan, Inc., from *The Manager as Negotiator: Bargaining for Cooperation and Competitive Gain* by David A. Lax and James K. Sebenius. Copyright © 1986 by David A. Lax and James K. Sebenius)

What is more, where authority and resources for given tasks are shared but accountability appears to be concentrated, the manager's degree of direct control is less than his or her degree of accountability. Examples abound of indirect management situations. A large British brewing organization manufactures in one division, sells and promotes in a second division and advertises in yet a third. A voluntary organization such as Oxfam has a professional management which has to achieve results with a largely volunteer staff. In the US Aid to Families with Dependent Children programme members of Congress held the Department of Health and Human Services strictly accountable for the so-called 'error rate' (i.e. error of overpayment of welfare pay-outs to ineligible persons).

Production takes place across organizational boundaries. When an organization, confronted by a 'make or buy' decision, decides to buy, the buyer's ability to manipulate the managerial systems in the seller's organization is restricted at many points. Such lack of control is important when what is being procured is reasonably easy to specify. However, for procurements such as weapons systems, even specifying performance, let alone design, can be difficult. The inaccessibility of the supply contractor to the procuring organization can present a problem, especially when the buyer is accountable for results. The problem can be compounded where part of the supply is by sub-contract. Where co-operative arrangments exist to obtain business unlikely to be obtained by individual organizations, as where consortia were set up to compete for the radar and weapons systems of the projected European Fighter Aircraft (EFA), the problems of control are multiplied by the need to communicate with the participants across languages, cultures, countries and even continents.

As organizations have become more complex in terms of structures, so the ease of applying traditional notions of accountability has diminished. With the acceleration of technological and market change have come stresses and strains on existing organizational forms. This has been reflected on the growing focus on the difficulty of reconciling the need for specialization with that for co-ordination and integration of effort. As these trends gather even greater momentum, it has to be expected that there will be a further blurring of traditional methods of contact.

The manager is likely to see his or her job as an integrator and co-ordinator becoming more and more significant. In such circumstances managers involved in making interaction work must shepherd their tasks or projects through many organizational units or even organizations, and coax agreement and co-ordination from them while lacking the line authority associated with the responsibility of getting things done. Such requirements of managers call for tools and skills beyond the traditional administrative ones. Formal authority will be insufficient, orders given are likely to go unheeded and the culture existing in the manager's organization or department is unlikely to be meaningful across boundaries.

Managers often rely on people outside their own function or department to get things done. Just as they negotiate for resources through networks of connections and relationships, so they also seek to assist the co-ordination of activities necessary to carry out a task effectively by developing and calling on similar networks. As a consequence of this, the manager's job is more closely defined by these relationships, and the tacit or explicit agreements which link them, than by boundaries within an organization or between organizations.

The interaction of hierarchies and networks

The following excerpt from Bradford and Cohen's book *Managing for Excellence* is in fact an illustration of how a manager develops his subordinates' competences. It is a useful illustration of the day-to-day interactions in which managers at different levels are involved in the implementation of inter-organizational commitments within an organization, and represents an episode in what is an ongoing negotiation of relationships. It involves communicating vertically with superiors and subordinates, laterally with members of internal networks and also communicating with people in external networks who can assist in resolving problems.

Attempting to resolve a   *Comment*
delivery problem via networks

Subordinate: We're having trouble delivering disposable widgets to Techcorp.

Manager D: Oh-oh, that doesn't sound good. What's going on? Can I be of any assistance?

Subordinate: Well, I thought I'd let you know about it and run through the actions I've taken already. I think I know what to do, but I don't want to miss any bases.

Manager D: Fine. Go ahead.

Subordinate: I got a call from Dan saying we couldn't make schedule. When I asked why, he gave me a song-and-dance about poor materials. Since I know he likes to use that as an excuse, I called Ellen in purchasing, who told me the stuff was exposed to excess moisture while Dan was storing it. He, of course, denies it.

Different functions have a different focus and view of things. The materials may or may not have been exposed to excessive moisture but that was the way the purchasing manager viewed it. People tend to support their own positions when reacting to issues.

Manager D: So what did you do?

Subordinate: I haven't done anything about that part of it yet. I don't think we should get directly into a confrontation with Dan, do you?

Confrontation is a last resort because it tends to destroy relationships, particularly if one party loses face as a result.

continued

continued

Manager D: That depends on what our options are. In general, it's not a good idea to make anyone lose face, but let's see if there are any other choices. We've got to find a way to meet our commitments or we'll lose our edge as the most reliable manufacturing unit in the business. What else have you done?

On what we do inside an organization, and how well we do it, rests our reputation and ability to implement our commitments.

Subordinate: I checked with Techcorp's purchasing agent about why the pressure. Turns out that their people made some promises to one of their customers without checking on actual availability. She's going to see whether she can get the customer to allow some slippage.

Problems of implementation inside the organization can sometimes be partly resolved outside the organization through the network of external relationships, in this case key people in the customer organization.

Manager D: Will they accept a looser tolerance on the widgets? If they would, would that help us?

Subordinate: She's going to check that too. Then we'd have to fight with our quality-control people. If I need you, would you talk to Ted's boss to pave the way?

A further example of the interaction of external and internal factors.

Manager D: You expect trouble from Ted?

Subordinate: He's done it before.

Manager D: How would you approach him?

Subordinate: I've always tried to play it straight and tell him what our needs are. But he's a stubborn old coot.

Manager D: What do you suppose his interests are?

Subordinate: I don't know; I've never thought about that—I suppose he's very proud of our quality and doesn't want his reputation to be hurt.

Underlines the different viewpoints that emerge in different parts of the organization. The fact that the quality-control people have a commitment to quality is a strength. The problem now is to reduce that quality to meet the needs of the customer

continued

continued

Manager D: Besides he's been at that job a long time and is likely to be there forever.

and the supplier organization (cf. Juran's classic definition of quality as 'fitness for purpose'), without Ted thinking that quality is being undermined.

Subordinate: Yes, and I suppose he needs to feel valued and recognized. If I involve him in deciding how much tolerance the product can take, he'd respond better, and we'll come up with something reasonable.

It is an essential feature of interpersonal skills that you involve people at an early stage if you want their support in a course of action.

Manager D: That sounds on target. Do you suppose it would help to reinforce with him the organization's theme of dependable and reliable service?

Subordinate: I think so, especially if I put it in that light. In fact, I've got another idea. I'll call him and get him together with the Techcorp buyer. That would be exciting for him, I'll bet.

Given that different functions may have different rationalities and logics, then the way to communicate meaningfully with a member of one of these functions is in their own terms. In this instance the argument is that a looser tolerance in fact reflects the company's theme of reliable and dependable service.

Manager D: Sounds good. When you put yourself in the shoes of someone who gives you a hard time, it's amazing how different things look. What else?

If you want to influence someone, first of all see the problem through that person's eyes. It is only in this way that you can address his or her interests.

Subordinate: It just hit me; there may be some way to reschedule some other production so we can concentrate on widgets. I know how to proceed now. I'll touch base this afternoon. Thanks.

Manager D: [Smiles]

(Dialogue from Bradford and Cohen 1984, reproduced by permission)

Co-ordination and Implementation

Networking

Large organizations have reached such a size and complexity that reshuffling of role relationships and responsibilities does not have the effect of increasing significantly organizational effectiveness. Industrial cultures are 'over-differentiated and under-integrated'.

While the attempts to reconstitute organizational structures represent a manipulation of organizational geometry, the social networks already alluded to in considering resource allocation are relatively disorderly. Mueller (1986) sees organizational effectiveness as partly, at least, the function of such networks. To get things done, individuals in larger organizations supplement conventional and bureaucratic systems with the influence of internal and external human networks.

Such networks are used to improve communications by helping individuals, teams and task groups to expand their boundaries. They exist at different levels. Company presidents or chairmen can establish contact at high government level by persistent lobbying to get a particular viewpoint accepted (for example, by advocating action to remove or mitigate the effects of 'unfair' foreign competition on their company's or industry's business) or by exercising the greater power available through joint action with others (for example, through an employers' federation). Strong representations can be made with a greater possibility of success: for instance, in resisting a proposed piece of legislation, the high cost of which might make a particular industry less competitive, such as where effluent requires to be treated to a required purity before discharge into river systems.

General managers and others, if they are wise, get around their domain, making and maintaining informal contacts in the organization that give early signals of problems which, in turn, trigger actions to contain them. They can have similar contacts outside the organization which can precipitate action by providing hitherto unknown information on competitive developments (for example, by membership of a trade association). Membership of professional institutions provides readymade networks of experience and knowledge which can be tapped into; similarly, belonging to less formal or *ad hoc* groups such as quality circles, export clubs or other associations of specific interests can facilitate exchange of information, action contacts and access to specific expertise. Organizational events often provide the social cement that binds together peers in the organization with mutually impinging interests, such as where marketing and accounts have a vested interest in pricing.

The company secretary or finance manager can and should have contacts with banks (including merchant banks), finance houses and credit insurance firms, and can be a useful point of contact in organizations for sales staff operating on long-term credit in the high-value capital goods sector. Buying managers in organizations have their connections within their own professional institution and outside it. These can keep them up to date in order to anticipate gluts and shortages of critical materials or supplies in the market, which keeps them abreast of product developments and price trends, terms and discounts and other factors affecting price such as terms of payment and delivery and developments in materials and methods. They often develop a facility in maintaining relations with principal suppliers such that they can demand favours such as rush orders, deliveries at short notice, preferential treatment when there is a scarcity and deferred payment terms when there is a cashflow problem.

Networks help the effectiveness of manager members in complex organizations by providing the knowhow contacts when they take the matter of action into their own hands in circumstances where more formal mechanisms fail. Networking is seen as an opportunity for managers to exercise leadership through the agency of strong peer relationships, their power base arising from common interests, ideology or social position.

Bridging the Power Gap

In addressing the management of the problems arising from interdependence and diversity in organizations, Kotter (1985) identifies a built-in gap between the power one needs to get the job done and the power that automatically goes with the job. He observes that resolving conflicts in a way which pulls people together instead of driving them further apart and which produces creative decisions instead of destructive power struggles involves high-level leadership skills. This requires sufficient power to fill the gap inherent in leadership jobs and the willingness to use that power to manage all the interdependencies in as responsible a way as possible.

At the heart of the creation of resource networks, good working relationships, personal skills and information power is a detailed understanding of the social reality in which the job is embedded. It means knowing the different perspectives of all the various interest groups and realizing where these perspectives are in conflict. It means knowing, too, what power sources are available to each group in the pursuit of its own interests and to what extent they are prepared to use that power.

Such information is necessary to identify whose co-operation will be needed to implement an idea, whether they will be amenable to complying, and if not immediately amenable, how strongly they are likely to resist. Information, however, is never enough of itself. It also requires the power associated with credible relationships with bosses, subordinates and those people reporting to them, peers in other parts of the organization, suppliers and customers. Such relationships are based on some combination of respect, admiration, perceived need, obligation and friendship. These are reinforced by good track records.

The main link between vertical and lateral relationships lies in obtaining the support of bosses. This does not happen automatically. It has to be managed by each individual who has to take responsibility for making it happen. Kotter sees the principal task during a manager's early career as developing the power sources he or she will eventually need for leadership. It takes time to obtain the support and influence to develop the reputation, business knowledge, relationships and interpersonal skills that represent the power to bridge the gap between authority and responsibility.

Networks in Action

Managers find themselves charged with executing plans which the organization may not have the structural arrangements to facilitate. In a ground-breaking piece of research, Bonoma (1985) addressed the much-neglected implementation end of strategy and identified the four key skills of interacting, allocating, monitoring and organizing. Interacting skill relates to a personal and informal application of talents in managing one's own and others' behaviours in a way that may run counter to the reporting hierarchy as formalized in the organization. Allocating skill is the art of shifting small amounts of discretionary money from here and there to make strategy work, despite the budgetary allocation system; it is also about getting a proportion of the time of people, already allocated to specific tasks, to give attention to a problem in hand. A problem identified through the manager's external network might relate to the product. His internal network might allow him to obtain assistance of an individual in R&D to address an emerging problem. The skill is to get this addressed within an identified timescale through his peer relationships in R&D.

Monitoring skill is an intrapersonal one of the manager which can be invoked to reconstruct degraded company information and control systems. The fourth skill of organizing or networking is the one which facilitates the accomplishment of the other three. It is the skill to create afresh an informal organization, both inside and outside, to match the job that needs to be done at any given time. Good managers fashion it to make good execution easier to achieve.

By such means, a dysfunctional formal system can be patched up to work nicely through the use of the networks that have been created. The allocating and monitoring skills are those which might be called technical. These are the abilities to identify problems, whether through formal systems or the informal controls represented by monitoring, and to see what is required to be done in order to obtain a short-run workable solution. Interacting and networking are the true managerial skills whereby these solutions can best be effected. The networks which are established are the necessary framework within which the interacting skills can be employed. It is implicitly understood by people who are good interactors that compromise, trade-off and the principles of exchange are what dominate managerial life. In Bonoma's study successful managers treated their peers like customers to get things done.

This exchange viewpoint served the good implementers well in their intra- and extra-firm relationships. They were quick to realize that sales force management might allocate more time to a well-supported product than those that were poorly supported, and that a liked product manager has more leverage with the sales force than one regarded neutrally. They were not averse to providing something in exchange for another's co-operation to get a more equitable effort, and indeed saw that process as a fundamental principle of management action.

There is support for this view from research in economics. Using the tools of neoclassical economics, Breton and Wintrobe (1982), in their model of public and private bureaucracy, show that relations between superiors and subordinates are governed by exchange. Whereas exchange relations between organizations have legally supported property-rights market systems, those within organizations are characterized by trust-supported property-rights network systems. Within organizations, then, informal negotiation replaces the formal, often ritualistic, bargaining found between organizations, and trust replaces the legal bonds. In the process, subordinates exhibit 'selective behaviour', i.e. they choose to deliver efficient or inefficient informal services. These are analogous to co-operative and competitive behaviour, as illustrated in Figure 6.4. While addressing relationships between superiors and subordinates and between subordinate peers, lateral relationships are implicit in the Breton and Wintrobe model. The work was carried out in the early 1980s, when parallel research into what managers do had not yet made an impact on the management literature.

SUMMARY OF MAIN POINTS SO FAR

1   Different specializations often generate different cultures and rationalities, and these inevitably come into conflict. This is highlighted by the fact that functions are interdependent. If decisions are to be made that enable the whole organization to perform satisfactorily, then these conflicts have to be resolved.

2   Because the self-interests of groups, functions and factions are facts of organizational life, such groups seek to acquire power selectively or the support of other groups that allow them to reinforce that power and so

make others dependent on them. This power is exercised to obtain resources such as an increased share of the organizational budget to further group ends. It calls on managerial actions outside normal line management structures, sometimes referred to as 'indirect management'.

3   Indirect management is also used to co-ordinate specialized activities in a way that meets what the organization is setting out to do in terms of performance. It is necessary since control and accountability are not matched because of the nature of modern organizations. In other words, managers often have to rely on people to get things done outside their own function or department.

4   There are limitations on what changes in organizational structures can do to have a significant impact on organizational effectiveness. Increasingly, this effectiveness is the function of social networks which managers build up. These networks exist inside the organization where they may be used to harness support for some demand for resources or to obtain early identification of problems. They are also established externally to provide the knowhow contacts for managers to assist their decision making when more formal mechanisms fail.

5   Through their specialist skills, managers identify problems through formal and/or informal means and see what is needed to be done. Where the formal system is inadequate, as it often is, good managers use their networks and interacting skills to get done what line management relationships cannot do. Successful managers use compromise, trade-off and the principles of exchange to make good the deficiencies of the formal system.

COMMUNICATION AND THE MANAGEMENT OF CONFLICT

The Nature of Conflict

It has been shown that differing perspectives, practices and perceptions have to be accommodated, or otherwise made productive, in order to meet an organization's overall goals. These differences can, depending on the circumstances, be covert or overt. They can take place between superiors and subordinates in a hierarchical structure and, perhaps even more importantly, take place across functional structures and sometimes across organizations.

In the great majority of situations conflict is either present or threatens to be present. Even where a co-operative relationship exists, there will always be a compelling need to be competitive if only to emphasize the importance of a certain position on an issue under consideration.

To enable people to communicate in a way which effectively handles such conflict it is useful to know something about the studies in conflict which have been made. A useful framework is that of Pondy (1967), who saw conflict as having a number of distinct phases. The first phase is *latent conflict*, in which two or more parties co-operate with each other and compete for certain rewards. This could be measurable in terms of bonuses or effectiveness benchmarks. For example, if sales targets seem to be within grasp and productivity targets look like falling short this might be seen by production as a possible threat to their reputation or to year-end payoffs. A remedial measure might be for the production manager to seek the sales manager's co-operation for a greater emphasis on the sale of standardized products during the remainder of the review period to enable him to reach his target and achieve the bonus figures. Equally, rewards could apply to intangible factors such as status, respect or autonomy, as where a subordinate is seeking more elbow room and decision-making authority in fulfilling his or her role. Where people are interdependent and in regular contact, conflict will inevitably arise, and every situation contains the seed of conflict.

The second phase is *perceived conflict*. Where, for instance, groups rely on each other and one believes that the other is pursuing a course of action which is harmful to its members, conflict is perceived to exist. One department may feel that it is not getting an equitable share of the budget due to what they think are the machinations of the head of the other department and/or his subordinates. Sometimes such perceived conflicts are defined in ways which are either easier or more difficult to manage. Definitions which facilitate conflict management are those which see a positive outcome for both parties as distinct from those which view conflict as a situation in which one gains at the other's expense. Conflicts in which the parties define the situation from the other party's as well as from their own viewpoint are more manageable than where at least one of the parties sees a situation entirely through its own frame of reference. Possibilities are good where the conflict is seen by both parties in a broad organizational context rather than from the much narrower context of their own individual or group viewpoint. Other, more easily handled situations are those where the issues are problem centred rather than ideological, as in the case of many disputes between management and organized labour.

The third phase is *felt conflict*, in which differences of interests and opinions are given expression in specific issues which take on an added significance because they symbolize how the parties feel about each other. It is at this stage that people as managers start to make choices. How they define the situation may be a conscious or unconscious choice, depending on the manager's awareness of the alternatives and the forces at work on him; how they orient themselves in terms of degree of assertiveness and co-operativeness will influence the ease with which conflict can be managed.

These definitions and orientations influence the course the conflict will take and the communication strategies which should be used to manage it.

Pondy's next phase is *manifest conflict*, which arises after a conflictual situation is activated. Such behaviour can be seen in the making of coalitions to resist the forces of opposition and organizational strife.

The final phase is the *conflict aftermath*. This consists of the results of conflict seen in terms of the likelihood of future conflict. If one of the results was restructuring of the situation through integration or personnel were changed to achieve integration more easily, then there would presumably be some reduction in the latent conflict. The outcome of any episode shapes the input affecting future latent conflict.

Communication Strategies for Conflict

When conflicts become overt their development and outcomes are not within the control of any one participant. Conflict issues are expressed in terms of response and counter-response. Depending on the way the parties define the situation, the conflict-handling modes which they adopt and the communication strategies they select will determine the effect they have on each other. Outcomes are dependent on the interactions of the parties. There is always a danger that these interactions will degenerate into self-perpetuating and self-reinforcing cycles. Such response and counter-response are best described as escalating attack/defend spirals. Individuals may enter into conflict interactions with the intention of reaching a certain outcome. Yet such are the dynamics of conflict that these spirals get out of control and inhibit agreement, even though the desired outcome is still technically possible. An understanding of this process and its connection with communication is a significant preliminary to being able to make an appropriate approach.

The available communication strategies have been well summarized by Conrad (1985), and these are shown in Table 8.2. The *avoidant strategies* may be appropriate where issues are trivial or where potential losses from an open conflict may outweigh possible gains. Nevertheless, they merely put off confrontation. There is no resolution of differences, no matter how temporary. It may have the effect of causing the other party to become frustrated or more hostile, which can only reduce the possibility of creative management of the conflict.

Delaying strategies of the 'I don't have time to talk about it now' variety can be used or, more subtly, procedural rules can be manipulated to delay or subvert protracted confrontations. *Structuring strategies* may be important in situations where individuals in an organization find conflicts ambiguous and complicated. People tend to become defensive under such conditions and to start communicating in ways which lead to escalating conflict spirals.

Table 8.2. Communication strategies in conflicts. (Reproduced by permission of Holt, Rinehart and Winston from Conrad, 1985)

Avoidant strategies	Structuring strategies	Confrontive strategies
(1) Delay/procrastination Manipulating procedures 'Putting off' communication Focusing on rules of interaction	(1) Definition of issue Initiating focal or new issues Focusing issues through repetition or classification Modifying the scope of the issue (enlarging, narrowing, fogging) Attaching emotional labels to the conflict or to the positions taken	(1) Coercion: overt displays of power Formal rank Coalitions Expertise
(2) Regression	(2) Establishment of evaluation criteria Exclusion of alternative criteria	(2) Coercion: threats or promises
(3) Commitments to revenge	(3) Manipulation of relationships Bribery Altercasting Predicting self-feelings Altruism Appeals to guilt	(3) Personalization Moral accusations Ad hominem Revelation of secrets
(4) Refusing to admit existence of conflict		(4) Toughness Pure form Reformed sinner

By focusing on a particular issue and repeating or clarifying it, attention is diverted from the complexity of the situation. By such activities structure is given to the conflict. Such strategies are used most successfully by managers in a position of some authority in the organization which gives them an opportunity to define or redefine conflicts. People listen to powerful people and behave as if they perceived situations in the same way.

Power can also be related to another kind of structuring strategy, namely establishing evaluative criteria. These are not imposed on the conflict; they arise from the use of structuring strategies. For example, A is a contender for the job of district sales manager. He has an excellent sales record and has been reported on well by various supervisors for whom he has worked. However, he would be reporting to the regional sales manager who, while acknowledging his capabilities, feels threatened and tries to put a block in the way of his promotion. To do so he has to dismiss past sales performance as a criterion. This he can do by highlighting A's few administrative errors, e.g. in sales reports and journey planning. This could be used to devastating effect by arguing that the district sales manager's post is so basically different in its requirements that past sales record is irrelevant to his selection.

Other strategies can relate to defining a conflict in personal terms, as where interpersonal relationships are appealed to: 'We have worked together for a long time and in all that time I've never asked a favour. For once . . .'

Where avoiding or structuring strategies are not alternatives, resort can be had to *confrontive strategies*. Threats and promises come into this category. The difficulty in using them is that people's perceptions of what is credible, equitable and appropriate differ. Another strategy in this category is taking a hardline position. Where one party to an interaction takes this kind of stance, the other party, even if he wishes to be co-operative, will require to take such a competitive stance himself if he is not to lose out. If the parties have the skills not to get into hardline positions from which they find it progressively more difficult to disengage, they are eventually forced to search for a mutually acceptable solution. This will tend to be more of a compromise than a creative solution, with the parties involving themselves in trade-offs.

These communication strategies are not used alone. People at various levels in organizations employ a complicated combination of them. They may seek to operate within a co-operative relationship but be forced to be competitive to make cogently their strong preferences on a particular point in contention. They may try to manipulate the agenda to establish a principle which bears advantageously on an issue which comes later in the proceedings. The most important point that emerges is the importance of not becoming trapped in escalating attack/defend spirals.

Conflict Prevention

It is always better to prevent conflict where possible than to have to exercise skills, time and energy seeking to resolve it. The conflict-handling communication strategies examined above are those which are used to secure preferred outcomes by parties to a dispute. Together, with their formal and legitimate authority, the qualities and abilities they bring to the job and the access to information and technical and human resources on which others depend, these strategies represent the exercise of overt power to achieve preferred outcomes.

Bachrach and Baratz (1970) developed the idea that power is not only invoked within conflictual decision-making situations it is also exercised to use mechanisms to squeeze people out and confine decision making to 'safe' issues. It assumes that absence of grievance and manifest conflict means consensus. Others have since tried to show that political acquiescence can be the result of fashioning people's understanding, perceptions and preferences in such a way that they accept their role in the existing order of things. Symbolism is used to manage meaning in achieving this. It embraces language, ritual and myths.

The significant aspect of symbols is that they stand for something other than themselves—the meaning is in the society or organization, not in the symbol. Language can be used as a device to cloud issues or quieten opposition, as we saw. Myths emphasize the importance of the past and of tradition. They are used mostly to legitimize existing power positions. Rituals, ceremonies and settings are the more physical aspects of symbolism. For example, meetings can take on a ritual character in order to convey messages to the participants. In a medium-sized family-owned engineering firm with three divisions but shared production facilities, a weekly meeting of the managing director (who was also production director) and heads of divisions debated priorities in relation to delivery to customers, who were all in process industries, susceptible to consequential losses if deliveries were not kept. The message which the institutionalization of this process spells out and reinforces with every meeting is that the customer's interest is paramount.

These means of manipulating people to secure preferred outcomes by presenting conflict from arising has been called *unobtrusive power* (Hardy, 1985). Hardy opposes Pfeffer's (1981) view that symbolic power is only used to legitimize outcomes already achieved from a position of power. If symbolic power is used to legitimize outcomes in advance, then the use of conventional power could conceivably be unnecessary in some circumstances because outcomes are deemed to be legitimate and acceptable by the people involved. This view was first articulated by Lukes (1974).

Power and Outcomes

At the heart of unobtrusive power is the ability to give meaning to events and actions so that those affected by it remain unaware of the implications of political outcomes or view them favourably. Unobtrusive power is thus founded in the ability to define reality for others in the way it is defined for oneself. Hardy has developed the relationship of overt and unobtrusive power and the effect of that relationship on outcomes. This shows that power, which is given effect through communication strategies, has two dimensions in use which interact to produce outcomes. Much of the literature has so far concentrated on the overt use of power. Figure 8.1 shows how these two aspects of power can be combined to produce desired outcomes. It represents an integration of the rhetoric of bureaucratic control shown in Figure 7.1 and the concepts of overt and unobtrusive power.

Figure 8.1 illustrates the numerous and complex relationships involved in the overt and unobtrusive aspects of power:

1 Overt power is based on the control of scarce resources and resource interdependencies. Success depends upon more than the mere ownership of these power bases; they also have to be brought into action through a process of power mobilization.
2 The mobilization of overt power sources enables managers to achieve the substantive outcomes they desire, for example in the form of budget or resource allocations, decision outcomes and implementation. Overt

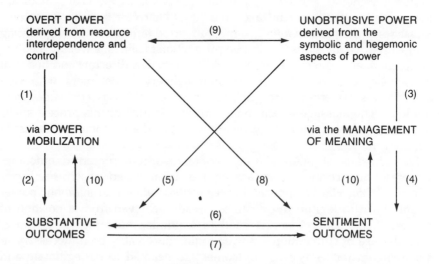

Figure 8.1. *The overt and unobtrusive aspects of power. (From Hardy, 1985, reproduced by permission)*

power is mobilized by those having the authority in their attempts to secure these outcomes in spite of opposition and conflict.

3   Unobtrusive power is derived from symbolic sources which are brought into play to legitimize outcomes in a process called the management of meaning (see page 126).

4   Unobtrusive power can be employed to influence sentiments with the use of such mechanisms as symbols, language, rituals and culture. It can also be used in conjunction with overt power—the one producing the desired substantive outcome, the other creating favourable feelings towards the outcome.

5   Unobtrusive power can produce substantive outcomes directly. Factors such as the institutionalization of power, ideological authority and the bias of the system ensure that certain demands and challenges are never made.

6   Unobtrusive power can be consciously used by people in organizations to achieve outcomes. In this case, mechanisms are used to legitimize and justify desired outcomes, producing favourable sentiments and removing the threat of opposition—steps are taken to 'persuade' other groups to accept certain outcomes though they may have been unaware of this.

7   There may be a relationship between substantive outcomes and sentiments—some outcomes may be so unpalatable they automatically produce hostile feelings.

8   The use of overt power may influence sentiments if, for example, it is excessively coercive.

9   There may be a relationship between the two types of power—for example, the use of overt power may preclude the use of unobtrusive power, for people in authority in organizations may have to possess the bases of overt power before they can try to use unobtrusive power.

10   There will be feedback from the outcomes into the power systems. The existence of certain physical outcomes and sentiments may, for example, increase or reduce the power sources of the groups involved.

SUMMARY OF COMMUNICATION AND THE MANAGEMENT OF CONFLICT

1   Almost every organizational situation contains the seed of conflict. Where conflict is perceived, it is more manageable where seen by both parties in a broad organizational context rather than within their own narrower frames of reference.

2   If a situation reaches the stage of active conflict this is signalled by such actions as the making of coalitions to support a party's position. When

conflicts become overt and people take up and strongly support what are seen to be extreme positions, there is a tendency for them to degenerate into attack/defend spirals.

3   Various communication strategies for handling conflict are available. Avoidant strategies only put off confrontation. Structuring strategies are often used in ambiguous or complex situations. Structure is given to a conflict by such actions as focusing and developing a particular issue (to divert attention from other issues), by establishing evaluative criteria (to devalue other possible criteria) or by calling on interpersonal relationships. Confrontive strategies may be used where avoidant and structuring strategies are not alternatives. Threats and promises, tough talking and personalization of the conflict are all possibilities. Threats, personal attacks and tough talking can be counterproductive if they lead to attack/defend spirals.

4   The above communication strategies represent the exercise of overt power to achieve desired outcomes. Unobtrusive power is about the management of meaning so that those affected by it remain unaware of political outcomes or view them favourably as a result of such mechanisms as symbols, language, rituals and culture.

COMMUNICATION AND FUNDAMENTAL ORGANIZATIONAL CHANGE

Action for Change

Changes are sometimes necessary for the survival of an organization. These are often more basic and far-reaching than the changes sought in managing conflict, where discrepant views occur in daily interactions. Major strategic decisions sometimes have to be taken adjustment of the organization's *modus operandi* and consequent attitudes, beliefs and values opposed to the traditional ones. The privatization of British Telecom is a case in point. From an organization that grew out of the British Post Office where profits had to be made but were often less than what were possible due to the perceived necessity to attend to social aspects of the service it provided, it became overnight an organization which was profits driven. It will require fundamental rethinking at all levels of the organization to establish whether resistance to the new values arise from these values being at odds with basic assumptions. If so, the organization will have to consider encouraging new assumptions congruent with values. This will be at the cost of jettisoning previous ideology and the strength that this represents.

One of the problems facing organizations is that in striving to become more efficient they introduce appropriate systems and procedures. In the very process of striving to become efficient they lose the flexibility they had as young and thrusting organizations and the effervescence, adaptability and creativity of personnel. The system has certain requirements which tie managers to them and discourage effort outside that required to make the system work. Most private sector firms lie on a continuum between the young, dynamic and flexible and the system/rule bound and inflexible. It is in this grey area that Bonoma's (1985) good implementers take action through networks of internal and external contacts to overcome barriers in the system to achieve results. In the process they manage to shift resources to needed areas which the system decrees are not transferable, and obtain the temporary service of individual specialists whom the system declares should be used elsewhere. Unobtrusive power, which we saw illustrated in Figure 8.1 concerning the prevention of conflict, is part of the answer to the problem of achieving change in the organization trapped in its own bureaucracy.

In the final analysis, to win support for a specific organizational action involving fundamental change requires a combination of motivation, expectations and commitment. These three factors interact to produce the conditions for organizational action (Brunsson, 1985). The stronger those three factors are, the greater the likelihood that people will participate in the action. Motivation tends to influence commitment, expectation influences motivation and commitment affects expectations. Brunsson's researches in Sweden showed that starting from motivation, which is where rational decision making would have us begin, produced little in the way of commitment and expectations. Starting with the formulation of expectations, it was difficult but not impossible to create commitment and motivation. Starting from commitment proved to be the most effective way of generating the determinants of action, mainly because commitment has a powerful impact on both expectations and motivations.

Commitment differs from expectation and motivation in that the latter can arise without there having been any intervening social process. Commitment, on the other hand, is a social activity, and commitment to anticipated actions can be created by social processes before any action takes place. By formulating and gaining acceptance (for example, for standard operating procedures), organizations can create commitment which is the initiator of specific organizational actions in anticipated situations. Where situations are not anticipated, it cannot be created in advance. But expectations and motivations can. Establishing common expectations and motivation is the function of organizational ideologies, which has little to do with objective reality but much to do with unobtrusive power.

These ideologies embody a set of values and beliefs which can serve as a guide and a way of dealing with the uncertainty of uncontrollable or difficult events. If these values and beliefs are not based on prior cultural learning they may come to be seen only as what Argyris (1982) has called *espoused theory*. It may predict what people will say but not what they will do. If espoused values are consonant with the underlying assumptions in an organization, then the articulation of these values in an operating philosophy or ideology can be helpful in bringing a group together, serving as a source of identity and core mission. These underlying assumptions are solutions which have worked repeatedly and have come to be taken for granted. A course of action which was at one time only an idea or a value was to be treated as a reality. Such basic assumptions are Argyris's *theories in use* which, if they match espoused theory or what people actually do, enable aspirations for the future to be pursued with some confidence.

It is these patterns of basic assumptions, claims Schein (1985), subsuming the ideologies that we have been discussing, which constitute organizational culture. These basic assumptions are:

> invented, discovered or developed by a given group as it learns to cope with its problems of external adaptation and internal integration and have worked well enough to be considered valid and, therefore, to be taught to new members as the correct way to perceive, think and feel in relation to these problems.

It is the consistency of the ideologies that provides a basis for common motivations and expectations. If members of a group, section, department or faction hold widely divergent concepts of what to look for and how to conclude results, they cannot develop co-ordinated action. If, on the other hand, ideologies are strong they will tend to give a clear result when used to evaluate a proposal for action, and this tends to lead to the same action ideas in similar situations.

Some Limitations on Action

If ideologies rather than rational processes drive people in organizations to pursue action in the implementation of organizational aims it would nevertheless be a mistake to assume that the development of the language which evokes the 'right' approach, the creation of the symbols which reinforce this and the progressive recording and reiteration of suitable myths is the end of the story. These processes can be shaped in small or young organizations, although even in the latter there is some indication that the range of choices of the founder(s) is constrained by the organization's evolution towards bureaucracy. In large firms it is much more difficult to achieve, although this has been claimed for organizations such as Hewlett Packard, IBM and some other non-unionized companies.

In the great majority of large organizations where history has assisted the emergence of organizational cultures it is more likely that a pluralist culture

Table 8.3. Unitary pluralist and radical frames of reference. (From Morgan, 1986, reproduced by permission)

Organizations can be understood as mini-states where the relationship between individual and society is paralleled by the relationship between individual and organization. The unitary, pluralist and radical views of organization can be characterized in the following terms:

	Unitary	Pluralist	Radical
Interests	Places emphasis on the achievement of common objectives. The organization is viewed as being united under the umbrella of common goals and striving towards their achievement in the manner of a well-integrated team.	Places emphasis on the diversity of individual and group interests. The organization is regarded as a loose coalition which has just a passing interest in the formal goals of the organization.	Places emphasis on the oppositional nature of contradictory 'class' interests. Organization is viewed as a battleground where rival forces (e.g. management and unions), strive for the achievement of largely incompatible ends.
Conflict	Regards conflict as a rare and transient phenomenon that can be removed through appropriate managerial action. Where it does arise it is usually attributed to the activities of deviants and troublemakers.	Regards conflict as an inherent and ineradicable characteristic of organizational affairs and stresses its potentially positive or functional aspects.	Regards organizational conflict as inevitable and as part of a wider class conflict that will eventually change the whole structure of society. It is recognized that conflict may be suppressed and thus often exists as a latent rather than manifest characteristic of both organizations and society.
Power	Largely ignores the role of power in organizational life. Concepts such as authority, leadership and control tend to be preferred means of describing the managerial prerogative of guiding the organization towards the achievement of common interests.	Regards power as a crucial variable. Power is the medium through which conflicts of interests are alleviated and resolved. The organization is viewed as a plurality of power holders drawing their power from a plurality of sources.	Regards power as a key feature of organization, but a phenomenon that is unequally distributed and follows class divisions. Power relations in organizations are viewed as reflections of power relations in society at large, and as closely linked to wider processes of social control, e.g. control of economic power, the legal system, the education.

will evolve in which sub-cultures proliferate. Because organizations tend to be a conglomeration of sub-cultures and may also have a discernible total organization culture if it has had a long enough history, it is necessary that they should be managed for multiple realities rather than in spite of them. Table 8.3 illustrates how different kinds of ideology are characterized in terms of 'unitary', 'pluralist' and 'radicalist' frames of reference (Morgan, 1986).

The implication is that for most organizations managers have to address conflict arising from these different realities in ways that will benefit the overall organization or, more selfishly, in ways that will promote their own interests within it. While conflict energizes an organization and counters tendencies towards lethargy, staleness and unquestioning compliance, it still requires to be managed in order to derive maximum benefit in terms of the quality of decision making.

Those managing in such situations have to maintain just the right level of conflict. The communication strategies essential to achieving this are those shown in Table 8.2.

SUMMARY OF COMMUNICATION AND FUNDAMENTAL ORGANIZATIONAL CHANGE

1 As organizations strive to become more efficient they introduce appropriate systems and procedures. Such systems limit the flexibility of organizations in seeking to adopt and implement new strategies to meet changes in the organization's environment.

2 It is non-rational ideological approaches rather than rational processes that drive people to pursue action in the implementation of new strategic aims. Commitment is the starting point to give effect to the other determinants of action, namely, expectations and motivation.

3 These processes can be directed in small and new organizations but are more difficult to shape as organizations evolve towards bureaucracy.

4 In the great majority of large organizations it is more likely that strong sub-cultures will proliferate. These have to be managed for multiple realities. The handling of conflict and the communication strategies to assist this remains a significant requirement in organizations.

REFERENCES

Argyris, C. *Reasoning, Learning and Action: Individual and Organisational*, Jossey-Bass, San Francisco, CA (1982).
Bachrach, P. and Baratz, M. S. *Power and Poverty*, Oxford University Press, London (1970).

Bonoma, T. V. *The Marketing Edge: Making Strategies Work*, The Free Press, New York (1985).

Bradford, D. L. and Cohen, A. R. *Managing for Excellence*, John Wiley, Chichester (1984).

Breton, A. and Wintrobe, R. *The Logic of Bureaucratic Conduct: An Economic Analysis of Competition Exchange and Efficiency in Private and Public Organizations*, Cambridge University Press, Cambridge (1982).

Brunsson, N. *The Irrational Organization: Irrationality as a Basis for Organizational Action and Change*, John Wiley, Chichester (1985).

Conrad, C. *Strategic Organisational Communication: Cultures, Situations and Adaptations*, Holt, Rinehart and Winston, New York (1985).

Doyle, P. Management structures and marketing strategies in UK industries. *European Journal of Marketing*, **13**, No. 5 (1979).

Hardy, C. The nature of unobtrusive power. *Journal of Management Studies*, July (1985).

Kotler, P. *Marketing Management: Analysis, Planning and Control*, Prentice-Hall, Englewood Cliffs, NJ (1985).

Kotter, J. *Power and Influence*, The Free Press, New York (1985).

Lax, D. A. and Sebenius, J. K. *The Manager as Negotiator: Bargaining for Co-operation and Competitive Gain*, The Free Press, New York (1986).

Lukes, S. (1974) *Power: A Radical View*, Macmillan, London (1974).

Morgan, G. *Images of Organisations*, Sage, Beverley Hills, CA (1986).

Mueller, R. K. *Corporate Networks: Building Channels for Information and Influence*, The Free Press, New York (1986).

Peters, T. J. and Waterman, R. *In Search of Excellence*, Harper and Row, New York (1982).

Pfeffer, J. *Power and Politics in Organisations*, Pitman, London (1981).

Pfeffer, J. and Salancik, G. R. The External Control of Organisations, Harper and Row, New York (1978).

Piercy, N. *Marketing Budgeting: A Political and Organisational Model*, Croom Helm, London (1986).

Pondy, L. R. Organisational conflict: concepts and model. *Administrative Science Quarterly*, **12**, No. 2 (1967).

Van Maanen, J. and Barley, S. R. Culture and organisation: fragments of a theory. In Frost, P. J., Moore, L. F., Louis, M. R., Wiendberg, C. C. and Martin, J. (eds), *Organisational Culture*, Sage, Beverley Hills, CA (1985).

Schein, E. H. *Organisational Culture and Leadership*, Jossey-Bass, San Francisco, CA (1985).

Spillard, P. *Organisation and Marketing*, Croom Helm, London (1985).

Wildavsky, A. *The Politics of the Budgetary Process*, Little, Brown, Boston, MA (1979).

9
Communication Problem
Solving Between Organizations

Just as the achievement of organizational goals is assisted by integration of specialized activities within an organization, so is it also helped by the co-ordination of specialized activities between organizations. This co-ordination is seen to operate within formal structures and also on an *ad hoc* basis. Typically, where the arrangement becomes a repeated or ongoing one, organizations develop a range of linkages which bind them together. They evolve a network of interdependent relationships. As such, there are always likely to be conflicts within areas of common interest.

Conflict is best handled by influence strategies, political strategies, problem solving and negotiation in order to achieve acceptable outcomes. Whatever strategy or combination of them is used, it is individuals who make decisions. The way they behave to each other will be affected by the internal dispositions of the parties and the emerging group phenomena. Common ground only begins to be found when one party has the ability to hear the other's values with empathy. The relational language used by the participants is crucial, as it has to complement the language content for maximum effectiveness.

ORGANIZATIONS AND INTERACTIONS

The focus of people in organizations is very much the organization itself, which gives them a context in which they live out their day-to-day activities. It is the principal milieu in which individual and group dramas are played out, where organizational direction provides opportunities and frustrations, where people pursue common and self-interests, have regular exchanges with bosses and subordinates and others outside the immediate authority structure, hold values or change their values and perceptions, experience fears, exhilaration and doubts, obtain psychical as well as tangible rewards, exercise their expertise, indulge their prejudices and display non-rational behaviour.

There is little doubt that many of the studies on organizations are related to this focus. Hence the emphasis on factors such as motivation, power, influence and the politics of management; on the workings of groups and the people within them; on what people believe in and what the organization wants them to believe in; and how order is created and co-ordination achieved out of the specialized activities of so many people.

Because organizations loom so large in the lives of people working in them, organizational life appears to bring about concentration on internal activities. Yet organizations exist to serve society and only remain in existence as long as this function continues to be carried out. In pursuit of this purpose, they make available to their customers acceptable products and services, are customers themselves of other supplying organizations who, in turn, have to make their own purchases. To give them a competitive edge they often have part, or even all, of what they supply made or provided by other organizations because these other organizations have the resources to manufacture more cheaply, better or more quickly.

Additionally, organizations, whether as suppliers or customers or as participants in some joint activity, require the services of a wide range of other organizations, which help them to achieve their primary purpose of serving their customers well. As an extension of their activities they often operate through intermediaries and partners on both the supply and demand side in order to achieve their goals. They therefore require of their managers a facility in managing negotiated relationships in respect of agency, distributorship, licensing, franchising, joint venture and other arrangements (McCall and Warrington, 1989). These inter-organizational linkages are established to reduce, within the context of resource constraints, those ambiguities faced by an organization arising from the dynamic, and hence uncertain, conditions in its environment. These are dependency relationships. Such interdependencies can bring further uncertainty if co-ordination of activities in the interest of acceptable organizational performance cannot be achieved. This is sometimes caused by too great a proliferation of inter-organizational linkages in terms both of numbers and complexity (Stearns *et al*, 1987). Whether or not these factors moderate environmental conditions as determinants of organizational performance, these interactions require to be managed. Organizations, and specifically those members involved in boundary-spanning activities, are in continuing interaction with their dependencies. This is not only with the traditional two-way dependencies such as suppliers, customers, banks, insurers and transporters but also with newer interests, such as consumer groups, community and environment groups and government-regulating agencies.

The Significance of Inter-organizational Relationships

What goes on in organizations shapes, and is shaped by, events in the organizations with which they constantly interact. Bonoma (1985) illustrates this nicely in one example he gives of reallocation of effort done with people and time without formal reorganization or rewriting of job descriptions. The head of production engineering in a firm in which the management felt that the power concentration between design and production had become a block to the firm's ability to listen to its customers and dealers was asked to spend three months on special assignment to the commercial products division. An additional reason for the move was to help reinforce the fledgling sales group's efforts, which involved a large element of custom design. In such a process it is highly likely that some customers will become more dependent on suppliers and, as a result, suppliers find a stable market on which they come to rely.

Inter-organizational interdependence tends to increase with the degree of innovation present. A link is also suggested between complexity of an organization and the external orientation of its members. Such mutual dependence is reflected in what has been called 'the customer-active paradigm of innovation' (von Hippel, 1982).

By the very fact of aligning themselves with other organizations in a relationship of dependence, organizations commit themselves to co-operative activities. Such co-operation often takes the form of fulfilling a role in the channel of distribution. This usually stems from negotiations in relation to the functions to be carried out and the rewards for performance. It is, in effect, a code of conduct which lays down the contribution of the channel member as expected by other channel members. Communication is central to the management of such relationships.

The Establishment of Relationships

Good, long-standing relationships resulting in the co-ordination of activities to mutual ends are often seen to consist of formally structured arrangements (for example, in dealership and franchising agreements). Yet an even larger amount of co-ordination occurs in the form of *ad hoc* efforts at co-ordination between pairs of organizations. In the first instance, they specialize to obtain the reduction of costs and increase of efficiency which such specialization enhances, and enter into trading relationships with other organizations to meet their specialized needs. When a course of dealing has been established, procedures are built up which facilitate the exchanges by which needs are satisfied. When two or more organizations acknowledge that it is in their long-term interests to perpetuate a relationship this is normally an indication that a channel of distribution has emerged. Such arrangements may then be formalized in terms of agreement.

Not all *ad hoc* arrangements result in formal agreements or long-term understandings. 'Open' or 'free-flow' channels of distribution can sometimes embrace a single transaction or take the form of short-term contracts to supply and to purchase. There is no expectation of further business when the sale is complete or when the short-term contract expires. Procuring organizations are at liberty to find other suppliers who can meet their immediate or short-term needs, either on grounds of price or other considerations. Nevertheless, it is these *ad hoc* efforts which often represent the embryonic stage in the development of inter-organizational relations out of which grow more permanent and structured arrangements. These have been noted as an increasing trend and to be likely to become the rule rather than the exception (Bowersox *et al.*, 1980; Spekman and Strauss, 1986).

Formally Structured Relationships

Organizations seek mutual gain from their relationships and wise personnel who have to forge and nurture relationships try to establish that common interests and goal congruence are sufficient for satisfactory operation. Communication should be aimed at extracting information which will confirm or confound the existence of goal congruence. Given a decision to enter a formal agreement (for example, in relation to joint research or advertising, distributorship or licensing), it does not follow that goals will be aligned. It is often, however, impolitic or difficult to ascertain at an early stage of relationship whether or not an organization is what it claims to be.

It is therefore in the process of operating agreements that companies learn a great deal about each others' real needs and preferences. Openness of communication, when it is allowed to develop, will highlight each party's need for the other and subsequent co-operative action will determine how problems will be resolved.

Informally Structured Relationships

Sometimes no formal agreement is envisaged but a close working relationship is desired. Where a manufacturer sees a desirable long-term market in the purchase needs of a target organization and that organization hopes for the possibility of a competitive edge through dealing with that particular manufacturer, the communication approach is critical. While it may be important to sell the organization to the other party in formally structured relationships, it is indispensable in informally structured ones.

Whatever value a supplying organization provides its buyers, it is often difficult for those buyers to assess this value in advance, even after careful inspection of the product or process. A buyer's incomplete knowledge may be partly corrected for him by how he infers value (Porter, 1985). In making a decision to purchase from a supplier for the first time, buyers use such indicators as advertising, reputation, professionalism, appearance and personality of supplier employees and the information provided in sales presentations to infer value. Porter terms such factors employed by buyers to infer the value a firm creates as *signals of value.*

Although not all the factors embraced by signals of value are under the control of the communicating company's representative, a significant number of factors remain in fact under his control, such as his professionalism, the way he talks about his company and the assumptions he makes and reinforces in his sales presentations. If, in addition, he can find out by advance preparation what the principal logics used by the buyer organization are, he can make himself acceptable to it as representing an organization fit to do business with by aiming his presentation to suit these logics. For example, many small-to-medium-sized firms often take decisions dictated by the whims of the chairman, managing director or dominant power group. Such a company might operate on a 'seat of the pants' decision-making process or personality logic as distinct from a rational/economic approach. In such a case an emphasis on the relationship rather than on the task might have a more favourable outcome.

Interaction of Organizations and Development of Relationships

Inter-organizational relations grow incrementally. As resource transactions come to be perceived as equitable and fruitful, subsequent transactions reinforce this belief and eventually develop a web of interdependencies.

The interaction of buying and selling organizations has been well illustrated by the work of the IMP Group. This group of researchers, based on five West European countries, has developed an interaction model (see Figure 9.1) which has grown out of inter-organizational theory and a microeconomic approach characterized as the 'new institutionalists' (Hakansson, 1982). The model depicts an interaction process between parties in a dynamic relationship in organizational markets and identifies four basic elements:

1 The interaction process;
2 The participants in the process;
3 The environment in which the particular interaction takes place;
4 The atmosphere affecting and affected by the interaction.

The interplay of the elements is conceptualized in terms of the complexity of the episodes and the extent of relationships, the structural fit between the parties and their knowledge of each other, the degree of homogeneity and dynamism of the market, and the relationship of atmosphere to these. The inter-organizational personal contact patterns are explored in terms of roles such as information exchange and social enhancement. Progressive institutionalization of these patterns is reflected in the expectations built up of the frequency and style of contacts. It becomes increasingly difficult in the

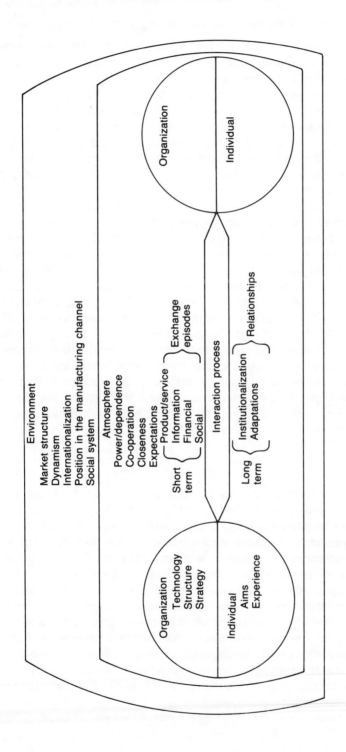

Figure 9.1. The IMP interaction model

face of intercompany dialogue becoming incorporated into the procedures of the separate companies for one party to withdraw from these arrangements. Interdependence becomes a way of life.

The interaction approach is extended by combining it with a systems analysis approach resulting in the concept of markets as networks (Stidsen, 1979; Hammarkvist, 1983). Here the company resources are not confined to the organization itself but also to other supplier and customer organizations in surrounding networks. Suppliers can include the providers of services (for example, financial) which enable organizations the better to meet the needs of client organizations. The perspective is one which views the development of relationships with other organizations as a necessary condition for the harnessing of resources across organizations.

This approach is reinforced by the concept of value chains developed by Porter (1985), whereby a systematic way of examining all the activities a firm performs and how they interact is derived from analysing the sources of competitive advantage. The value chain 'disaggregates the firm into its strategically relevant activities in order to understand the behaviour of costs and the existing and potential sources of differentiation'. A firm's value chain is embedded in what Porter calls a *value system*. A firm gains competitive advantage by performing these strategically important activities more cheaply or better than its competitors. To achieve this, it requires to interact with the value chains of suppliers, customers and channels of distribution. The interdependencies arising from these interactions are the source of competitive advantage, and, as such, inhibit withdrawal from evolved arrangements.

Organizational Bonds

Relations between companies in interacting networks, as shown above, tend to bind organizations together, and these bonds typically get stronger as time goes by (Hammarkvist, 1983). These can be *technological bonds*, where companies become technologically bound to each other (for example, where there is co-operative research and development). In order to reduce the tying up of capital, producers often keep down the costs of materials and components to a minimum, trusting that suppliers will deliver on time. This leads to *time-based bonds* between companies in a network. As relations develop, each organization learns progressively more about each other's strengths and weaknesses, processes and procedures. A purchasing organization gets to know about its supplier's abilities, while the supplier learns how the purchaser uses the product or service.

This learning about each other can be seen as an investment in the relationship which creates *knowledge-based bonds* between the organizations. Finally, there are *financial and legal bonds*, as where a manufacturer buys a share of the equity of a supplier company to guarantee a critical source of raw materials or of a customer company to ensure the stability of a market. Equally, it could apply to the establishment of a joint venture to exploit an opportunity or to the contractual nature of distributor- ship agreement where the manufacturer provides off-the-shelf facilities for the distributor or the distributor has to invest in specific equipment in support of the agreement.

In addition to these bonds, there are *social bonds*, which develop between individuals who span the boundaries between organizations and ensure the smooth functioning of what amounts to an inter-organizational unit. When these have been established over and above the other bonds a cohesion between the organizations involved is provided which can only be broken by some crisis to which one party has not been perceived to act adequately (for example, when a supplier has increased his price sub- stantially without apparent justification and in breach of the trust implicit in the social bonds).

Stages in the Development of Relationships

Relationships take place between two active parties each of whose actions is likely to impact on the other, and who might at least consider the likely reactions of the other party in relation to any action implying change which they may make. The closeness of the relationship is likely to be determined by the nature of the product and technology as well as by the amount of competition in the market.

Relationships are also likely to be close and long-term arrangements entered into where the procuring party can obtain benefits in the form of cost reduction, increased revenues and enhanced product differentiation. The existing relationship will have a bearing on any episodes/transactions with which the relationship is punctuated, just as an episode may change the nature of the relationship and bear on the next episode.

It is the episode or transaction which is the focus of the economics of Williamson (1980), who develops the useful notion of transaction cost analysis to guide the strategic selection of exchange partners. In the process, he addresses the 'hard' concerns inherent in any discussion of inter- organizational behaviour. In particular, his concept of *transaction-specific investments* captures the idea of mutually beneficial long-term arrangements. These are long-term investments in durable and human assets that are specific to the relationship and not readily redeployed or realized, making dissolution of the arrangement a last resort. Such investments mark the commitment of the buyer or seller to the relationship. They can vary from a supplier developing a special product for a customer or a buyer modifying his product, process or procedures to suit the seller's product, to a supplier who locates his main store adjacent to a major customer. Both have a vested interest in the perpetuation of the arrangement—the supplier to maintain his market and the buyer to maintain cost or other advantages.

Such long-term relationships have been conceptualized in terms of phases or stages (Ford, 1982). There is no inevitability about the development of relationships which will depend on the actions of either party or of other buyers and sellers. If, however, the relationship is allowed to develop, the stages identified can be examined in relation to uncertainty, commitment, distance and adaptations (see Table 9.1). The stages are examined as follows.

Stage 1: Pre-relationship Stage

Internal *ad hoc* efforts by an organizational agent or 'entrepreneur' is aimed at setting activities in motion to gain support, co-operation or resources from a number of other organizations in pursuit of a particular objective. The stage is characterized by social, cultural, technological and geographic distance.

Stage 2: The Early Stage

Considerable management time is needed to resolve issues such as quality, changes in design and scheduling of activities. This investment in time helps the parties to begin to acquire experience of each other. Relationships are organizational rather than personal. Lack of social relationships means that there is little to reduce the cultural distance. Differences between companies' product or process technologies tend to emerge at this stage.

Stage 3: The Development Stage

With increased experience of each other's operations, social and cultural distance is reduced. The adaptations which the companies make to each other bring a closer match of processes, with savings for one or both parties and a reduction of uncertainties. Perceptions of commitments by each party emerge as adaptations begin to be made and companies evaluate future possibilities.

Stage 4: The Long-term Stage

This stage is characterized by the companies' importance for each other. It is reached after a period of continuous dealing or after some major installation of works or product. Personal relationships have been established, uncertainty

Table 9.1 The development of buyer–seller relationships in organizational markets. (From Ford, 1982, reproduced by permission)

	(1) The pre-relationship stage	(2) The early stage	(3) The development stage	(4) The long-term stage	(5) The final stage
	Evaluation of new potential supplier	Negotiation of sample delivery	Contract signed or delivery build-up	After several major purchases or large-scale deliveries	In long-established stable markets
Experience	Evaluation initiated by: —particular episode in existing relationship —general evaluation of existing supplier performance —efforts of non-supplier —other information sources —overall policy decision	—Low	—Increased	—High	
Uncertainty		—High	—Reduced	—Minimum development of institutionalization	Extensive institutionalization
Distance	Evaluation conditioned by —experience with previous supplier —uncertainty about potential relationship —'Distance' from potential supplier	—High	—Reduced	—Minimum	
Commitment	Commitment —zero	Commitment Actual—low Perceived—low	Actual—increased Perceived—demonstrated by informal adaptations	Actual—maximum Perceived—reduced	Business based on industry Codes of Practice
Adaptation		Adaptation High investment of management time. Few cost savings	Increasing formal and informal adaptations. Cost savings increase	Extensive adaptations. Cost savings reduced by Institutionalization	

is at a minimum and the institutionalization of the arrangements is begun. Commitment has been demonstrated and reinforced.

Stage 5: The Final Stage

This stage is reached in stable markets over long periods of time. It is marked by an extension of the institutionalization process to a point where the business is conducted on industry codes of practice, i.e. good business practice (for example, avoidance of restrictions on changes in the respective roles of buyers and sellers).

In view of the above, a company cannot treat its buying or supplying market in some general way. Its potential market is a network of relationships. Each of these has to be assessed in relation to the opportunity they represent and the closeness of relationship sought. Strong relationships in an organizational market represent a powerful barrier to the entry of a competing company.

Whatever the nature of the interaction between organizations, if these are on a continuing basis then the element of interdependence is present to a greater or lesser degree. Even where the basic relationship is co-operative such circumstances will inevitably lead to conflict which has to be resolved, however temporarily, in the interests of the maintenance of relationships. These relationships are vital to the achievement of organizational objectives.

SUMMARY OF MAIN POINTS SO FAR

1 In order to achieve its purposes an organization requires to work with those other organizations that can best enable it compete on cost or differentiation by performing those operations which the organization cannot do or perform as well, as quickly or as cheaply. Inter-organizational interdependence arises from such linkages.

2 Relationships are central to the co-ordination of activities for mutual ends and communication is central to their management. They develop incrementally and, typically, are reinforced by technological, time-based, knowledge-based, financial, legal and social bonds.

3 Long-term relationships are often characterized by transaction-specific investments in assets not readily redeployed or realizable. Such investments mark the commitment of the parties to the relationship.

4 If relationships are allowed to develop, stages can be identified in relating experience to uncertainty, distance, commitment and adaptations of products and processes. Strong relationships reflected in the latter stages represent a powerful barrier in commercial relationships to the entry of a competing organization.

MANAGING COMMUNICATION CONTENT AND STRUCTURE

Interests and Conflicts in Inter-organizational Relations

Interdependence is a basic concept requiring the management of a number of important behaviours. By aligning themselves with other organizations in a relationship of mutual dependence, organizations are in a resultant power relationship. Inter-organizational relations are more likely to be characterized by unequal than by equal power. One party to a power relationship will therefore enjoy a relative power advantage. Under such conditions of unequal distribution of power, conflicts are certain to arise between organizations and the people in them who handle the relationships.

This one-sided imbalance of power distribution is not a permanent feature of the inter-organizational scene. Often it derives from factors in the environment which can shift and therefore alter the distribution of power between parties, as where deregulation of financial services or transport creates a completely new situation in terms of market structure. It can change, too, depending on the actual situation in which the parties find themselves. For example, an appointed distributor might be found to have a special relationship with customers, or have particular abilities, such as being able to raise special finance for customers, thereby altering the relative power balance between manufacturer and distributor in the latter's favour.

When a purchaser establishes that a supplier is short of orders, he increases his power, as does a supplier when he finds that his product is urgently needed by his customer or is the only one to meet the customer's specification. The relative power balance can also change through efforts of one of the participants to restructure the power balance, as where one of the parties in a cross-licensing agreement significantly improves his product and supports it with strong patents.

The fact that conflicts between organizations can arise even where co-operation is the preferred form of behaviour means that the exchange is either a voluntary relationship or is one derived from the exercise of power in a conflict situation by the party holding the relative power advantage. This is consistent with the view that inter-organizational relationships should be viewed in a way that integrates exchange and power-dependency relationships, and suggests that these relationships are mixed-motive situations in which each organization behaves in accordance with its own self-interests (Schmidt and Kochan, 1977). The conflict motive has been handled in the literature by four power-related processes, namely, influence strategies, political strategies, problem solving and negotiation.

Influence Strategies

If relationships, as illustrated above, operate in an environment in which parties have different perceptions of how to reach a goal that is to the advantage of both, this is a situation that has to be handled with some care and circumspection. The strategies used by a company's personnel in their attempts to influence target firms assume a considerable significance.

In order to co-ordinate company strategy and tactics, both in existing business relationships and in attempts to initiate new business, an organization's boundary personnel must be aware of, and be able to employ, available influence strategies; they should also be able to evaluate both short- and long-term implications in interactions between organizations.

Personnel responsible for administering various forms of joint activity between organizations such as franchising, agency, sales/purchase and other less structured activities aimed at creating sales usually possess a considerable latitude both in the way they promote their company's interests and communicate the target firm's needs to others within the company. Frazier and Summers (1984) examined the influence strategies adopted by boundary personnel responsible for customer service and territorial management. They identified two general influence approaches, (1) strategies based on seeking to *alter directly* the perceptions of the target firm to effect some modification of that firm's behaviour, and (2) doing this indirectly through altering the target firm's perceptions regarding the *inherent desirability* of the intended behaviour. While each of these approaches suggests different specific influence strategies, it is likely that two or more strategies of those indicated below might be utilized within the same interfirm interaction or within a series of interactions over time.

Strategies for Altering Perceptions Indirectly

Such strategies are seen as appropriate in situations where the particular behaviour can reasonably be expected to have positive implications for the attainment of the target firm's goals as well as those of the company seeking to change the behaviour. Under such conditions, real benefits will accrue to both organizations, and will result in a stronger relationship between them. There will be a higher dependence of the target firm on the relationship and a greater credibility for the company seeking the behavioural change. This has certain beneficial effects. The greater credibility should, in turn, increase the company's ability to influence the target firm. Also, overseeing the target firm's activities by the company should be unnecessary, and this could be expected to continue to be so because the target firm's motivation is independent of the company.

The two principal influence strategies based on this approach are *information exchange* and *recommendations*. Information exchange is the strategy where the company uses discussions on general business issues with the target firm to alter the target firm's general perceptions of how it might most profitably be operated. The assumption is made that these changes in the operating philosophy or decision-making processes of the target firm will be translated into a broad set of preferred responses. Recommendations are that strategy by which the company's boundary personnel predict that the target firm will be more profitable if the company's suggestions are given effect. This strategy clearly requires that the company identify and communicate the detailed behaviour to be performed by the target firm. The latter strategy is more specific than the former and requires less time and effort. It could be perceived for what it is, that is, an attempt to influence the target firm's autonomous decision making.

There is, however, another group of strategies not based on changing perceptions which can be adopted, particularly where prompt compliance is required or where the company needs to influence the target firm to take an action not basically in the target firm's best interest. A situation in which they could apply is where a main contractor wants a sub-contractor to bear a proportion of a customer's claim for corrosion damage on the customer's site, despite the sub-contractor's meeting the main contractor's packaging requirements.

Strategies for Altering Behaviour Directly

Strategies in this second group are not based on altering perceptions. They merely induce the required behaviour. These include promises, threats, legalistic strategies and requests. In a *promise strategy* the company undertakes to give the target firm a specific reward contingent on the target firm's complying with the company's stated wishes. Company policy and legal constraints place limitations on boundary personnel in the rewards they can offer, as do negative perceptions of reward on the part of the target firm. Under a *threat strategy* the company communicates to the target firm that it will apply negative sanctions should the target firm fail to perform the desired action. The long-term threat strategy will be determined by the relationship between the threat messages and corresponding subsequent events. It is a high-cost influence approach in that the coercion involved is seen by a number of authorities to magnify conflict as well as to reduce the effectiveness of other influence strategies based on mutual trust, such as information exchange and recommendations. A *legalistic strategy* relies on the legality of agreements. Where there is a mutuality to the agreement and it is seen as fair, long-lasting compliance is likely to result. Where it is viewed in operation as biased to the company or vague, it is likely to be resisted. It has to be noted, however, that in places like East Asia the principle is more important than detail.

Request strategy exists where the company informs the target firm of the actions it would like to take without implying consequences for compliance or non-compliance. This strategy would appear to be most applicable in situations where an easy, co-operative relationship has developed and the value to the company of the target firm's compliance exceeds the target firm's corresponding costs. Mutual trust and personal identification between the boundary personnel of the two organizations is promoted by this strategy. As such, it should have positive implications for the future effectiveness of the information exchange and recommendation strategies.

Using these categories, Frazier and Summers' research into the use of influence strategies in the motor car manufacturer/dealer relationship revealed the frequency of the use shown in Table 9.2. The research also

Table 9.2 *Frequency of use of influence strategies. (From Frazier and Summers, 1984, reproduced by permission of the Journal of Marketing)*

	Mean use (%)	Most frequently used (%)	Tied for most frequently used (%)	Never used (%)
Information exchange	49[a]	62[b]	6	8
Requests	27	13	7	11
Recommendations	19	8	7	23
Promises	15	4	9	37
Threats	10	1	5	53
Legalistic pleas	6	0	3	59

[a] To be read: The information exchange strategy was used in an average of 49% of typical monthly contacts across all dealerships.
[b] To be read: The information exchange strategy was the one most frequently used in 62% of the dyadic relationships.

determined the following, which confirmed hypotheses based on analysis of available literature:

1 In interfirm relationships where interdependencies are high, the parties seek to develop and monitor a co-operative atmosphere to facilitate the co-ordination of their marketing activities. In this situation organizations will rely most heavily on information exchange to gain their influence objectives. While recommendations are sometimes used successfully, the successful employment of information strategies over time reduces the need to use recommendation strategies.
2 Request strategies can be effectively used in relationships characterized by both high interdependencies and low conflict. These are much more likely

to be employed than other strategies not based on altering perceptions, i.e. threats, promises and legalistic pleas.

Apart from being effective in choosing among the available influence strategies, successful influencers anticipate the need to work at establishing those conditions that will assist positive outcomes for their influence attempts at the lowest possible cost. For example, they increase the effectiveness of the request strategy by being alert to opportunities to perform favours for others at little cost to themselves but which are greatly appreciated (Kotter, 1977). They continue to create the impression of experts in particular areas to enhance their ability to make use successfully of information exchange and recommendation strategies.

Deciding on the issues on which influence attempts should be instituted can be just as critical as selecting the influence strategy in developing and maintaining a successful relationship. Generally, influence strategies should be initiated where there is good reason for believing that the contemplated action will be of benefit to both the target firm and the company. Where perceptual biases exist in the target firm, the company has to decide whether to risk irritating the target firm by persisting in pressing an issue when the opening gambits have been turned down. When the contemplated action is not desirable from the target firm's view point, the company has to exercise particular care in deciding whether an influence attempt is warranted.

Problem Solving

Problem solving involves basic assumptions. One is that even if an organization's secondary objectives raise issues of conflict, the parties involved have common primary objectives. A second assumption is that a solution can be found within the framework of these common objectives. By using the common objectives a more efficient flow of communications can be devised to assist interacting organizations in their search for a solution. In many cases of organizations operating under a formal arrangement such as specialization, joint and contract product research, joint purchasing and joint advertising and promotion agreements, experience accumulated in operating the agreement eventually identifies and/or resolves difficulties arising from differences in philosophy and approach not necessarily identifiable when the agreement was made.

For example, the interests of a manufacturer seeking the widest possible distribution through an agent may conflict with an agent's view which sees the sale of only one or two items a year from a wide number of agencies as a factor which can produce the maximum profit from minimum resource commitment. Expectations of manufacturers in terms of market information may be seen as an unnecessary requirement or unprofitable, resource-consuming activity by a distributor.

Once resolved, such basic differences allow the parties to concentrate their energies on solving the problems to their mutual advantage. In sales/purchase situations where episodes take place within extensive relationships and are therefore analogous to formally structured agreements, problem solving can also be the preferred communication approach. Where the relationship is limited, the episode has to be treated as a totality in itself, the parties not being able to rely on implied agreements as they do in extensive relationships. Where the episodes are complex, there is a clear requirement for both parties to organize the problem-solving process in an efficient way (Hakansson, 1982).

Political Strategies

By the development of conditions to alter the power structure within a channel of distribution, organizations seek to obtain a political solution to problems associated with conflict. An example of this would be where small firms get together to compete more effectively with larger ones and induce a change towards indirect influence strategies in the larger organization and a shift from acquiescence to a reciprocal exchange in their own case, enabling them also to use a wider range of influence strategies.

Political solutions are also obtained by inducing the processes of arbitration and mediation, as where commercial disputes are submitted to an independent arbitrator either by direct negotiation of the parties or arising from the agreement to which they are party. Industrial relations disputes, once taken outside the firm to the wider union setting, can be referred to conciliation and mediation processes.

Another political solution is where a distribution channel member in a position of relative power *vis-à-vis* another channel member exercises that power to resolve an issue. The channel member influenced by that solution will normally agree with it because the benefits of doing so exceed the costs of breaking off the relationship. It is usually resorted to only when other, less confrontational, alternatives are rejected or are not available.

Negotiation

The basic objective of negotiation in commercial relationships is to initiate, maintain, alter or terminate a particular arrangement or arrangements between organizations. As indicated above, these may be formally structured or *ad hoc* arrangements which, if mutually beneficial and acceptable, become more formally constituted or are perpetuated by implicit agreement. They take place within the communication framework of Figure 6.1 and the Negotiation Skills Model in Table 6.2.

Establishing Agreement

The fact that long-term relationships are envisaged in original agreements means that any action by one or other of the parties perceived as undermining the trust condition implied in co-operative behaviour would seem a threat to, and a bad omen for, the establishment of a relationship. Nevertheless, with new agreements the co-operative nature of contracts for long-term relationships (for example, licensing, distributorship or joint-venture agreements) does not mean that there cannot be a competitive element to the interaction. What might be an outrageously demanding proposal in the operation of mature agreements can be viewed more tolerantly when the parties are strangers to each other and neither party has yet ascertained its stake in the relationship. To that extent, there is a scope for settlement within a bargaining range by reducing the other party's aspirations. This is particularly true of sales/purchase negotiations where the parties have not met before and where the possibilities of future business are limited.

In defence of his position, a negotiator can plead limited authority. One of the difficulties confronting high-level negotiators is that, while they have more discretion which they can exercise, they are less able to appeal to limited authority as a source of bargaining power. Restrictions on authority such as budget, commission, credit and cash discount limits, fair trading laws and constraints on authority to agree specification changes all give their user negotiation strength and hence a better opportunity of achieving preferred outcomes.

A different approach to establishing agreement is advocated by Fisher and Ury (1983). They maintain that the best way to handle opposing negotiators is by what they term a 'principled' approach. In this, they identify four key actions. One is to separate the relationship from the problem. This entails accurate perception of the problem or conflicts which lies not in objective reality but in people's heads—their fears, hopes and emotions. Any solution has to address this in terms of the opposers' needs. In the process, the problem should be separated from the people (for example, by not saying 'That is totally unacceptable', but by articulating in a much more self-directed manner 'I am very concerned that we seem to be so far apart on . . .'. The second key action is to focus on interests, not positions. Negotiators can be just as hard talking about their interests as about their positions. It is the combination of support and attack which is most effective in achieving satisfactory outcomes; support in terms of trying to meet both parties' interests which may be related to their security, recognition and the sustenance of self-image; attack in terms of fighting hard on the substantive issues.

The third key action is to invent options for mutual gain. This is the creative aspect of negotiation and seeks to broaden the options of the parties. Table 9.3 shows the characteristics of agreements of different strengths that can be invented in case the sought-for agreement is beyond reach.

Table 9.3 *Varying the scope of possible agreement. (From Fisher and Ury, 1983, reproduced by permission)*

Substantive	Procedural
Permanent	Provisional
Comprehensive	Partial
Final	In principle
Unconditional	Contingent
Binding	Non-binding
First order	Second order

The fourth key action is to insist on objective criteria. This focuses on principle, not pressure, and involves a joint search for objective criteria which would include fair standards and procedures. It produces wise agreements and protects a relationship that would be threatened by an approach in which there is a constant battle for dominance.

Maintaining and Revising Agreement

The self-determination of the parties which exists when original agreements are made is complicated by factors of commitment and performance once it has been operationalized. The original objectivity is clouded by the history of the growing relationship and subsequent negotiations that take place within the original agreement made and the relationships formed. The parties involved create rules for their joint working and define roles that are to be played by personnel as they increasingly acquire knowledge and understanding of each other's needs in the relationship.

When one party to a long-term agreement confronts an issue in contention from a position of perceived weakness, that party will attempt to keep the communication medium as informal as possible in order to take advantage of the relationships formed. In these circumstances, it is less easy for the stronger party to maintain a strict line and refuse concessions. In such eventualities the negotiators would be chosen on the basis of the closeness of their existing relations with the other party's representatives (Morley and Stephenson, 1977). Conversely, where a negotiator is in a strong position he can prevent his position from being eroded by maintaining a social distance between himself and his opposer, or preferably by introducing someone more senior to the proceedings which will help to provide the social distance without harming the relationship on which his more junior colleague will hope to draw in the future.

If, in the course of an agreement, a party finds that his opposer, in his view, is making unfair demands of him, he may appeal for redress to some form of legitimate power or moral rules related to the agreement, social norms of equity, equality, need, opportunities, equal concessions and historical precedent (Magenan and Pruitt, 1979). Such appeals are emotional and may have some effect if the interpersonal relationship is a close one.

The principled approach of Ury and Fisher can equally be utilized in negotiations arising from the operation of mature agreements. For example, the problem can be separated from the people by not saying something like 'You broke your word'. Rather, by playing down the extent of disagreement and eliminating the personal nature of the comment by revealing or appearing to reveal what is going on in the negotiator's mind, as in 'I feel let down', the disagreement is stated in the least competitive and personal terms.

Terminating Agreement

Such is the dynamism of the marketplace that relationships between organizations are never static. Changes in the balance of advantage will be tilted one way or the other as a result of technological, strategic and market developments. Economic and political factors change outside the control of the organizations affected by them; changes in legislation can affect the relative power balance between organizations, as can changes in the perceived strengths of the parties concerned as the organizations get to know each other better. These changes can result in issues for negotiation, if not settlement, which require adjustment to the agreement in respect of service/product, price, distribution and promotion. Where the conflict issues represent a divergence of objectives and one of the parties feels that the gap can no longer be bridged, withdrawal from the formal or informal arrangement becomes a strategic decision. A similar situation involving termination may be brought about because market factors are such that a new form of distribution is important. For example, what might have been suitable in terms of distribution in Spain may no longer be suitable with Spain's accession to the European Communities and the increase in market potential involved.

The communication approach in such cases is to ensure that costly litigation is avoided. This involves legal information and advice so that a threat of litigation can be seen for what it is, and that, very often, is a bluff, certainly in the European scene, although litigation is a much more common factor in American commercial relations. The approach also has to handle what are often residual problems from the agreements which have to be negotiated away. A distributor carrying stocks, for example, may, on the termination of the agreement by his supplier, wish the supplier to repurchase them or otherwise recompense him; a supplier will want to terminate in a way that the outgoing intermediary assists in the transfer of stocks, customer enquiries and, if possible, information on markets to the new intermediary or other form of organization. The approach therefore has to be one which facilitates the resolution of such termination issues and involves the maintenance of relations that will provide an atmosphere in which the outgoing intermediary will try to comply.

SUMMARY OF MANAGING COMMUNICATION CONTENT AND STRUCTURE

1 Under conditions of mutual dependence one party is likely to have a relative power advantage over another. Such relationships are rarely equal. Under such conditions conflict is bound to arise within the overall common interest.

2 Conflict is handled by four power-related processes. These are influence strategies, problem solving, political strategies and negotiation. They are not mutually exclusive and may be combined as appropriate.

3 Influence strategies are used to influence parties in other organizations in order to reach a mutually advantageous outcome in situations where the means of arriving at it are perceived differently. Direct influence strategies induce the required behaviour. Indirect influence strategies seek to alter the perceptions of the other organization regarding the desirability of the required behaviour.

4 Problem solving operates on two basic assumptions. One is that even if organizations' secondary objectives result in conflict, the parties have common primary objectives. The other is that a solution can be found within the framework of the common objectives.

5 Political strategies often provide preferred solutions by altering the power structure within a channel of distribution or other relationship by inducing third parties to assist in reaching agreement, or by the exercise of the relative power which a party to a business relationship may hold.

6 Negotiation strategies are those lines of action which are aimed at identifying common ground whereby parties in different organizations with both common and conflicting interests can agree to the form of any joint action they may take in pursuit of their individual objectives which will define or redefine the terms of their interdependence.

7 Negotiations have the basic aim of establishing, maintaining, altering or renewing or terminating a particular agreement. Effective support is provided by a principled approach, by appeal to limited authority or

some form of legitimate power, by co-operative rather than competitive behaviour as the relationship strengthens, and by formal or informal stances.

MANAGING INTERPERSONAL COMMUNICATION

From Inter-organizational to Interpersonal Communication

The various bonds which link one organization to another are reinforced by the social bonds arising from the development of interpersonal relationships. One of these social bonds is investment, as in the specific adaptations made by seller or buyer firms either in terms of product/process or of precise procedures. Investment can be considered a social bond, because it is undertaken only after a careful assessment of the relationship and in the light of previous successful exchanges. Other examples of investment of a personal nature are where time and energy are expended in furtherance of a relationship. In these circumstances, what started out as a business relationship often turns into friendship. Business or friendship, it is individuals who make decisions. Their behaviour to each other will be affected by the internal dispositions of the parties and, perhaps more importantly, the emerging group phenomena.

The way to a successful and productive interpersonal relationship is beset by a host of problems which interacting organization representatives have to avoid or resolve. The more complex their problem, the greater the need for mutual knowledge. Boundary spanners have the responsibility of identifying the blocks to relation development and the organization the responsibility for ensuring that they receive the appropriate training.

Openness and trust

These grow out of the social and economic exchanges between members of different organizations. It is important to understand that openness is not an absolute value in face-to-face relationships. For some purposes it is better not to reveal exactly where one stands, such as where a seller has empty order books and needs the business, or where a buyer has a great need for the seller's product or service. One of the ways that relationships become more intimate is through successive minimal self-revelations which constitute interpersonal tests of acceptance (Schein, 1981): 'If you accept this much of me then perhaps I can risk revealing a bit more of myself.' Total openness may be safe and creatively productive when total acceptance is guaranteed. It can become highly dangerous when goals are not compatible and acceptance is therefore not guaranteed at all.

Taking the Other's Perspective

Organizations are often characterized by differences in the values to which they adhere. These different values are reflected in management style and language. Members of different interacting organizations could not really understand each other if they did not have the ability to put themselves in the place of the person in the other organization.

We could not develop judgements, standards and morals without the ability to see our own behaviour from the standpoint of others. This gives us the capacity to develop repair strategies where some disruption of the relationship threatens or has taken place. Unfortunately, the majority of people fear loss of position or image, particularly if they have no strong concept of themselves. Some sense of one's own commitments is necessary so that defensiveness and denial can be reduced. It is only when people have the ability to hear others' values with empathy that they can begin to find common ground. We cannot hear others if we cannot accept ourselves.

Beyond Communication Content

Even with the ability to hear others, people involved in communication situations, and, by association, in inter-organizational communication situations, usually do not say all they mean and usually hear more than was said. When trying to interpret the communication behaviour of another person an individual communicator does so by going beyond the information given. How actual meaning is interpreted cannot be explained by the content of a message. The concept which addresses this question is *relational communication* (Watzlawick *et al.*, 1967). This refers more to the form than to the content. The content of communication comprises words and sentences and may describe anything, whether the information is true or false, valid or invalid. Relational communication, on the other hand, relates to how the message is intended; it serves to enable communicators to negotiate their relative positions and hence to define their relationship.

Mangham (1978) makes the point that what others do (and relational communication conveys very much what they do or are perceived to be doing) are important clues to the definition of the situation. If a communicator puts together a string of linguistic and other behaviours he is presenting himself and creates a part in the developing interaction for the person representing the other organization. What he is saying, in effect, is 'This is who I want to be taken for and this is who I take you to be'. The other's interpretation of the situation consists of attempting to take the communicator's role and in understanding the implications for himself just as the communicator has to define the other's behaviour and intentions. From this stems patterns of behaviour and the imputation of roles for both parties. Such mutual roletaking is a function of relational communication as a necessary element in successful interaction.

Various combinations of the relational communication behaviours of dominance, deference and equality can be classified as to whether they represent agreement or disagreement (Soldow and Penn, 1984). This is shown in Table 9.4.

When one of the communicating parties takes a dominant stance and the other a deferent one (for example, in cases B and D in Table 9.4) the interaction is characterized as one of agreement. Since there is a co-ordination of the skills of the communicating parties, there is little likelihood of discomfort and lack of harmony. Similarly, when both parties communicate equality, as in case I, agreement is said to exist. There is also a fit here of the skills of the parties. However, when both parties take a dominant stance, as in case A, or a deferent stance, as in case E, the relationship is characterized as one of disagreement. There is a conflict of techniques resulting in lack of fit.

By definition, combinations which are characterized by relational agreement require less effort devoted to the relationship than to cases characterized by relational disagreement. Nevertheless, where agreement is required in the interest of organizational effectiveness, the communicator may require to adjust his or her behaviour as necessary and so accommodate in the interest of meaningful interaction.

Language has to be used in different ways according to the categories a communicator wishes to adopt. There are many possible verbal indicators and many situations to which they can be related. Table 9.4 includes a buyer/seller example, but it could embrace alternative interactive situations, as between licensors and licensees, manufacturers/retailers and intermediaries, etc.

Content and relationship aspects are not mutually exclusive. They are, in fact, complementary. It is therefore insufficient to rely on one of those dimensions alone. A combination of the two will lead to better preparation for communicators, whatever their organizational role, for effectiveness in interactions.

Co-ordination of Interfirm Activities

Since interfirm relationships on a continuing basis have, to a greater or lesser degree, an element of interdependence, it is necessary to develop and maintain a co-operative atmosphere in order to facilitate the co-ordination of intercompany activities. This has to take place very often against a background of differing viewpoints and behaviours. The extreme is when these differences are characterized by covert conflict or when the differences

Table 9.4. Relational communication behaviours and how they combine to give agreement or disagreement. (Adapted from Soldow and Penn (1984), by permission of the American Marketing Association)

		SALESPERSON	
	Dominance	Deference	Equality
BUYER — Dominance	A − *Salesperson:* 'You are the most knowledgeable buyer I've met.' *Buyer:* 'Actually I know very little.' Initiation/disconfirmation	B + *Buyer:* 'Your prices are really quite high.' *Salesperson:* 'Do you really think so? I suppose they are.' Initiation/question, confirmation	C − *Buyer:* 'Your prices are really quite high.' *Salesperson:* 'Yes they are but so are everybody's in this inflationary economy.' Initiation/extension
Deference	D + *Salesperson:* 'You are the most knowledgeable buyer I've met.' *Buyer:* 'Do you really think so?' Initiation/question	E − *Buyer:* 'Your product really meets our needs.' *Salesperson:* 'Do you really think so?' *Buyer:* 'Yes, don't you?' Support, question/support, question	F − *Buyer:* 'Your prices are really high.' *Salesperson:* 'Yes, they are, but so are everybody's.' *Buyer:* 'do you really think so?' Extension/support, question
Equality	G − *Salesperson:* 'You are the most knowledgeable buyer I've met.' *Buyer:* 'Thank you, I've had 17 years' experience.' Initiation/extension	H − *Salesperson:* 'You are the most knowledgeable buyer I've met.' *Buyer:* 'Thank you, I've had 17 years' experience.' *Salesperson:* 'Oh really:' Extension/question, support	I + *Buyer:* 'Your product really meets our needs.' *Salesperson:* 'Your right, it's beautifully designed.' *Buyer:* 'Yes. So is most of your line.' Extension/extension

Key: + Agreement regarding the definition of relationship.
     − Disagreement regarding the definition of relationship.

break into open conflict. In order to handle these situations and achieve necessary co-ordination, influence strategies must to be used in the case of moving an individual, and through that individual the organization, to a different point of view.

Conflict may be resolved by means of a direct problem-solving approach, a political approach or perhaps most often a negotiation approach on the part of the communicating parties. By the appropriate use of one approach, or a combination of them, people communicating across the boundaries of the organization can seek to maintain that co-operation which is the touchstone of co-ordination. Co-operation can be assisted by adaptive behaviour along the relational dimension of communication. This can nurture the social bonds that provide the inter-organizational cohesion which can only be broken by some crisis that one of the parties has precipitated or to which it has not responded appropriately (for example, by exploiting the relationship in the interest of an individual or organization, or by failing to implement agreement, such as where a new product is inadequate for a partner's purpose).

SUMMARY OF MANAGING INTERPERSONAL COMMUNICATION

1 Openness and trust characterize relationships only where total acceptance is guaranteed. It can be highly dangerous when goals are not compatible and acceptance is therefore not guaranteed at all.

2 It is only when parties have the ability to put themselves in the place of the person in the other organization that they can begin to find common ground. People who have a strong concept of self are not exposed to the defensiveness and denial that prevent people from hearing others.

3 Even where people have the ability to hear others, what is said and heard do not convey the idea of how a message is sent and interpreted. Relational communication relates to how a message is intended and received and how it serves to define a relationship.

4 Relational communication behaviour most readily facilitates agreement where one of the parties is dominant and the other deferent or where there is equality in the interaction. Communicators may need to adjust their behaviours in the interests of reaching agreement and achieving through it the co-ordination necessary to meet organizational objectives.

REFERENCES

Bonoma, T. V. *The Marketing Edge: Making Strategies Work*, The Free Press, London (1985).

Bowersox, D. J., Cooper, M. B., Lambert, D. M. and Taylor, D. A. *Management in Marketing Channels*, McGraw-Hill, Maidenhead (1980).

Fisher, R. and Ury, W. *Getting to Yes: Negotiating Agreement Without Giving In*, Hutchinson, London (1983).

Ford, D. The development of buyer–seller relationships in industrial markets. In Hakansson, H. (ed.), *The International Marketing and Purchasing of Industrial Products: An Interaction Approach*, John Wiley, Chichester (1982).

Frazier, G. L. and Summers, J. O. Interfirm influence strategies and their applications within distribution channels. *Journal of Marketing*, Summer (1984).

Hakansson, H. (ed.) *The International Marketing and Purchasing of Industrial Goods: An Interaction Approach*, John Wiley, Chichester (1982).

Hammarkvist, K.-O. Markets as networks. In Christopher, M., McDonald, M. and Rushton, A. (eds), *Back to Basics: The 4Ps Revisited*, Proceedings of Marketing Education Group 16th Annual Conference, Cranfield School of Management (1983).

von Hippel, E. Get new products from customers. *Harvard Business Review*, March/April (1982).

Kotter, J. Power, dependence and effective management. *Harvard Business Review*, July/August (1977).

Magenau, J. M. and Pruitt, D. G. The social psychology of bargaining. In Stephenson, G. M. and Brotherston, C. J. (eds), *Industrial Relations: A Social Psychological Approach*, John Wiley, Chichester (1979).

Morley, E. and Stephenson, G. M. *The Social Psychology of Bargaining*, Allen and Unwin, London (1977).

Mangham, I. H. *Interactions and Interventions in Organisations*, John Wiley, Chichester (1978).

McCall, J. B. and Warrington, M. B. *'Marketing by Agreement: A Cross-Cultural Approach to Business Negotiations*, John Wiley, Chichester (1989).

Porter, M. *Competitive Advantage: Creating and Sustaining Superior Performance*, The Free Press, New York (1985).

Schein, E. H. Improving face-to-face relationships. *Sloan Management Review*, Winter (1981).

Schmidt, S. M. and Kochan, T. A. Interorganisational relationships: patterns and motivations. *Administrative Science Quarterly*, June (1977).

Soldow, G. F. and Penn, G. P. Relational communication: form versus content in the sales interaction. *Journal of Marketing*, Winter (1984).

Spekman, R. E. and Strauss, D. An exploratory investigation of a buyer's concern for factors affecting more co-operative buyer–seller relationships. *Industrial Marketing and Purchasing*, **1**, No. 3 (1986).

Stearns, T. M., Hoffman, A. N. and Heide, J. B. Performance of commercial television stations as an outcome of inter-organisational linkages and environmental conditions. *Academy of Management Journal*, **30**, No. 1 (1987).

Stidsen, W. Comments on Arndt, J., Towards a theory of domesticated markets. *Journal of Marketing*, Fall (1979).

Watzlawick, P., Beavin, J. and Jackson, D. *Pragmatics of Human Communication*, Norton, New York (1967).

Williamson, O. Transaction cost economics: the governance of contractual relations. *Journal of Law and Economics*, **22**, No. 2 (1980).

10
Cross-border Communication Problem Solving

Once communication has to cross national boundaries there is an added dimension to conveying and interpreting meaning. The speech and the culture of the countries will differ, even where they purport to use the same language. The difficulties of decoding speech and behavioural patterns are multiplied by the number of countries in which people are required to interact.

If we can classify these countries in a way which simplifies the process of understanding how people behave; if we can obtain insights into their thought processes and communication styles; if we can gain some familiarity with the texts and rules which govern life in these countries, then we are in a strong position to communicate meaningfully and effectively.

This chapter sets out to give the frameworks which will assist people whose work entails communicating across national borders, to persuade, negotiate and generally interact in a positive and sensitive manner in business and social encounters.

PROBLEMS OF COMMUNICATING
BETWEEN COUNTRIES

The world of business becomes increasingly international. In the industrialized countries there is a realization that, in order to establish competitive advantage or to generate the returns required to justify investment in the first instance, it is necessary to operate on an international scale. Newly developing countries have come to learn that to develop their economies, and even to survive, they need to find market outlets among the advanced economies and to purchase there the goods and technologies necessary to their perceived well-being. We now take in each other's washing on an international scale.

This situation is paralleled in public administration. Transnational organizations force different country nationals to communicate with each other; the European Community is the example *par excellence*. Joint military development demands a joint purchasing structure in which a balance of different nationals is sought. Local authorities and state governments become involved in finding foreign sources of finance just as they do in national policies of open procurement and sourcing. Their communications have to reach beyond local and national boundaries.

As a result, it becomes increasingly difficult to avoid having to communicate with people from other countries and cultures. As overseas activities expand, organizations develop new strategies and seek means of acquiring new products and services or of putting them on the market which match these strategies. International operations imply contact with foreign intermediaries in their country and one's own; transfer of technology involves people in the production process who would not otherwise have worked outside their own production units; the setting up of overseas facilities in order to hold and develop markets involves negotiating and co-operating with foreigners; public administrators have to produce rules and regulations which facilitate and control these activities within the limits described by public policy. All such activities expose those responsible and their staffs to people in other countries who speak a different first language and whose behaviour is influenced by different cultural assumptions and priorities.

It is not only the so-called boundary spanners who have exposure to people who talk, think and act differently in given situations. Large-scale immigration brings individuals with strong cultural roots in ethnic groups which seek to maintain their often very distinctive culture in social and employment situations in their host country. It is those people, however, who are increasingly required to visit or work overseas, who are exposed to the problems of what they come to realize can be great divides.

As we saw in Chapter 8, individuals can have the utmost difficulty communicating with others for reasons of personality and personal values and interests, and because of group identification and the interests and priorities of the group. As mentioned in Chapter 5, people in different cultures do not perceive situations, issues or problems similarly due to the way in which their languages classify and label knowledge. The problem is compounded in organizations which, apart from receiving an imprimatur from the wider culture, develop a language of their own which categorizes the organization's experience in a particular way and evokes specific responses to issues and problems in terms of organizational members' perceptions.

It should already be clear that if you do not share another person's assumptions of what is important and relevant, you are in danger of sending messages which are not taken as intended, or of drawing meaning from messages received which was not the intention of the sender.

To span different languages and cultures, and achieve a fuller understanding, the organizational member communicating internationally has to interpret the cultural patterns and concepts of one country in terms of the patterns and concepts of the other. If communicators, because of lack of cultural awareness, can easily misperceive words, actions and other clues in international business encounters, there is a need for approaches which will assist perception.

The tall poppy syndrome

Communicating across cultures can involve risk for many people of low cultural awareness. Their own sense of propriety may be very dissimilar from that of host-country nationals.

'In many Western countries, there is something of a taboo on verbal self-presentation. While Australians have been observed to have an achievement motivation, they also have the "tall poppy syndrome"—one must not take too much credit for one's accomplishments or be seen to stand out above the crowd. Observers have noted a similar attitude in Sweden to setting oneself apart from others in terms of what is said and done. In places like India and the Middle Eastern countries, such behaviour is quite acceptable. People are not forced back into non-verbal signals as in these Western and Australasian cultures. An understanding and acceptance of these different clues can direct verbal and non-verbal behaviour in a way which smoothes the communication process.'

(From McCall and Warrington, 1989, reproduced by permission)

Cultural Bias

What has been illustrated above are in-built hurdles to bridging the culture gap. Hall (1976) has argued that words, actions, posture, gestures, tone of voice, facial expressions, the way he handles time, space and materials, and the way he works and plays, all give man his identity. All these are communication systems with meaning which can be interpreted correctly only if he has a familiarity with the behaviour in its historical, social and cultural contexts.

Yet, everything man does is modified by learning. Once learned, habitual responses gradually sink below the surface of the mind and operate from the depths of the unconscious. Man's nervous system is so constructed that the patterns which govern behaviour and perception come into consciousness only when there is a deviation from a learned pattern. He tends to form judgements against these patterns and is easily led into attitudes of cultural bias, a process sometimes referred to as *projective cognitive similarity*, or the self-reference criterion.

The only way to transcend this bias is to achieve awareness of the structure of one's own system by interacting with others who are not members of it.

This is assisted by the acquisition of the relevant language and of conceptual frameworks, as indicated below. Given the achievement of this awareness, one is in a position to exercise the cultural sensitivity necessary for successful interactions with members of other cultures and organizations.

A FRAMEWORK TO DIRECT BEHAVIOUR IN INTERCULTURAL ENCOUNTERS

National and Organizational Value Systems

In chapter 5 we saw that there was a strong relationship between the way people behave in the wider culture and their conduct in organizations. If we are to learn to communicate well, either as an organizational visitor to an overseas country or as a semi-permanent resident in an organization overseas, then the better the frameworks we have to assist us, the better will our performance be.

One such framework is that of Hofstede (1984), mentioned on pages 22 and 74. We shall now look at his four-dimensional framework more closely. Based on considerable and sophisticated research, Hofstede named his four dimensions:

1 *Power distance*: This is concerned with authority and the extent to which members of a society accept that power in institutions and organizations is distributed unequally. An index is derived from country mean scores on perceptions of a superior's style of decision making, colleagues' fear of disagreeing with superiors and subordinates' preferred type of decision making in their superior. Prior to this research, it had been widely held that in interpersonal relationships between superiors and subordinates the superior would always seek to maintain or increase the extent to which he could influence subordinates, while subordinates would always seek to reduce it. The level of power distance at which these tendencies will be brought into balance is seen to be determined by the particular society and culture.

   In high power distance countries, subordinates do what the superior wants them to do. Because they have a certain fear of disagreeing with superiors, they tend to accept authoritarian attitudes. In low power distance countries, on the other hand, the individual has far greater room to meet explicit or implicit objectives in his or her own way.

   It will be seen from Figure 10.1 that countries such as Malaysia, the West African group and Mexico typify the high power distance countries, while Scandinavia, New Zealand and Israel are among the lowest.

2 *Uncertainty avoidance*:,This is the degree to which members of a society feel uncomfortable with uncertainty and ambiguity, which leads them

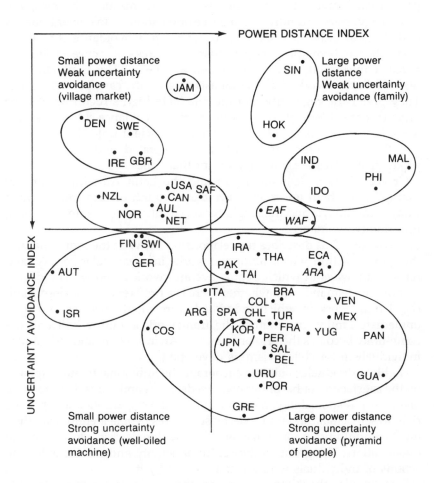

Figure 10.1. *A power distance × uncertainty-avoidance plot for 50 countries and three regions. ARA Arab countries (Egypt, Lebanon, Libya, Kuwait, Iraq, Saudi Arabia, UAE); ARG Argentina; AUL Australia; AUT Austria; BEL Belgium; BRA Brazil; CAN Canada; CHL Chile; COL Colombia; COS Costa Rica; DEN Denmark; EAF East Africa (Kenya, Ethiopia, Zambia); ECA Ecuador; FIN Finland; FRA France; GBR Great Britain; GER West Germany; GRE Greece; GUA Guatamala; HOK Hong Kong; IDO Indonesia; IND India; IRA Iran; IRE Ireland; ISR Israel; ITA Italy; JAM Jamaica; JPN Japan; KOR South Korea; MAL Malaysia; MEX Mexico; NET Netherlands; NOR Norway; NZL New Zealand; PAK Pakistan; PAN Panama; PER Peru; PHI Philippines; POR Portugal; SAF South Africa; SAL Salvador; SIN Singapore; SPA Spain; SWE Sweden; SWI Switzerland; TAI Taiwan; THA Thailand; TUR Turkey; URU Uruguay; USA United States; VEN Venezuela; WAF West Africa (Nigeria, Ghana, Sierra Leone); YUG Yugoslavia. (From Hofstede, 1985, reproduced by permission)*

to support beliefs promising certainty and to maintain institutions which protect conformity. This is coped with in organizations by means of technology, rules and rituals. Using rule orientation, employment stability and stress as indicators, an index of uncertainty avoidance is built up.

Members of high uncertainty avoidance cultures experience anxiety and perceive uncertainty as a threat to their well-being. This is evidenced in fear of failure at work and an emphasis on security, career structure, etc. They prefer the regularity and the relatively high structuring of large organizations. Members of weak uncertainty avoidance cultures tend to agree implicitly with the biblical saying 'Sufficient unto the day is the evil thereof'. Dissent and conflict are tolerated and even seen as productive. Roles are more important than rules.

Greece, France, Belgium, Japan and the Latin American countries exemplify the high uncertainty avoidance countries. Singapore, Hong Kong, Scandinavia and the Anglo-Saxon countries are examples of weak uncertainty avoidance.

3 *Individualism*: This describes the relationship between the individual and the groups within which he or she works in a particular society, and reflects the ways in which people live and work together. The degree of individualism indicates whether there is a preference for a loosely knit social framework in which individuals care for themselves and their immediate family, or whether the framework is tightly knit and the community becomes the primary concern. An index in relation to country individualism (or collectivism) is developed.

Highly individualist cultures encourage the individual to put emphasis on the satisfaction of his or her own needs. He is ambitious, likes to work on his own responsibility, has a life outside the organization and has the right to self-actualization. In collectivist cultures people identify with their own community or organization. Private life is tied closely to the organization. The group is the centre of activity and the focus for the actions of individuals who are constrained by it.

Scandinavia, the Netherlands and the Anglo-Saxon countries, for example, are all high on the individualism index, while Portugal, Pakistan and the Latin American and West African countries are all low.

4 *Masculinity*: Depending on the society one is in, sex roles will differ, sometimes quite considerably. Men and women tend to have different goals based on sex differences. A masculinity index measures how far people tend to embrace goals more popular among men or women. In a masculine society, even the women prefer assertiveness, at least in men; in a feminine society, even the men prefer modesty.

In strongly masculine cultures sex roles are clearly differentiated. Values such as decisiveness, assertiveness and an ability to accumulate material wealth are approved or applauded. In feminine cultures, members place emphasis on co-operating with others rather than on competing with them. Elitism and the acknowledgement of individual achievement are perceived negatively.

The Anglo-Saxon countries have masculine cultures, varying from strong in Australia to weak in Canada. Japan is, from Hofstede's research, the most masculine country. Countries with a feminine culture include Scandinavia, Thailand and Yugoslavia.

Culture and What People Think an Organization Should Be

These value dimensions affect both people and organizations. On the power distance × uncertainty avoidance plot (Figure 10.1) we see that different combinations of the two dimensions lead to different implicit models in people's minds of what an organization should be. Hofstede argues that large power distance plus strong uncertainty avoidance leads to people viewing an organization to be what he characterizes as a 'pyramid of people', that is, a hierarchical bureaucracy typical of France and other Latin and Mediterranean countries. When small power distance and strong uncertainty avoidance are combined, this leads to viewing it as a 'well-oiled machine', that is, an impersonal bureaucracy, typical of West Germany and other central European countries. Small power distance plus weak uncertainty avoidance leads to viewing it as a 'village market', that is an *ad-hocracy* (typical of Anglo-Saxon and Nordic countries). Lastly, large power distance plus weak uncertainty avoidance leads to viewing it as a 'family', that is, a personnel bureaucracy of the kind that might be found in India, West Africa or countries with a strong Chinese influence. In this latter type, the organization is built round a strong leader, rather like entrepreneurs in the West, who, in the early stages of organization, control directly and are assisted by aides who carry out such tasks as are given to them.

Such implicit models cannot depend on nationality alone. They are also affected by the purpose of the organization. A hospital will always be like a pyramid of people, an advertising agency like a village market and a corner store like a family.

Using these characterizations, it is possible to foresee some of the communication problems that are likely to arise between people of different cultural backgrounds. African sports council members against apartheid (family) lobby their UK counterparts (village market) to exercise their personal authority to prevent a group of athletes competing in South Africa. The Africans go away feeling that the British are not really interested in campaigning against apartheid, and the British wonder why it is that the Africans think they are magicians or have authority beyond what they have ever imagined. An Austrian (well-oiled machine) is appointed to set up and run an agricultural project in India (family). He will establish rules and procedures, only to discover that nobody keeps them and that his physical presence is required to get the job done. A doctor from Hong Kong (family), hoping to overcome the uncertainty of his future when Hong Kong is returned to Chinese rule in 1997, gets a job in an American hospital (organizational pyramid, national village market). He will expect structures to give way to the personal authority of bosses and it may take him some time to understand the rigidity of the bureaucracy and how it can, on occasion, be replaced by personal relationships.

Culture and the Self-concept in Organizational Settings

Individualism versus collectivism and masculinity versus femininity affect a person's self-concept. If a person is from a culture where individualism is low, that person will see himself as part of the community or organization. The individual counts for nothing without his or her in-group. To be effective, a work group has to be composed of in-group members or must be receptive to new ones. If individualism is high, the person will pursue his or her self-interest and will seek self-actualization. Others, at least in theory, should be treated equally, irrespective of the groups to which they belong.

Where masculinity is high, women are expected to be self-effacing and men to carry out the function of ego-boosting. If masculinity is low, these actions are carried out by both men and women. In such circumstances, people would prefer to see themselves as relating to others rather than competing with them.

By referring to Figure 10.2 it is possible to predict the problems of self-concept confronted by a person of one culture when entering an organization in another.

In 1974, six US automobile workers from Detroit (two women and four men) worked for three weeks in the Saab-Scania plant in Soededtaelje, Sweden, where a new 'humanized' system of group assembly had been installed. At the end of their visit five out of the six Americans rejected the Swedish system (the one who preferred it was a woman). The journalist who accompanied them reported that what seemed to be an attraction for a Swede was the very reason why an American disliked it. At Saab-Scania, workers have to collaborate with others, whereas in Detroit they are on their own and can set their own challenges. This reflects the difference between a masculine (achievement oriented) and a feminine (relationship oriented) culture. Which leads to a different philosophy of what represents 'humanization of work'.

(From Hofstede, 1985, reproduced by permission)

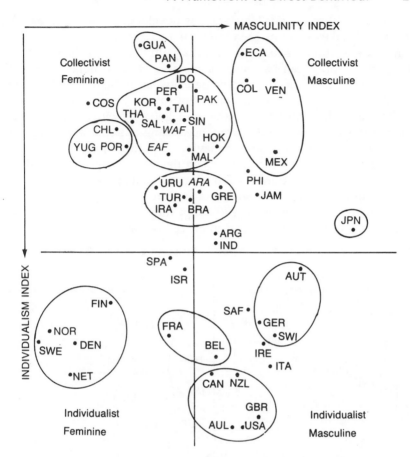

Figure 10.2. *An individualism–collectivism × masculinity–femininity plot for 50 countries and three regions (From Hofstede, 1985, reproduced by permission)*

Culture and the Motivation of the Individual

Figures 10.1 and 10.2 provide people about to enter into communication with organizations overseas with an invaluable starting point for their dialogue. Cultural characteristics persist, although there will always be individuals who do not have the cultural traits to the extent of the majority. It is part of the information-seeking behaviour of communicators to establish when this is so and to adopt other suitable tactics.

Hofstede has also drawn other correlations of the indices developed. The interaction of uncertainty avoidance and masculinity. for example, challenges the universality of Maslow's hierarchy of needs, Herzberg's two-factor theory and McLelland's achievement theory and suggests that they are all culture-bound. Hofstede has developed a 'motivational world map' which takes account of cultural characteristics that depend on the degree of uncertainty avoidance and masculinity (Figure 10.3).

From this plot, it can be seen, for instance, that in negotiating with a Frenchman (strong uncertainty avoidance/weak masculinity) it would be advisable to make a proposal which appeals to his defensive and risk-avoiding culturally induced behaviour. In negotiating with a person of British nationality (weak uncertainty avoidance/strong masculinity) an appeal to risk-taking, recognition-seeking behaviour would be preferred.

The cultural clusters which have been developed from combinations of the indices provide, within this four-dimensional space, categories which serve to simplify managers' thinking on cultures. They give communicators a point of reference from which to adapt their behaviour in the interests of accurately communicating and interpreting meaning.

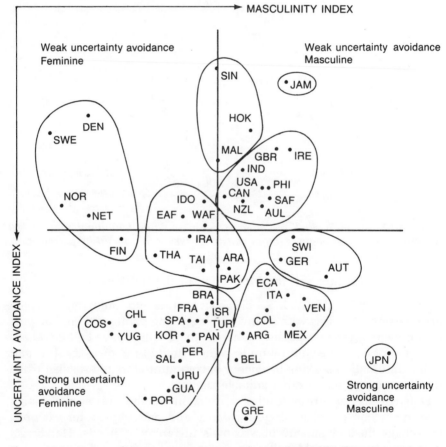

Figure 10.3. *A masculinity × uncertainty avoidance plot for 50 countries and three regions (Adapted from Hofstede, 1983)*

The Hofstede research did not include the Eastern European countries as his sample frame included only employees of IBM internationally. It is interesting to compare West and East Germany which share a common language and culture. Despite this commonality, 40 years of living under Communist rule have made East Germans more dependent on state institutions. No longer does the German language usage there distinguish between authority and power. People have expectations of being told what to do. Some of the refugees who have gone to West Germany in the past, have returned to the East because they could not take the openness of West German society (Henry, 1989). Openness implies responsibility and this trait has been eroded during these 40 years.

It is therefore to be expected that East Germans will not have the same degree of individualism as their West German counterparts. Power distance is likely to be greater in East Germany as a result of prolonged exposure to the bureaucracies and hierarchies imposed by the system. This is a problem currently confronting other East European countries in the convulsions they are now undergoing.

LANGUAGE AND INTERCULTURAL COMMUNICATION

While the general frameworks we have discussed above give us an understanding of how an overseas counterpart views the world and provide us with clues as to how we should couch the general tenor of our communication, they give us little guidance on how we should address such people and the pitfalls that await us when we are addressed. Language and the understanding of it often give rise to miscommunication. If a foreigner speaks in English to a native speaker, meaning is sometimes concealed because the listener applies the tests he or she would make when talking to a fellow national. For instance, it is not always easy to spot that a foreigner is upset of embarrassed. Indeed, it is not uncommon to assume that a foreigner is being belligerent or sullen on the basis of his or her tone of voice. The temptation is to respond in like manner. For example, flat, level tones in English are associated with boredom or sarcasm. In some Slavonic languages, on the other hand, the level tone is used much more widely with a natural interpretation. Russians, for instance, will tend to speak English with too many level tone endings for the English ear. To their own ears the sentence sounds neutral, but to an English listener it can sound uninterested and boorish. The English speaker communicating in a foreign language—assuming he or she can indeed speak it—has, by the same token, to ensure that he or she uses the pitch, degree of loudness, speed and rhythm associated with the meaning it is intended to convey.

Whether to use the other's language to communicate depends on a number of situational factors. If the communication is important, then the communicator should consider whether he should use the language at all if he does not have a reasonable command of the language. In most countries, an honest effort to speak the language is usually well received and is often a breaker of ice, which produces an interpreter or induces the other party to change to the speaker's language.

French people do not like to hear their language abused, however well meaning the speaker, and sometimes do not hesitate to indicate their feeling. On the other hand, in the former French overseas territories lack of fluency can be an advantage. French has lost the stigma associated with it because of colonial experience. The majority of Algerians and Tunisians recognize the practical necessity of some French, but see it as a tool that does not necessarily have to be learned perfectly. French also allows Algerians and Tunisians to maintain social distance in certain situations. A similar distancing effect has been observed in the use of English by Indians when addressed in Hindi, which is reserved for social relationships (Gumperz, 1966).

The English-speaking nations have never been renowned for their ability to speak foreign languages, with certain honourable exceptions. Yet we have seen that in many countries relationships are important, and ability to speak a language is one way in which a relationship can be cultivated. The effect of a good relationship on communication outcomes has been demonstrated. Those who claim that English is an international language and see a language facility as a competence which rates below many other skills are mistaken. Research by the IMP Group into managers' perceptions, attitudes, opinions and beliefs in five European countries concluded, among other things, that the British were, despite their own views on the matter, less than adequate to discuss technical and commercial matters because of shortcomings in their ability to communicate in the language of the other four countries (Turnbull and Cunningham, 1981). French buyers had particular difficulties in making social contact with British and West German suppliers.

Ideally, the best way to overcome the language barrier starts with mastery of the language. Cultural aspects are then more easily assimilated and appropriate foreign-language behaviours facilitated within the communication process. There are occasions when the intellectual investment in a language is too heavy and the cultivation of cultural skills becomes a priority. With languages such as Japanese and Chinese, the inputs required of learners is so great that other aids to communication are necessary for the great majority. There is a view that mastery of the foreign-language component of communication raises listeners' expectations in respect of cultural behaviour. Argyle (1983) reports how American servicemen in Turkey, having acquired linguistic skills, were then expected to act culturally.

Cultural Aspects of Language Use

All speech acts in a dialogue are characterized by breaks, however short, between the time when one speaker finishes what he or she has to say and another begins. Among the Japanese, there are frequently long silences between speech acts. This has been ascribed to the fact that the Japanese savour an undefined quality best described as 'sincerity'. Virtue and integrity are said to reside not in a man's heart but in his stomach. Between men the most meaningful understanding is one which needs no words. The Japanese call this 'stomach talk'. Such is their emotional sensitivity that there is no urgency for words.

Westerners often feel awkward in long silences and seek to fill them with unimportant chatter. This is viewed by Japanese as a form of behaviour aberration. It should be clear to both Westerners and Japanese that an understanding of the difference in perception of silence can be used to advantage by them as communicators by adjusting their behaviour to make the dialogue easier and more acceptable to the other party.

It frequently happens that interpreters have to be used because neither party has sufficient knowledge of the other's language to carry out the object of their meeting. This does not normally present difficulties. Business executives report, for example, that they check that much more carefully if they have to use interpreters to ensure that both parties take away the same understanding. Even so, they would be most reluctant to accept agreement in Arabic, as that language is so flexible in translation that such agreement would be ill advised.

In Chapter 7 we saw that in Arabic, exaggeration and over-assertion become natural means of expression. As a result, simple statements in Arabic cannot be translated into English without losing some of their meaning. If an Arab does not over-assert and over-exaggerate, there is a strong likelihood that another Arab will misunderstand him. If an Arab says 'No' without embellishment it may be taken as a sign to continue rather than as a direct negative.

Such a linguistic tradition can lead to misunderstanding when non-Arabs are involved. Similarly, Arabs can fail to realize that others mean exactly what they say when a statement is made in a simple, unelaborated manner. In a Scottish court, an Arab student new to the country was charged with harassing a young woman who had politely declined his advances! Perhaps the matter would not have needed to come to law had the young woman said 'No, no, a thousand times no' or used an unlady-like term to reinforce the declined invitation.

We saw in Chapter 5 that when a Japanese says 'Yes' he means 'No' or, at best, 'Maybe' as a way of avoiding confrontation which, in a society which seeks to maintain harmony in a system of vertical organizational relationships, is considered good linguistic behaviour.

A cross-cultural scenario

This imaginary encounter attempts to create an amusing scenario which will make the characteristics of the Japanese and Arabs easily remembered.
Japanese do not like confrontation which threatens loss of face. They therefore tend to say 'Yes' when they mean 'Maybe' or 'No'. In spatial terms, they like to maintain a similar distance between each other as North Europeans. In terms of gaze, they tend to avoid direct eye contact which symbolizes confrontation in a culture which needs harmony to maintain vertical relationships. They have long silences between turns of talking which can be discomfiting to the uninitiated.

Arabs have a language which is expressive and beautiful but is classical in its origin, which lies largely in the *Koran*. It is therefore not particularly suited to nuances of meaning. Arab language requires exaggeration to convey everyday meanings and cannot be translated into English without losing some of that meaning. Within their own countries, Arabs need to make strong assertions or over-exaggerate in order to communicate meaning to other Arabs. Thus, when an Arab says 'No' another Arab may not accept this as a direct negative if he does not support what has been said with flowery, expressive words as embellishment. They also like close physical contact—there is a classic photograph of President Kennedy and Nasser in which Nasser is half-facing Kennedy and has a hand on his (Kennedy's) knee. Associated with this proximity is a tendency to direct eye contact—they are a perfect example of a people who believe that the eyes are the windows of the soul. This reflects their warmth and spontaneity. Such characteristics leave little time for silence.

We now have a picture of a Japanese who says 'Yes' when he means 'No' talking to an Arab who says 'No' when he means 'Yes'; a Japanese who likes to maintain good physical distance between himself and another and an Arab who prefers a close contact; a Japanese who avoids gaze and an Arab who likes to hold it; a Japanese who likes to leave long silences and an Arab who loves to fill them.

Differences in the Way Different Peoples Solve Problems

The effect of language on the way people classify and label experience and knowledge was illustrated in Chapter 5. It was also shown that there is a relationship between language and the way different nationalities interact. The Japanese, for instance, have a language which, whether cause or effect, reflects their vertical relationships and emotional nature. This is exemplified by the way in which they go to great lengths to avoid confrontation by the use of affirmatives as negatives.

These vertical relationships and the behaviours which sustain them are a positive disadvantage when solving problems. The logical or dialectic style is guided at all times by the interpersonal relations between the speakers. The premises underlying thesis–antithesis are parity and confrontation on an equal footing which will develop into, or permit the possibility of, synthesis. Because of the lack of discipline for relationships between equals, the Japanese do not practise these three basic steps of reasoning and have to overcome this great handicap in order to advance any issue brought under discussion.

The Japanese overcome this problem by seeking answers to all sorts of questions and apparently building up a kind of composite picture. Their questions are innumerable, and any responses they make to questions directed to them are ambiguous. This ambiguity appears to stem from the concepts of *tatemae* (truthful) and *honne* (true mind). It is important to the Japanese to be polite and communicate the *tatemae* without giving offence, withholding the possibly offensive but informative *honne*. Americans view this as a double standard. It offends their belief that everything should be open and that sincerity, spontaneity and candour are the most desirable characteristics in any communicator. They are reassured in the presence of a sincere person that nothing is being withheld, or masked by irony, understatement or wit. It is worth noting that these are the principal modes of European discourse. The Japanese view American frankness with discomfiture and are likely to react to it with silence and withdrawal.

The Chinese, who have the same roots as the Japanese if we go back far enough, exhibit a similar behaviour in relation to the apparently endless search for information. Communicating with Orientals therefore has to take these characteristics into account. One way of doing so may be to persist in the asking of questions until satisfied that as much information as possible has been uncovered in relation to the issues.

Cultural Rules

Every culture has certain rules, the origins of which have been lost, but which become the norm for acceptable behaviour. Communicating with people of these cultures is eased if foreigners know the rules.

When introductions are being made in Denmark, for example, both the person being introduced and the person to whom the introduction is made are described by the sponsor in sufficient detail for the proper relations to be made quite clear. This occurs in Danish ritual before either of the people being introduced has spoken. It is an example of the determination of the distribution of deference, which is a crucial understanding in those cultures that are more than usually occupied with the establishment of relative status (for example, most of Western Europe, East Asia and the Americas).

In many areas of the world it is customary to pay a commission to people responsible for a purchase or who have facilitated a preferred outcome in a particular situation, despite the fact that they are already receiving a salary for doing that as part of their job. It is in some countries necessary to mark certain occasions with gifts. These can vary, from presenting a small bunch or spray of flowers to the hostess when invited out to dinner in countries such as France or Poland to donating a trophy to symbolize a mutual business relationship. Other rules exist concerning eating and drinking, how late (if at all) to keep an appointment and where guests should be seated at dinner.

Sometimes it is necessary for the foreigner to conform to rules—for example, in eating and drinking. At other times the rules may conflict with his own values or the practice of his own organization or his country's laws. There may be no easy solution to such problems. It is important, however, to recognize what the rules are, as conformity or avoidance of an embarrassing or offensive situation can ease the communication process.

Different cultures, different rules

Peter L is general manager for India of a company offering technical design and consultancy services to the chemical industries. He indulges in the practice, common in India, of dressing in open-necked shirt and trousers. It is people in the lower echelons of management there who are formally attired.

Because of his wide experience in the industrial processes involved, Peter is asked to go on assignment to Mexico to discuss the design and operation of a new refinery near Mexico City for which an affiliate company has been invited to tender. He is met at the airport by the head of the family-owned business pursuing the project. This man is immaculately dressed as, in his perception, befits the occasion, and takes umbrage at the apparent slight by the visitor who was so brash as to arrive dressed informally.

The relationship never fully recovers from the initial setback and the group managing director who is in London decides, on this being reported to him, to drop what he is doing and flies out to Mexico City to appease the aggrieved clients.

Styles of Persuasion

It is only a short step from different ways of solving problems and the application of cultural rules to the styles of persuasion employed by different national cultures. Generally, people know how to influence others of their own culture and what behaviours are unacceptable. When confronted with an unfamiliar culture they tend to be unable to interact effectively unless they have been specifically prepared for it.

Light has been shed on the way in which different people communicate from studies on social issues which helpfully classify the cultural styles when a communicator seeks to meet his instrumental purposes in different cultural settings. There are basically three styles (Brislin, 1982):

1 *Factual–inductive*: This style is common in West Germany, the United States and the United Kingdom. Indeed, it is evident in all English-speaking countries. In considering issues of conflict, people move from salient facts to conclusions. Fisher (1988) claims that salient facts include persuasion by expert opinion, and that this 'hard' evidence will be used in communicating a position or viewpoint. By finding similarities or points that can be discussed with the other party they can proceed to draw conclusions, such as a range of action alternatives.

2 *Axiomatic–deductive*: This style is to be found in France, the USSR and China. In this mode, communicators move from a general principle to particulars which can be easily deduced. Such deductions should be easily understandable within these principles, on which the reasoning process should be based. When this reasoning process has started it becomes relatively difficult to introduce new information or facts. When, for example, an American seeks to persuade a Frenchman, he has to overcome this barrier and vice versa. It is not too difficult to put the salient facts within a framework of principles or apply the principles to salient facts.

3 *Intuitive–affective*: This style is to be seen in the Arab countries and also in many Latin American and African ones. People express their positions through appeals and emotions. Mexicans are not likely to be impressed by hard evidence and rational argument. They tend, as in other Latin American countries, to start with a principle, like the French and the Russians. Thereafter, all is different. The French pursue the logical reasoning which makes the introduction of new facts difficult; the Mexicans seem to place more emphasis on feelings and intuition.

Mexicans, then, if they wish to persuade Americans or British, Canadians or Australians should address the available facts, look for cause and effect and generally get on to problem solving in the American mode. Americans and other Anglos, if they wish to influence Latins, should first determine what their feelings are and address them.

CULTURE AND NEGOTIATION

As discussed in the previous chapter, negotiation takes place against the background of problem solving and style of persuasion reviewed above. No transaction is carried out without acts of persuasion normally being involved. It is part of the negotiation interaction. We are always concerned to lower the other side's aspirations so that we are in a better position to obtain more advantageous outcomes. To that extent, we project certainty of our expertise or concern about an issue, or we appeal to norms of reciprocity or to our reputation. If we refer to the negotiation skills model shown in Figure 6.6 we see that, depending on the cultural environment, certain stages of the negotiation process are de-emphasized while others have an enhanced importance.

Pre-negotiation stage

We know that the higher an offer is pitched, the higher the level of settlement is likely to be; it is also true that the higher the level of offer, the less likely it is that there will any agreement at all. High initial offers will be considered unacceptable if there is evidence of a willingness to make relatively large reductions or concessions in the course of a meeting. Finns and Norwegians come into this category.

West Germans appear to make their offers after extensive preparation and tend not to be open to compromise. To an Arab there is a market price for everything, and a seller, for example, putting forward a well-inflated price may not be considered serious.

Getting to the Negotiation Table

In the so-called 'high-context' countries an appeal to the profitability or wage benefits of what is being offered may be unimportant compared to, for example, level of sales or tenure of employment. In many underdeveloped countries a product may be chosen because it matches national aspirations rather than economic or performance criteria.

Face to Face

Establishing rapport takes different forms in different countries. Japanese and Arabs spend more time on this than Europeans and Americans. The rule should be—do not rush from the hospitality to the business; wait for the indication if you wish to increase acceptability and start out well in the building of a relationship.

Relationships are important for negotiations in many parts of the world. The Arab businessman often bases his buying decision on the personality of the salesman rather than on the quality of the product. Brazilian negotiators, like all Latin Americans, prize continuing relationships and dislike those who, in their view, are overly concerned with their job. West Africans see friendship as an element of the business relationship and are likely to suspect a foreigner's motives if they feel they are being hurried through negotiations without regard to local custom. In Latin America, black Africa and the Arab countries the use of family and friendship ties is widespread, and is a necessary and successful means of doing business.

The visitor has to accommodate to this where, for instance, family matters intervene in the business discussion.

Distributive Bargaining Stage

This stage facilitates an exchange of information and defines the negotiating range. The hard line witnessed in this stage in most Western countries is often bypassed when a relationship has already been established, the parties have a knowledge of each other's styles or where the nature of the agreement is basically co-operative, as in agency and joint-venture arrangements.

The stage is de-emphasized in some cultures. As indicated in Chapter 5, Far Eastern people feel uncomfortable when exposed to confrontation which carries the implication of loss of face. They seek to obtain and exchange their information at the next stage, which better suits their cultural characteristics.

Getting Movement

When relationships are co-operative, as when the participants have experience of each other, respect each other's interests and have had prior satisfactory outcomes, the distributive stage tends to be short and to comprise their basic positions. They can then move easily into the integrative bargaining stage.

Otherwise, conditional concessions are employed. Where one of the parties has a different culture, language or political ideology, then the time taken is likely to be much longer. Cues tend to be more specific unless one of the parties is skilled in the language or culture of the other. Where a specific cue is required, this can sometimes be indicated by conceding a 'straw issue', using a minor point as a negotiating counter.

Integrative Bargaining Stage

As negotiators move into this stage and attempt to persuade each other of the issues that are important to them, and to test assumptions made, the ability to understand and communicate without distortion is crucial. It is also important to ensure that actions which build barriers to listening or speaking freely are avoided. The use of Hindi to address indigenous Indians is usually met with a reply in English, being a mild rebuke for adopting, however well intentioned, an intimate status. To understand this, it is helpful to know something of the nature of social relationships and how they are marked linguistically. Indians will tend to speak English to foreigners to mark personal distance. Only when the relationship has become less formal can the language use change.

In some areas of the world (for example, Austria, Czechoslovakia, West Germany, Hungary and Italy) it is customary to overstate a case. In others (Britain, Scandinavia and Australia) it is normal to understate it. By attributing his own linguistic customs to the other party, a communicator can perceive a violation of his expectations. There is a need, therefore, to develop familiarity with the culture with or within which a person is interacting (Clyne, 1977).

Differences in expectations are at the heart of communication breakdown in intercultural situations. A good example is given in Negandhi (1980). He examined expectational differences between multinational companies and host governments, and found that differences in expectations contributed significantly to conflict, unlike other MNC attributes such as size of investment, sophistication of technology and period of operation. The company focus on their task environment conflicted with the host government's emphasis on wider issues such as political needs and national aspirations. The message that this research underlines is that care and repetition in the indication of expectations should go a long way towards reducing tensions.

Bargaining Away the Unacceptable

Once commitment has been demonstrated and tested, trading-off may begin on terms which will provide each side with the satisfaction that they have achieved their objectives. Within different cultures, different values will be reflected in what is considered important. A Saudi buyer, for example, will tend to put a high value on contract disputes being settled in local courts under local law as compared to a European counterpart. On the other hand, he is unlikely to put as much emphasis on aspects of safety.

Trading-off is preceded by assessment of worth, which takes account of all the factors affecting outcome, including cultural ones. The price, the commission, the royalty and downpayment arrangements and the anticipated individual pay-offs from joint operation will reflect the value the parties eventually place on these exchanges.

It is by the moves and countermoves they make that negotiators manage to resolve their difficulties. This is when they have to put together all those items they have promised to 'consider', 'bear in mind' and 'take account of' and put forward a package for consideration by the other side.

Decision Making and Action

West European and North American negotiators tend to use a tone of voice indicating absolute finality and words which show the absence of bluff. They also use more intimate behaviour, such as an increased rate of smiling, taking the other party by the arm and the use of friendly language.

In Eastern cultures signals may not be so apparent. Chinese negotiators do not appear to telegraph their next move through a show of emotion. The level of friendliness remains the same, whether negotiations are approaching agreement or failure. In consequence, there seems to be an element of surprise when negotiating with the Chinese. As they move from the integrative stage to decision in one well-considered step it is not surprising that there is a lack of finality about such agreements, for the intuitive method cannot guarantee that parties dealing with the Chinese will make agreements that stick.

The system is effective because changes can be made after the agreement has been struck. The implications of this for people communicating with the Chinese is that they should not hesitate to ask for preferred changes after agreement has been reached. The Chinese will not hesitate. The way is smoothed if a memorandum of agreement is drawn up indicating the heads under which agreement has been recorded as a preliminary to the formal contract. The Chinese have no proper contract law and the Japanese one reflects the requirement of the negotiating parties to come to agreement among themselves.

In European and American transactions, negotiations are often brought to a conclusion by one or other of the parties summarizing the position they have reached or by making a final concession, usually associated with language which links the concession to a corresponding concession by the other side. The completion of agreement is often symbolized by handshakes, more informal intercourse and even photographs.

East Asians have less feeling for the drama of the agreement than do Westerners. Like the Greeks and many Latin Americans, they view a formal contract as the start, or the re-expression, of a relationship rather than the conclusion of a commercial process. The spirit of the agreement is more significant than its observation to the letter.

Legalistic approaches, for historical and cultural reasons, are strongly entrenched in countries such as the USA, West Germany and, to a lesser extent perhaps, the United Kingdom. Such approaches make relationships more difficult to establish. Yet, in order to be effective across different national borders, negotiators have to adapt suitably to the country concerned. Communication lies at the heart of negotiation and successful negotiators are competent communicators.

A concluding quote

'In England, that which is not forbidden is permitted; in Germany, that which is not permitted is forbidden; in France, everything is permitted, even that which is forbidden; in Russia, everything is forbidden, even that which is

continued

continued

permitted, and in Japan, everything, whether it is permitted or forbidden, is subject to negotiation.'

Anon, quoted in Robert Akroyd, *A Guide to Contracting, Negotiation and the Law*, Routledge and Kegan Paul, Sweet and Maxwell, 1987)

SUMMARY

1   Because of increasing exposure to international influences, organizations in private and public sectors increasingly have to interact with people from other countries and cultures. In order to communicate clearly with each other they have to interpret the cultural patterns and concepts of one country in terms of the patterns and concepts of the other. Otherwise cultural bias creeps into the interaction.

2   Hofstede's four-dimensional approach of power distance, uncertainty avoidance, individualism and masculinity help us to understand how and why people think and act in organizational settings in different countries. Plots of 50 countries on the interaction of different elements provide us with implicit models of how people behave, giving us ways of understanding them and hence of communicating with them.

3   While these frameworks give us guidance on how to couch our general communications with a person from another culture, we have to know something of that person's culture and the characteristics of his or her language because these can affect meaning for us if we are unaware of them. Simple words like 'Yes' or 'No' can have different meanings depending on the culture involved.

4   The logical approach or dialectic is not used in the major East Asian countries and their approach to problem solving has to be understood in order to communicate effectively. Also, every country has rules, with origins often lost in antiquity, which require to be learned before a foreigner is accepted and hence more easily communicated with.

5   Different ways of problem solving and different cultural rules lead to different styles of persuasion which characterizes all communication. These have been classified into the factual–inductive, the axiomatic–inductive and the intuitive–affective. They provide us with general frameworks for persuasive communication with people in each category. This includes informal negotiation.

6   Inter-organizational or interfactional negotiation across countries, which is subject to formal and ritualistic processes, is open to different cultural

influences at each stage of negotiation. Some stages are de-emphasized in the process, depending on the cultural context, while others are heavily emphasized. It is only through acquiring knowledge of these that one can become a successful communicator and hence a successful negotiator.

REFERENCES

Argyle, M. *The Psychology of Interpersonal Behaviour*, Penguin Books, Harmondsworth (1983).
Brislin, R. W. *Cross-Cultural Encounters*, Pergamon Press, Oxford (1982).
Clyne, M. International communication breakdown and communication conflict. In Molony, C., Zobl, H. and Stölting, W., *German in Contact with Other Languages*, Scriptor, Kromberg (1977).
Fisher, G. International negotiation. In Samovar, L. A. and Porter, R. E., *Intercultural Communication: A Reader*, Wadsworth, New York (1988).
Gumperz, J. Linguistic repertoires, grammars and second language instruction. *Monograph No. 18: Report on the Sixteenth Annual Round Table Meeting on Linguistics and Language Study*, Georgetown Press, Washington, DC (1966).
Hall, E. T. *Beyond Culture*, Anchor Press/Doubleday, New York (1976).
Henry, T. Interview on BBC1 'Today' programme, 21 October (1989).
Hofstede, G. The cultural relativity of organizational practices and theories. *Journal of International Business Studies*, Fall (1983).
Hofstede, G. *Culture's Consequences: International Differences in Work-Related Values*, Sage, Beverly Hills, CA (1984).
Hofstede, G. National and organisational value systems. *Journal of Management Studies*, **22**, No. 4 (1985).
McCall, J. B. and Warrington, M. B. *Marketing by Agreement: A Cross-cultural Approach to Business Negotiations*, John Wiley, Chichester (1989).
Negandhi, A. R. Multinational corporations and host government relationships: comparative study of conflicts and conflicting issues. *Human Relations*, **33** (1980).
Turnbull, P. W. and Cunningham, M. T. *International Marketing and Purchasing*, Macmillan, London (1981).

11
Training and development for effective communication

Having identified the skills of communication within and between organizations, these have to be transferred to people whose performance requires to be improved. This chapter examines the training implications of the previous chapters and seeks to derive a basis from which the skills identified can be built into a management development programme.

MANAGING AND THE SKILLS OF COMMUNICATION

The previous chapters have indicated how different the traditional and normative picture of managerial behaviour is from the descriptions evident from research. Management is not a planned and orderly activity, and is now seen to be fragmented, reactive and intuitive, requiring managers to think on their feet and be advocates, persuaders and negotiators. From a view of management which has focused on working within established relationships with a boss and subordinate, there is an emerging focus on recognizing the importance of lateral relationships. Decisions of any importance are almost certain to affect people outside the manager's own function or organization who may have the power to block a preferred course of action should they so desire. Therefore there is a need for sound and flexible reciprocal relationships requiring the development of skills, mainly interpersonal communication ones, which assist in establishing, maintaining and nurturing relationships necessary for effective action across organizational, cultural and national boundaries. This change implies moving from an understanding of managerial behaviour as non-political with decisions taken rationally from information provided by formal systems to a view of organizations as political systems in which information is used for group or personal advantage, with decisions often being taken using information provided by informal communication networks. The general perspective on managerial behaviour seems to have moved from people trying to meet organizational objectives to a view which sees individuals seeking to pursue their own goals or those of their work group as far as possible. It is implicit in these shifts that managers, to be effective, will need to learn how to trade, bargain, persuade and compromise.

What has emerged from the research into the managerial role is a picture of managers who, as they climb the managerial ladder, live in a political world. It is a world where they must learn to influence people other than subordinates, to manoeuvre for position and to enlist support for what they do. At the heart of all these activities is communication, and managers will spend the greater part of their time communicating with other people who will often be other managers. It is within this context that this final chapter will develop some ideas on how managerial communication skills can be developed, with the ultimate intention of relating the conceptual framework which will assist managers in understanding the complexities of their communication situation and the issue of training.

Initially, the chapter will review in broad terms some of the most commonly used approaches to the development of communication skills. This will then be linked with the associated notions of what managers actually do and how they learn. Finally, an attempt will be made to synthesize current thinking on the development of managerial communication skills in the light of the emerging model of management.

There is a substantial amount of knowledge and advice on the nature of relationships within and across organizations. Various approaches have been developed with the express intention of changing the behaviour of managers. These approaches tend, as a rule, to provide managers with sets of general guidelines about what they should do to improve relationships and concentrate on the improvement of specific skills, i.e. motivation, listening, group problem solving, giving instructions, delegating authority, counselling, negotiating, chairing meetings, making presentations, using the telephone and selling skills and team development.

Most of the available training methods seem to have certain common elements, although the detail of their application and their conceptual backgrounds is very different.

Common elements of communication skills training

1 Based on discovery and experimental learning. Learners are encouraged to experiment with new behaviours.
2 Learners receive feedback from each other and trainers on their performances.

continued

continued ──────────────────────────────────────

3 Groups of learners are led to provide mutual support, discussion and feedback.
4 Learners are provided with knowledge about the skill or skills prior to their practising it/them.
5 The exercises, roleplays, case studies, simulations are as realistic and meaningful as possible to the learners. (It should be noted that some methods take an opposite stance, arguing that task relevance obscures issues of behavioural importance.)

Adair (1983) suggests that training courses for communication skills should go through four main phases:

1 Knowledge and practice on general skills;
2 Small group work and discussions;
3 Face-to-face exercises;
4 Discussions of workplace applicability.

There are a large number of experience-based training methods pioneered by Pfeiffer and Jones (1971) on structured methods. They recognized that experience could be shaped to fulfil definite learning objectives and is therefore structurable.

A recent study on the effectiveness of communication skills training, undertaken by the Department of Communication Studies at Sheffield City Polytechnic, generally found that many approaches received a low rating from learners and their organizations. Training, in a traditional course-based sense, was seen to be most effective in those skill areas which were relatively well defined, formal and which allow for preparation and scripting, with the manager being the initiator of information and thus holding a powerful role. Training was least successful when the focus was on what the authors called responsive communication and where substantial power lies with the other party, or parties, to the interaction. Perversely, this may lead to the conclusion that training which is seen as most needed according to the evidence of this book is that which can be least effectively taught using current approaches. An extreme example of this concerns the skill of listening, which is consistently rated by managers as having the greatest need for improvement but which may be one of the most difficult to learn. Similarly avoided, or done less effectively, seems to be training in the areas of communication which involve the exercise of interpersonal and organizational power and the probability of conflict involving managers in influencing and persuading.

Because of the relatively low effectiveness of training in high-need areas, then, organizations are either discouraged from offering communication skills training at all or concentrate their efforts on the lower-order, more predictable areas of communication skills training such as making presentations and handling selection interviews.

The basic problems in the delivery of the more complex communication skills revolve around the lack of realism and relevance of course content, particularly in the exercises and roleplays used as a basis for experiential learning, the lack of practical and managerial experience on the part of trainers and the difficulties involved in providing the training at the most appropriate point in a manager's career. The best approaches to the identification of managers who require this higher order of communication skills training may be through a process of self-analysis and self-nomination using self-ratings comparing the importance of specific skills with their current perceived competence.

APPROACHES TO COMMUNICATIONS SKILLS TRAINING

From the above outline it is apparent that there is a wide range of problem situations which have in common an interactive, interpersonal aspect. There is much advice available on the ways in which people's behaviour can be changed so that interpersonal relationships can be improved to a greater or lesser degree, concentrating on the communication aspects. For the purposes of review these have been separated into three broad areas—the thinking, doing and feeling approaches to interpersonal skills training.

The Thinking Approach

The thinking approach concentrates on providing learners with knowledge appropriate to the area of study, usually by employing learning methods based on lectures, discussions, case studies and guided reading. However, there is very limited evidence, if any, that increased knowledge in itself leads to more effective interpersonal skills. Skill acquisition is a function of translating knowledge into actual behaviour, and while it is necessary to understand the context and components of a skill before using it, only through practice can the skill be learned and eventually internalized into the behavioural repertoire of the learner. It would be unusual, but not unknown, for training programmes with a focus on communication to concentrate on the cognitive inputs to the exclusion of experiential elements.

The Doing Approach

The argument about skill acquisition requiring a substantial element of practice would suggest that any training programme with a focus on skills should include a carefully sequenced and relevant series of practical exercises for the learner to work through. Roleplays, simulations and games used within a workshop context form the basic material through which learners experience the situations in which new skills can be used; they experiment with them, and through a combination of practice and feedback integrate the new skills into their work behaviour. The context of the training should provide a safe environment where the incentive to learn new skills is encouraged and where the sharing of experience and work problems with other learners and trainers provides a stimulating and motivating influence to action. Roleplaying and behavioural simulation have been supported as techniques which, if used properly, can lead to highly successful skill acquisition. (Randell *et al.*, 1980; Drath and Kaplan, 1986). Roleplaying, involving learners in acting out roles varying from those loosely structured by a few lines of context to those comprehensively scripted, is open to criticism when the situations used are artificial and manifestly irrelevant to the learners' work situation. Learners may not feel that the exercises used by trainers have sufficient relationship to the real world in which they will have to operate and may be inclined to opt out or exhibit only the pretence of participation.

Behavioural simulation has been suggested as a way of recreating the experience of problem situations in organizations by placing learners in interrelated roles, staging the simulation in a realistic environment and allowing the simulation to run for several hours (Cousins and McDougall, 1989). In this way simulation attempts to overcome the contextual disadvantages of roleplay. However, the organizational requirements of simulation are similar to that of putting on a theatrical performance and usually filming it simultaneously for feedback purposes, an exercise not to be taken lightly or without access to appropriate resources and skilled tutors.

Wright and Talyor (1984) offer some guidelines and discussion on the issues and problems of tutoring roleplay exercises and emphasize the importance of the way in which the analysis of performance and feedback is handled. A key factor underpinning the effectiveness of any of the doing activities is the conceptual and behavioural framework which the trainer is using to make the feedback and guidance processes organized and meaningful. Overgeneralized approaches to the analysis and feedback processes in communication skills training have been criticized (Buchanan and Hucynski, 1986). They advocate having specific frameworks which managers use as guides to action in particular circumstances and outline an interrelated sequence of four areas of analysis:

1 Diagnostic skills to identify key aspects and the circumstance of the problem;
2 Awareness of the options—the behavioural repertoire that can be consciously selected and deployed to achieve the desired outcomes in specific circumstances;
3 Appropriate decisions concerning behaviour that fit the context;
4 Person perception which involves accurate evaluation of the attitudes, emotions, needs and potential responses of other people.

The emphasis on the decision framework has its heritage in the work of Honey and Rackham (1986), which uses methods of analysis and feedback concentrating on the actual behaviours of people in interactive situations and its external causes and effects.

The trainer's role using the methods of behavioural categorizing is to control and predict behaviours by helping the learner to interpret the connections between external events and observable behaviour. Table 11.1 illustrates a typical framework for behavioural categorizing which is used to help in the observation of learner interaction, in either a training or a real-life situation. The trainer records the interactions by categorizing the behaviour of individuals and using this information as the basis of feedback, discussions and analysis of the performance outcomes. Honey and Rackham argue that many interpersonal skills can only be defined in terms of the observable aspects of an individual's objectives. A focus on observable behaviour without too much attention being paid to the emotional and attitudinal state of the learner is the consequence and indeed central element in the behavioural approach.

The Feeling Approach

Feeling approaches to communication skills training regard behaviour only as an outward symptom, and attempt to bring a variety of techniques to concentrate on the internal causes of behaviour such as needs, motives,

Table 11.1 An example of behaviour categorizing. (From Honey, 1982, reproduced by permission)

Seeking ideas	Asking other people for their ideas
Proposing	Putting forward ideas
Suggesting	Putting forward ideas as questions
Building	Developing someone else's idea
Disagreeing	Explicitly disagreeing with something someone else has said
Supporting	Agreeing with something someone else has said
Stating difficulties	Pointing out the snags with something someone else has said
Seeking clarification	Asking other people for further information
Clarifying/explaining	Airing information

attitudes and feelings. Schein (1981) and Haney (1986), for instance, argue strongly that each party to a relationship must first achieve some self-insight, a sense of one's own commitments, for if we cannot accept ourselves we cannot hear other people. People only begin to hear and understand each other as they seek common ground around which common activities can be designed. In the USA much of the activity in interpersonal and communication skills training has been involved with inner-directed training techniques such as sensitivity training, T-groups, encounter groups, transactional analysis and Zen meditation. What they have in common is a focus on learning how to perceive oneself, others and the environment realistically, and to disengage, when appropriate, the analytical self in favour of the feeling self.

Haney (1986) develops the concept of an exceptionally realistic self-image (ERSI) as a necessary condition for individuals to perceive accurately. With an ERSI an individual is released from constantly defending an unrealistic self-image, more able to maintain a valid self-image, able to understand, predict and cope with others more effectively and better able to select realistic personal goals. A three-step programme is necessary to achieve the ERSI:

1   Make a commitment, decide that you really want to understand yourself better and that you are prepared to commit the necessary resources.
2   Learn to recognize and reduce defences against the cues from reality.
3   Receive and evaluate those cues in order to assess how your current self-image and your realistic self-image may conflict.

The cues from reality may come from verbal feedback from others, psychometric instruments (for example personality tests), reading and reflecting, watching video playbacks of interpersonal interactions and personal stocktaking techniques involving inventories and journal/diary keeping. It has long been known that our behaviour is a response to our perception of reality rather than some externally validated reality, and it is the objective of the feeling approach to put the learners in touch with their feelings and emotions so that their perceptions are based on a validated view of the external world.

The effectiveness of this group of techniques have been the subject of substantial research summarized by Argyle (1981). Sensitivity training and T-groups are based on creating a non-structured atmosphere in which people should feel free to give and receive feedback. Objectives for such activities vary, but tend to concentrate on improving individual ability to understand and predict their own and others' behaviour. Transactional Analysis (Berne, 1964,) is a technique geared to providing detailed means of analysis of interpersonal situations with a view to helping people cope better with each other. TA's central idea is that people have three ego states,

Parent–Adult–Child, and that it is the Adult state which should dominate the personality, while the domineering Adult or the lacking in confidence Child should be subjugated. Overall research results into the impact of these techniques on the quality of communication in interpersonal relationships is inconclusive. Some point to the worst excesses as being dangerous to the psychological well-being of participants. These techniques are also difficult to manage and control, with the outcomes for individuals and their organizations being very uncertain. Finally, question marks have been put against the ability of feelings-based approaches to sustain behaviour change for a meaningful period of time, and that once participants return to the organization, they revert to original and reinforced patterns of behaviour and communication. It may be worth noting, however, that the issue of learning transfer and the reinforcement of new behaviour is one that affects all the off-the-job techniques referred to so far.

TRAINING TECHNIQUES AND LEARNING

While there may be, at least superficially, a degree of common practice evident in the doing and feeling approaches, there is a substantial difference in the interpretation of cause and effect. The feeling approach concentrates on encouraging managers to review and, if appropriate, adjust their feelings, attitudes and needs so that they are motivated to act and communicate differently. The doing approach, in that it uses behavioural methods of analysis, would suggest that it is more practicable to construct training programmes so that the effort is put into actually changing behaviour as a precursor to feelings and attitudes being reviewed and adjusted as the results of the new behaviour are evaluated. Allowing for this difference, the question is how far these established (if not validated) approaches to interpersonal and communication skills training apply to a managerial world, where it is the development of reciprocal relationships within political systems that is the key to success. It is implicit in this shift in perception that managers have to learn how to trade, bargain and compromise. For many years trainers have been trying to develop methods which will develop these skills using the available knowledge about how individuals and, more particularly, managers learn.

At the cognitive level the learner exercises his mind to conceptualize, analyse and exercise logic in relation to decision alternatives, albeit according to criteria which are often culturally determined and specific. At the affective level the learner, by involvement with his own values, beliefs, feelings, attitudes and self-image, learns in terms more meaningful to himself. At the conative level the learner, by his interactions with others, will receive feedback by which he can, with the requisite intuition or skills, assess and

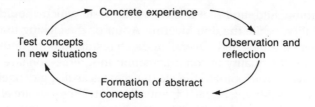

Figure 11.1 *The Experiential Learning Cycle (From Kolb et al., 1981, reproduced by permission)*

restructure his perceptions and so learn how to learn. This process is formalized and extended in the concept of experiential learning, which encourages the learner to sort things out for himself by the interaction of thinking and doing processes. Kolb *et al.* (1981) have represented this process as a learning cycle following a sequence of experience, reflection, conceptualizing and testing (Figure 11.1).

Honey and Mumford (1982) have developed a version of Kolb's model which, they believe, has improved validity in the eyes of managers as an instrument for the diagnosis of individual learning styles. The implications of diagnosing individual learning styles are shown in Table 11.2.

The emphasis on this work on the role that experience and conceptualizing have in learning is supported by Revans (1983), who over a long period of time, has advocated action learning approaches to development. Action learning involves giving managers unfamiliar problems to work on in unfamiliar organizations, and places them in a position where they must learn from their experience to achieve their task objectives. Much recent support has been forthcoming for managers learning from their experience of actually solving real problems (Mumford, 1980; Burgoyne and Stuart, 1976), not deliberately planned for learning purposes. The IPM's approach to Continuous Development echoes this theme of managerial learning being closely linked to the managers' real-life experience. This may lead to the questioning of off-the-job training approaches in themselves as solutions to the issue of developing interpersonal and communication skills.

Table 11.2 *Implications for developing managers of learning-style preferences*

1   It helps managers to know the stages in the process of learning from experience and how their learning styles help and hinder them.
2   It helps managers to work out how to improve underdeveloped learning styles.
3   It provides managers with resources where they can practise developing and help learning from experience to be a deliberate and conscious process.
4   It can help managers to identify learning opportunities in their current job and aid them in planning how to utilize them.

The idea of learning as a social and experiential process has added significance in that the greater the interpersonal competence of managers, the greater will be their capacity to learn with and from each other. The more a learning method engages the cognitive, affective and conative means of learning, the greater the feedback the learner will get, extending self-knowledge and encouraging self-actualization and self-development. It may be feasible to fit a learning method such as the case study into this learning mode. Normally a case study makes demands on the mental capacities of the learner. Data are given on the problem and events and learners are asked to analyse the case and make proposals for action. Usually a case study does not include or integrate feelings, values and attitudes, thus escaping using affective or conative modes, and learning potential is missed.

Case material can involve values and beliefs of some participants by the nature of the subject and the interpersonal requirements of the case analysis situation. A case involving decisions about withdrawing or maintaining stocks of ethical drugs for sale when research has cast some marginal doubts on their safety can engage all three learning modes and focus discussion on our propensity to be influenced in communication by supposedly objective information fed to participants by those in powerful roles. It must be recognized that not everyone is likely to be influenced by this process to learn something about their communication skills, as styles of learning vary considerably between individuals.

Affects and conatations as a means of learning are exploited to a greater degree by roleplays, particularly where the situation develops out of the learning group itself and becomes a 'here and now' situation. If this can be allied to some desired behavioural end then there is a chance that the full learning potential is being tapped. Roleplaying, allied to the case study, may go some way towards achieving a balanced approach, with the case emphasizing cognitive aspects and the roleplaying developing affective and conative ones. Learning which is itself negotiated is a further example of a vehicle for the development of skills related to communication. Learning contracts embody learners diagnosing their own interpersonal strengths and weaknesses and then negotiating for resources to achieve goals set out in their plans of action. This process introduces into learning activities experiences which will stand them in good stead when they have to perform managerial roles.

CONCLUSION

In the traditional model of management, where stable relationships were the norm and interpersonal exchanges took place through the hierarchy, communication skills and their development could be argued to be relatively straightforward. Report writing was of prime importance, as was the ability to make clear and brief presentations. These skills lend themselves to a training approach as the skill elements are easy to identify, and do not generally involve the kind of responsive interaction which requires a flexible and complex conceptual framework. With the newer, less comfortable model a wider range of interpersonal communication skills are required to cover a greater complexity of situations.

The experience gained by way of traditional learning methods is inadequate to handle the complexities of the new model of management and its associated communication skills. Training and development under conditions of change, ambiguity and complexity has to relate to acquiring a wider range of concepts to handle the complexity. Most of the skills required in the emergent model of management are based on concepts which can provide the manager with frames of reference through which past experience can be interpreted and used to think through unforeseen and novel situations as they arise. The old belief that skills could be perfected with practice is dead; experience alone is not enough. Ways will have to be found to integrate the conceptual framework outlined throughout this book into the training and development of managers so that they are equipped through their career to handle the complexities and uncertainties which they will undoubtedly face. Training and development must address issues of skill development at all three levels of learning to ensure maximum effectiveness, and managers must be given support and encouragement in learning about communication, both in training events and during their everyday experience of work.

REFERENCES

Adair, J. *Training for Communication*, Gower, Aldershot (1983).
Argyle, M. *The Psychology of Interpersonal Behaviour*, Penguin Books, Harmondsworth (1981).
Berne, E. *Games People Play*, Grove Press, New York (1964).
Buchanan, D. and Huczynski, A. A new approach to interpersonal skills development. *Journal of European Industrial Training*, **10**, No. 8 (1986).
Burgoyne, J. and Stuart, R. The nature, use and acquisition of managerial skill and other attributes. *Personnel Review*, **15**, No. 4 (1976).
Cousins, J. Y. and McDougall, M. A bridge to reality. Simulation training at the Glasgow Garden Festival. *Journal of Industrial and Commercial Training*, November (1989).
Drath, W. H. and Kaplan, R. E. Developing managerial skills through realistic simulations. In Lewis, L. H. (ed.), *Experimental and Simulation*, Jossey-Bass, San Francisco, CA (1986).
Haney, W. *Communications and Interpersonal Relations: Text and Cases*. Irwin, Homewood, ILL (1986).
Honey, P. Why I am a behaviourist. *Journal of European Industrial Training*, **6**, No. 4 (1982).
Honey, P. and Mumford, A. *Manual of Learning Styles*, Honey (1982).

Honey, P. and Rackham, N. *Interactive Skills Training*, Gower, Aldershot (1986).

Kolb, D. A., Ruben, I. M. and McIntyre, J. M. *Organisational Psychology: An Experimental Approach*, John Wiley, New York (1981).

Mumford, A. *Making Experience Pay*, McGraw-Hill, New York (1980).

Pfeiffer, M. and Jones, A. *Structured Experience*, Prentice-Hall, Englewood Cliffs, NJ (1971).

Randell, G., *et al. Staff Appraisal*, IPM, London (1980).

Revans, R. *Origins and Growth of Action Learning*, Chartwell-Bratt (Publishing and Training) Ltd, Bromley (1983).

Schein, E. S.M.R. forum: improving face to face relationships. *Sloan Management Review* (1981).

Wright, P. L. and Taylor, D. S. The development of tutoring skills for interpersonal skills training. *Journal of European Industrial Training*, **8**, No. 6 (1984).

Author Index

242   *Author Index*

Subject Index

245